FRACTURED HOPE

celebrating 20 years of democracy amid poverty and despair

SIPHO MZOLO

Order this book online at www.trafford.com
or email orders@trafford.com

Most Trafford titles are also available at major online book retailers.

Printed in the United States of America.

ISBN: 978-1-4907-1727-2 (sc)
ISBN: 978-1-4907-1726-5 (e)

Trafford rev. 12/23/2013

 www.trafford.com

North America & international
toll-free: 1 888 232 4444 (USA & Canada)
fax: 812 355 4082

Dedicated to the young people of South Africa

Today, young people in South Africa are negotiating a complex reality wedged between a brutal apartheid history they did not personally experience; a post-apartheid era where poverty and violence are their only experiences and the knowledge that they inherit a fractured future

CONTENTS

FOREWORD

2014 represents 20 years of democracy and freedom for the people of South Africa. Much was given in order for us to enjoy the freedom we have today. Tears, blood and sacrifices of many people across the racial and social divide made it possible for us to appreciate this freedom. The Arab Spring represented a time in history where Arabic revolutions sparked by restless youth who were tired of governments that held them hostage in their own backyards willing to die for a something they believed in. As a young man born in South African the same soil that has been soaked with the blood, sweat and tears of many people of my parents generations who fought against a regime that was immoral, I find myself together with my peers struggling to figure out our own identities in this new found freedom. We the youth have are asking ourselves what do we stand for and what defines our struggles and us? We live in a time where having 'swagger and street creed' expressed in the form of fancy cars, deep pockets of money, pretty girls and trendy clothes is more important than looking at ways in which we can contribute towards the advancement of our society. As we go through this book *South Africa Fractured Hope* we realise that the youth of South Africa have a new struggle in our hands and the sooner we identify it the sooner we can get a sense of direction. Sipho Mzolo could not have captured the times we live in more succinctly as he takes us on a journey that marked the genesis of our democracy and transporting us to a place where we envision our better selves in the country of our dreams. If the generation of Gandhi, Martin Luther King Jnr. and Mandela could transcend the social injustices of their era so that the generation after them could have a real chance to live in peace and freedom, then by all means let our generation do so for its own sake. Given the presenting evidence of unemployment, poverty, diseases and violence our hope may be dim and fractured nevertheless let us continue to keep hope alive, if not for ourselves then let us keep hope alive for those coming after us. Hope is the one thing we can hold onto even in the midst of the challenges.

Vusisizwe Mahlangu
Pastor: Temple of Grace, Kempton Park
National Youth President: International Assemblies of God, South Africa
December 2013

INTRODUCTION

In the book *Long Walk to Freedom* Mandela wrote, 'I have taken a moment here to rest, to steal a view of the glorious vista that surrounds me, to look back on the distance I have come. But I can only rest for a moment, and I dare not linger, for my walk is not yet ended.' Although Mandela's walk has now ended he was never alone on the walk, for we have all taken part in the long walk to freedom and now we need a moment to survey the journey covered thus far, and cherish whatever view there is. After the celebration of the arrival of democracy and in its second decade, it is a good place for us also to pause and reflect on the progress and poignancy of democracy. As we pause and consult our GPS, we acknowledge that even though we all come from different starting points our challenge remains that of finding a common path to the destination of our open shared South Africa. It is our time to accept Mandela's inheritance of humanity and courage to build a better nation and a better future for us all. It is not given to every generation that it should be present during and participate in the act of creation of a new era. We believe that ours is privileged to occupy such a historic space and because of this privilege, a sense of responsibility coupled with gratitude we pass this knowledge to our young generation.

On 27 April 2014 will be twenty years of democracy in South Africa. In 1994, the country had undergone a facelift along with a new name—*Rainbow Nation*—a raft of rookie leaders and a fledgling democracy. The enfranchised majority now votes frequently as a practice that underscores democracy but the much-vaunted freedom remains elusive. 'So, what has Mandela's South Africa done with its freedom' pops the question many would have liked an answer to, however, because we are looking to engage the reader with qualitatively intelligible discussion, a different question is better suited: has South Africa prospered under the ANC stewardship? Ordinary people in the streets of South Africa tell their story and their story is an honest assessment of the government's performance based on the track record of the two decades in office.

Twenty years after democracy the attention has firmly shifted to what the ANC has achieved, or failed to achieve, rather than its past as the liberator. The Mandela, Mbeki and Zuma leadership and the impact their leadership has had on the country's fortunes or lack thereof weighed in. There is a sense that much of what the government accomplished at the beginning of the journey was commendable but a lot that happened in the intervening period is inimical to the long-term interest of South Africa. Our examination zeroed in on whether the lived experience represented a dream deferred or hope of a better South Africa. We weaved the stories together into a tapestry of voices anchored on this lived experience. The analysis of facts culminates in a synthesis of the full picture of where we are as a nation and conclude that our nation is impoverished and it will take a different energy to pull it back from the cliff edge. South Africa is at cross road; black communities have emerged from a history of social and economic maginalisation and exclusion with little or no substantive improvement in 20 years. For the masses of people, life has become increasingly difficult. Urban ghettos are the way of life for the majority. Extreme levels of poverty and violence are on the rise. Where there is no education people sink deeper into the jaws of poverty, where there is no work people become corrupt and where hope is progressively diminishing, the nation experiences a catastrophe.

A fractured hope of the country of our dreams—what went wrong, if anything? We have had an opportunity to create a 'stretch mindset' rather than a 'fit mindset'. Stretch attitude accommodates all of us while a fit attitude accommodates only interests of those in power. We have considerably more to do to convert the opportunities presented by the advent of democracy into tangible achievements. When we come to the awareness of our power, we can examine ourselves and take the initiative to shape our society to one compatible with our dreams. As we become bolder and courageous citizens, we step into our power, start to participate in the affairs of the nation as empowered citizens whose presence matter, no longer prepared to settle for twaddle. Developing a positive consciousness about our future forces us to have a healthy outlook even in the face of setbacks; in essence, that is how transformation is birthed. For the nation to achieve any of this, all of our human potential must be fully accessed and our collective contribution maximised. In that sense, we enter the process of maturation as citizens that know, as opposed to objects that are controlled.

Hope is a single currency humans trade on amidst the drudgery of life's changing fortunes. Hope is positive expectation of receiving a promise fulfilled in our lives. Hope is a desire whose answer is found in the promises of God. Hope believes you can have it someday and faith transforms hopes into realities, in other words, hope is the raw material from which faith builds the house. This kind of hope entails pathways and thoughts to an intended goal. With the sense of hope come positive emotions such as joy, courage, and empowerment. Hope is not brought about by the acts or omissions of others rather something fuelled by an internal desire to accomplish something for oneself. Hope is an ontological need that demands an anchoring practice. It requires a practice for it to become edifying for it to become historical concreteness. The anchoring practice exercises positive emotions that are generated from one's cognitive, psychological and social space.

We asked the youth to transport us on their imaginative mind into the future, a glimpse of their envisaged selves became discernible and this gave us further inspiration to pen the words you are reading in this book. Discussing their experiences challenged the culture of silence and ignorance, which are the result of the past from which many of us emerged. On the occasion of the fifth election in 2014, we have 2.4 million first-time voters so-called 'born frees,' may you maximise the opportunity presented by your right to vote—as young citizens of this nation you too have a responsibility. To the 6.4 million youth not in school and not employed may you find both solace and inspiration in our words as well as courage to take a stand and change the course of your destiny. To Sfiso, Kgaugelo, Sigra, Siphumusa, Mfundo, Saroya, Masego and all their cousins far and near, our prayer is that may you live to the calling of your names and lead your generation with wisdom and humility for the glory of God.

We began researching material for this book in 2010 the actual writing commenced in 2013 and at the time of publication, we had barely touched the surface in terms of documenting the account of stories told by ordinary South Africans. In its presentation, the book is not data rich but provides empirical evaluation backed by thick analysis. Our method and epistemology was the interpretation of the observed phenomena. We looked objectively at the lived human experience in post apartheid milieu and generated explanations of the observed phenomena at the level of meaning rather than their cause and effect. By following a process of reflection, we look into history for the purpose of looking ahead more keenly because we believe reflection is an essential precursor of action.

It is not the intention of this book to criticise the ANC or trumpet its praises. In the pursuit of objectivity, we hold the belief that dispassionate reflection and scholarly enquiry should be at the heart of any intellectual endeavour and ours is no less so. Our research has uncovered a narrative that is both fascinating and deeply troubling. Even so, we do not claim that we know everything that is going on in South Africa right now. Nevertheless, we do know much and we will tell you the things you might not have heard. The story behind the lethal struggle between good and bad has not been told fully until now; at least that is the goal of this book. As we put together this story we are acutely mindful that to navigate the delicate balance between the polarized extremes in our society requires a clinical approach and healthy respect for the efforts others have made in contributing to the changing landscape. It also means we had to live out the practice of posting platitudinous parables, ass-kissing aphorisms and hackneyed self-help clichés.

For ease of reference, the book is divided into two parts. The first part presents facts on the 10 key areas in which major advances should have occurred and 10 key areas where challenges remain unresolved and attempt to distill what it all means using the tools of analysis. At the conclusion, we live the reader with some thoughts to reflect upon. It is certainly possible for each one of us to construct a path into the future that simply accentuates the negatives, which becomes a future of isolation, exclusion and narcissism that would invariably end up in what Gratton author of *The Shift* calls the *Default Future*. The tendency of many South African commentators and writers is to excoriate the ANC and decry its failures without offering alternatives is talk for the sake of talking not helpful to anyone. There is also a future where the positives can be harnessed to present a *Created Future*. In the stories of a crafted future people are experimenting with ways of working and learning from each other and rapidly adopting new ideas. These storylines shape things that transform lives and bring hope.

The second part begins with a discussion that looks at this possibility; in it we take a more discursive view of the emergent patterns of the future, which in our opinion is the undercurrent shaping the views and behaviour of generation Y and Z. In the penultimate chapter, we discuss the research findings; ideas that we believe if replicated on a large scale have the potential to help the entire generation of young people of South Africa. In this sense, the book brings real hope. The final chapter revisits pre-colonial history and asks what lessons are there for the renaissance millennium. By taking a historical perspective it is often useful in both creating a sense of momentum and velocity, thus provide a view of historical precedence reinforcing the belief that no matter how dark the nightfall may be hope abounds. We publish this book in the spirit of work in progress, a rough-hewn set of building blocks knowing that all writing in transformation is provisional anyway; future researchers may find it worthwhile to build upon the work we have begun. Ours is an open-ended ongoing inquiry in conscientious service of the truth. Thank you for reading it.

THANKING OUR COMMUNITY

A lifetime of relationships and a great deal of lived experience formed the raw material from which I have pulled together an articulation of what I have learned and hope that others will find worth reading. I learn in community, listening to others, reading widely and brainstorming with enthusiasm. Yet few pieces are mine. I am indebted to the influence of authors before me who became my mentors some I have met and others not, some are living and some are no longer with us. I acknowledge them individually for their influence on the development of my thinking of this work. I am grateful for the sacrifice and years that went into their teachings. In the 1980s, we were arrested and subsequently condemned into solitary life on Robben Island, a place of banishment where prisoners were isolated so that society may forget about them and in the event that they manage to come out alive, it was thought they would be pretty much worthless to the society. Condemned for furthering the aims of a liberation movement and under the laws existed then, we had to make peace with the knowledge that we called terrorists as uncomfortable as this was we carried our heads high. Our prison terms ranged between three and seven years. Vulnerable to a prison system that set about stripping black us of dignity instead taught us enduring lessons. However, in a bizarre twist of luck unbeknown to us the presiding Magistrate of the lower court as fate would have it had misdirected himself in rendering his judgement and on appeal the Justices of the Appeals Court, struck down both the conviction as well as the prison term and released us before completing full sentences.

I count myself privileged to have had the tutelage of distinguished heroes among others Dr. Joe Thloloe, Manthata Tsedu, Truman Mnguni, Thembinkosi Nonqgekele, Sipho Ngcobo, Nhlanganiso Sibanda, Bafelile Ramphele and Bafana Mtshali. Despite the harsh treatment we were subjected to during pre-trial custody, these men were very brave and humble at the same time that they would withstand torture and shameful humiliation without even as much resenting the tormentors. Sons of the Africa your indomitable spirit carried us through even when there was nothing left inside the little ones. This book is a tribute and recognition of your contribution to an open shared society. With high admiration of your courage, I stand in the shadow of your greatness!

Former colleagues at Sacwu present and those no longer with us (the late Lele and Masindi Mavhivha), Manene Samela, Tiny Ngcobo, Mike Tsotetsi, Leonard Mavuso, Vusi Nkosi, Majola, Humphrey, Jabu, Morgan, Phumzile, Deborah, Jacqueline, Nombulelo,

Bontle, Mandla, Bokman, Joe, Petros and those I have not mention by name but who somehow touched my life. Thank you for chiseling away the rough bits and pruning the wild until the best in me matured into a fruit at its prime. Because I have leant from each one of you, you have remained important to me thus my acknowledgement to you individually and severally.

The *Ayeye* crew was my virtual collaboration team that volunteered time to organize talk shows with students and township youths to participate in conversations and sent me tons of video images without you this project would have been an academic theory worth nothing. You are the other half of 'we' in the narrative, I could have never written this book on my own without you, you awesome and you rock man! Finally, I also thank Charlotte Stevens for her contribution in providing me with guidance on the semantic and technical aspects of the manuscript thus making the book more readable.

BOOK I

1994-2014
A HISTORIC MISTAKE

WHEN why
who when which
whose what where

CHAPTER 1

A Trip Down Memory Lane

Thousands of those who survived the mayhem, tormented by their wounds and hunger, searching for solace and comfort among the ruins of their homes, the church auditoriums, sometimes open veldt where wanton destruction was the heritage of the titanic battle for political ascendancy—to you the dream has not died and your hopes remain alive.

A survey of South African history reveals that black people's resistance to subjugation dates back more than three centuries, from the beginning of wars of primary resistance just after 1657, to the rise of early African nationalism in the late 1860s. In a more contemporary context of the 1980s, the struggle against white subjugation saw black resistance rising to new heights. All areas of life workplaces, in the community, in church and at schools became the terrain of political struggle, people sought to take control of their circumstances. Faith-based, community, students, youth and women's organisations sprang all over South Africa; these struggles were directly linked to the demand for freedom. This political consciousness rebirth morphed into a mass movement that became the seat for people's power. uMkhonto weSizwe (MK) and Apla armies intensified confrontation with the white security forces. ANC called on residents to render townships ungovernable by destroying Black Local Authorities. Councilors and policemen were called upon to resign; municipal buildings and homes of suspected collaborators were burned down. As the apartheid administrative system began to show signs of breaking down, people established alternative structures to run their communities, including street committees and people's courts in the townships. The democratic structures replaced the Bantustan appointed Chiefs in many parts of the homelands. A generalised atmosphere of mass insurrection enveloped the country in its entirety, mass based and armed struggles began to complement and strengthen one another. The freedom struggle shook the very foundations of the apartheid system. As people's resistance mounted, the white regime became extremely vicious.

Consequently, a series of states of emergencies were declared over many parts in black residential areas of the country beginning July 1985 and again June 1986, lasting until 1990. These states of emergencies were used as indiscriminate measure to silence struggle activists—as many as 300000 were detained, among them children as young as nine years.

At the height of things, the white regime tried desperately to save itself by supporting black vigilante groups and became extraordinarily brutal in their suppression of popular resistance in the land. However hard they tried, they failed. From this crucible emerged a rough and ready understanding between the oppressed on the one hand and the full might of state power on the other. These face-to-face engagements in the trenches were the birthplace of the resistance politics that eventually shaped the conditions that created the South Africa we have today. Zuma's ostentatious living may suggest oblivion of these history-making moments but people still living in the townships battling *Amaberethe* riot control squad in service delivery protests in the streets remember these times only too well. AfriForum too has learned that resistance from the tyranny of the government can deliver reasonably good results and as Samora Machele once said, 'the struggle continues' and so it is.

It is now a matter of public record that the negotiations for a constitutional democracy started much earlier than the actual unbanning of the liberation movements and the release of the political prisoners from Robben Island. While in prison, Nelson Mandela had conducted no fewer than 43 secret meetings between himself and envoys of the Nationalist Party government, solely by himself, before the ANC formally got involved in the talks. At one of the secret meetings then President FW De Klerk met with Mandela and informed him that he would be released over the weekend in Johannesburg. To De Klerk's surprise, Mandela balked and demanded a week to prepare for his release and that he preferred to take his first three steps to freedom from Victor Verster Prison in a symbolic gesture for the time he spent in prison. They compromised, the date could not be postponed but he could leave from the prison rather than the private guesthouse he lodged at during those exploratory discussions. The Dakar/Lusaka meetings between the envoys of the South African government on the one hand and the exiled ANC group on the other culminated in President De Klerk officially announcing the unbanning of the ANC, the PAC, the SA Communist Party and Black People's Convention. On the morning of Friday 2nd February 1990, on the occasion of opening of parliament the rescinding of the banning orders and the release of all remaining political prisoners was announced by De Klerk. On the hot summer afternoon of Sunday, 11th February 1990 at 16:00, a suited Nelson Mandela, at first unsmiling, his hand clasping that of his beloved wife Winnie, shadowing Bulelani Ngcuka on his right hand walked towards the prison gate. His life, he felt, 'was beginning anew, his ten thousand days of imprisonment were over'. Standing at the balcony of Cape Town City Hall flanked by Walter Sisulu and Cyril Ramaphosa, Mandela addressed the people of Cape Town. He began by declaring 'Friends, Comrades and fellow South Africans. I greet you all in the name of peace, democracy and freedom for all. I stand here before you not as a prophet but as a humble servant of you, the people. Your tireless and heroic sacrifices have made it possible for me to be here today. I therefore place the remaining years of my life in your hands . . .'

When Mandela became the president of the ANC, he led his organisation to the first round of official talks on 21 December 1991. The first round of negotiations took place under the aegis of the Convention for a Democratic South Africa (CODESA) held in Kempton Park. The parties agreed on a process whereby a negotiated transitional constitution would provide for an elected constitutional assembly to draw up a permanent constitution. The CODESA negotiations broke down, however, after the second plenary session in May 1992. One of the major points of dispute was the size of the supermajority that would be required for the assembly to adopt the constitution: The NP wanted a 75 per cent requirement, which would effectively have given it a veto power. In April 1993, the parties returned to negotiations, in what was known as the Multi-Party Negotiating Process (MPNP). A committee of the MPNP proposed the development of a collection of 'constitutional principles' with which the final constitution would have to comply, so that basic freedoms would be ensured and minority rights protected, without overly limiting the role of the elected constitutional assembly. The parties to the MPNP adopted this idea and proceeded to draft the interim constitution of 1993, which was formally enacted by parliament and came into force on 27 April 1994. The Interim Constitution provided for a Parliament made up of two houses: a 400-member National Assembly, directly elected by party list proportional representation, and a ninety-member senate, in which each of the nine provinces was represented by ten senators, elected by the provincial legislature. The Constitutional Assembly consisted of both houses sitting together, and was responsible for drawing up a final constitution within two years. The adoption of a new constitutional text required a two-thirds supermajority in the Constitutional Assembly, as well as the support of two-thirds of senators on matters relating to provincial government. If a two-thirds majority could not be obtained, a constitutional text could be adopted by a simple majority and then put to a national referendum in which 60 per cent support would be required for it to pass.

The negotiations took place against a backdrop of unprecedented internecine war in South Africa, especially in Gauteng townships pronounced more so in KwaZulu Natal between Inkatha warlords and self-styled ANC *amaqabane* (Comrades). In the middle of those negotiations, horrific events began to emerge marking the never-ending twist and turns that would constantly punctuate the drama behind closed doors of CODESA. The Boipatong massacre was the first grim news streaming through to the delegates seated at Kempton Park, thereafter train commuters butchered *en masse* by white men wearing black balaclavas, drive-by-shootings at taxi ranks in peak hours, Bantustan soldiers brazenly killing

ANC supporters in Bisho under Qgozo's command. The white right-wingers murdered Chris Hani uMkhonto weSizwe Commander. All these events happened nine months after the start of CODESA1 under FW de Klerk's watch. Mandela was pained by all of this; he expressed the wish that he were never released.

Simmering discontent had poisoned the well of initial goodwill that had greeted the unbanning of black organizations, the release of political prisoners as well as the beginnings of CODESA negotiations. The rumblings of grassroots rebellion in many ANC strongholds began to penetrate the confines of Kempton Park, much to the dismay of ANC negotiators. The need for transparency in the process was exigent. The 'tug-of-war' between factions in favour of a more aggressive, militarist approach to speed up the process and factions in favour of negotiations had reached serious proportions. The ANC had to stand back and reassess where it was going, how it was going to bring its constituency along with it, what bottom lines were simply nonnegotiable. What it was willing to concede to bring negotiations to an expeditious conclusion, as well as getting a grip on the spiraling violence before it could develop a self-sustaining momentum that would make the holding of elections and the transfer of power without the further spilling of blood impossible. Bilateral negotiations between ANC and NP in remote bush lodges pressed ahead despite the significant risks attaching because of the atrocities perpetrated by both sides. They were spurred even as they deadlocked occasionally then restarted again; at other times, contact between warring parties suspended then resumed. On the opposite side, a number of different dynamics were at work, often at cross-purposes. Once De Klerk had rid himself of the threatened white backlash, he should have been able to reach accommodation with the ANC on the outstanding issues. But the context of government's thinking had changed. It was no longer thinking in terms of the best deal it could reach from the ANC, and was no longer prepared to concede an outright victory to the ANC in a non-racial election. Rather it had begun to think in terms of building an anti-ANC coalition that would defeat the ANC. Hence, the need to appease the ANC was no longer essential in its strategic arsenal: it now began to lay the basis for a strategy that would take more heed of the parties it hoped to "woo" into the grand coalition it envisaged—parties which were already resentful of having to dance to the tune of the ANC/NP duet.

When CODESA II appeared on course, it reignited hopes of an end to the reigning chaos although its path too was topsy-turvy with many side dramas. A platoon of heavily armed Afrikaner Weerstandsbeweging (AWB) paramilitary commando, who through sheer desperation stormed the World Trade Center to deliver a short message 'we will stop these talks by any means necessary', occasioned an episode that would remain graphically etched in the nation's memory. Smashed their *Ratel* armoured vehicles through the reception hall of the negotiating chambers with precision of a sharpshooter; they disrupted the negotiation process only just. Incidentally, the negotiators had taken a recess and chambers were empty on that day, except for the cleaning and odd administrative staff attending to paperwork. The mediation process led by Eminent Persons Group between ANC and IFP came to naught. Further afield members of AZAPO so-called *Amazimzim,* killed in large numbers by members of ANC so-called *Amavarara.* A sister killed by a brother on suspicions of being a police informant and neighbours forced to drink cooking oil and washing powder for failing to support a consumer boycott here, or calls for random stay-away over there. Fathers sjamboked in full view of neighbours by 18-year-old children called *izikhonkwane* or *amaqabane,* depending on which part of the country, they were at that time. Friends would kill friends for supporting a 'reactionary force' (at that time township youths were instructed that the only black political organisation that had a license to operate was the ANC—all other black formations in the townships had to be silenced by all means necessary we suspect that is how the phenomenon of black on black violence fomented).

At low tide, news broke out that Oliver 'OR' Tambo, the acclaimed public face of exiled ANC had died, but the uplifting good news was far better—the Oslo Nobel Peace Committee honoured FW De Klerk and Nelson Mandela jointly with the Nobel Peace Prize for their efforts to bring about a negotiated political settlement in South Africa. Still, sentiments were at a boil bloodletting and mayhem continued unabated bombs thrown from both sides of the political divide. The SANDF army, *AWB, Apla, UmKhonto weSizwe,* SDU's *and Amabutho,* turned South African streets into a bloodbath reminiscent of the battle of Isandlwane. Worshipers murdered in temple sanctuary, nightclub revelers were not spurred death in Cape Town, Shell House massacre of IFP's *amabutho* by the *MK.* In a twist of irony, Bophuthatswana police lynched the *AWB Commandos* whom they sought to defend ostensibly against the ANC final onslaught. Meanwhile, across the length and breadth of the land the otherwise low-key civil war in the townships had reached a frightening new crescendo exerting maximum trauma on black people.

As the blood bath and wanton destruction worsened, the country dithered on the brink of full-scale civil war, the anger of the black youth in the townships was reaching boiling point the panic among whites was palpable; media fed on the frenzy and despair abounded. Thousands of those who survived the killing mayhem, tormented by their wounds, by hunger, searching for solace and comfort among the ruins of their homes, the church auditoriums, disued schools and even open veld which wanton destruction was the heritage of the titanic battle for political upper-hand in the townships. Biko's adage 'black man you are on your own' became as real at this time for most of us who were up to that point ambivalent about whether or not to join the liberation war, the luxury of fence-sitting was literally taken away. We found ourselves placed between the proverbial devil and the deep blue sea and became reluctant participants in the theater of war. At this time the country was truly ungovernable, anarchy reigned supreme, lawlessness and brutalisation of black people by De Klerk's war machines continued on the one hand and on the other the terrorising of black communities by the ANC self-defense units were intense, so much so that words cannot even begin to describe the pain we experienced. The Press simply headlined 'South Africa on fire'. The mayhem threatened to put an immediate end to the dream of a negotiated settlement stitched together in CODESA at the time. When South Africa had been on a knife edge after the assassination of Chris Hani, Mandela had been all that stood between it and mayhem. Mandela's fortitude and steely resolve of single-mindedness held a country on the boil firmly together. Truly, courage is not the absence of fear but rather the judgement of something else more important than fear.

Setbacks notwithstanding, negotiations culminated in the Record of Understanding that paved the way for a constitutional assembly and a five year Government of National Unity (GNU). At that point, the nation sighed a collective relief and many of us fell on our knees with gratitude to *Jehovah Nissi* the Lord our banner. That many were saved to live another day to tell the story to our children is in itself worth remembrance. To describe this short yet intense period of the South African political history, as a traumatic moment is to be sanguine, the memory is as vivid as it is palpable. For those of us who were in the trenches then we reminisce about the experiences of suffering at the hands of our oppressors, deep in our soul somehow we knew it was conceivable that blacks could one day forgive whites for the mistreatment and hate we had respectively for one another even as the nation experienced great trauma.

Seeking the healing of wounds inflicted by other blacks upon blacks would remain the most difficult of all experiences of that time. Is it any wonder to see many black adult folks still carrying emotional and psychological scars of yesteryear? Somehow, in the noon of this despair, the negotiation process was moving along swiftly—probably because the negotiators felt that they were overtaken by events on the ground and sensed an impending total loss of control. Driven by this urgency of the moment it was becoming all too apparent that the day was approaching when the politicians would wake up one morning and find no one left in the country over whom to govern. Hastily in the last ditch, effort to avert the collapse of the negotiations, 27 April 1994 was proclaimed as the date on which the one-man one-vote election would happen. This is the first ballot paper all South Africans black and white used to cast their first vote for a democratic dispensation.

The main point of settlement was lauded internationally for three reasons. The first, it was led by mandated leaders; at least this was true from the side of the white community (a year prior to the commencement of CODESA 1, two-thirds of the white population voted in favour in a referendum for new constitutional negotiations, effectively agreeing to surrender their political power to black majority). Second, it had a semblance of transparency to it (television cameras gave us snippets of what was going on inside the closed chambers and occasionally airing gibberish sound-bytes of grimace politicians, press reported regularly on the procedural matters but skipped the more substantive the juicy bits leading to finite text of the agreement hashed at remote bush lodges *bosberade*, we can never be sure). Despite its inherent weaknesses our process, unlike the 1980 Lancaster House Agreement of Zimbabwe was a home brewed model for which we remain immensely proud.

Broadly described, whites traded their racial state for assurances that political institutions would allow the disenfranchised majority to elect black leaders. Strictly speaking, the transition from apartheid to democracy occurred by way of a deal, not as a result of one protagonist defeated in war by another. The truth is that there were no victors in this sordid saga. Similarly, the post CODESA agreement whereby the-winner-takes-all system was equally premature for a society that has just emerged from a brutal and bloody conflict that decimated half the generation. History teaches that winners often gain access to state power and dispense patronage for supporters willy-nilly in order to ensure for themselves the continued stay in power. Losers are never accommodated—instead they are constantly humiliated in the long run eliminated. De Klerk and the surviving NP elites as well as the Pan Africanist Congress of Azania and Inkatha Yenkululeko Yesizwe (IFP) and the whole bunch of homeland politicians experienced this reality firsthand.

One of the regrettable features of the outcomes of the negotiations was a little known development called the *Pretoria Minute.* The Pretoria Minute contained among other things a secret agreement between the ANC and the NP in terms of which the apartheid principal architects were offered permanent immunity from future prosecution either in South Africa or at the International Court Tribunal for crimes against humanity, neatly circumventing several UN resolutions that declared apartheid a 'human rights crime.' This offer was in exchange for suspension of the otherwise ineffectual fantasy armed struggle by the MK.

The Pretoria Minute offered cover to people who were responsible for creating conditions of sufferings for millions of South Africans thus compromising the essence of the settlement outcome as well as the nation building efforts that would ensue. Principally, this private agreement served to undermine the sacrifices of black people who died for the freedom of South Africa. It is noteworthy that black people are a forgiving lot, baying for the blood of PW Botha and his ilk would have been out of kilter with the spirit of magnanimity of a black person. The TRC was not conceived as the Nuremburg type platform where the victors would seek retributive justice against the losers, rather, it was intended to be a forum for people to seek and receive forgiveness from one another and rebuild the ruins of their country both in the spiritual and political sense.

From the reconciliation standpoint the nation would have benefited enormously as this would have progressed a long way healing the rift between black and white. All there ever was to it was for the leaders of white apartheid to come forward and to explain to the commission why they fomented the hate that the Afrikaner community had for black people and the human suffering they subjected black people for as long as they did. The telling of their story would have made blacks to weep at first, but the tears would eventually dry and then the understanding of the psychology of their tormentors would emerge thus placing black people in a position where such abuse of one cultural group by another would never repeat itself.

Tragically, the nation missed an incredible opportunity to heal itself—instead a Band-Aid was placed over gaping wounds the wounds that would fester even as we look back two decades later. The Boeremag treason trial two years after the new democracy would underscore the reality of this folly. We can't say with certainty that this was a political suicide on the part of the protagonists, but political analysts have invariably interpreted this outcome as a reward for FW De Klerk for initiating political change and a self-congratulatory gesture by the ANC for the opportunity on its part to negotiate an end to the apartheid system. Whichever was the case it matters none because the people who bore the full brunt of oppression and the atrocities that accompanied it interpreted this agreement between political elites protecting one another as a travesty of justice and history will judge it as such.

A decisive moment, a historic turning point for the present-day democracy is firmly anchored on the 27 April 1994. Inspired leadership of Mandela pulled the country back from implosion at a critical moment in history. On this date a one-person one-vote was finally exercised and the African National Congress received an overwhelming support from the electorate, just few votes shy of the two-thirds threshold the constitution guaranteed any party to change the constitution by itself. On 9 May the ANC members proudly took their seats for the first time in the people's assembly and the following day Nelson Rholihlahla, the revolutionary godfather, was sworn in the first President of the people of the Republic of South Africa to the pomp and palaver attendant with royalty and glitz. Making his inaugural speech on the 10th April 1994, he gave the following prophetic message: 'We enter into a covenant that we shall build a society in which all South Africans will be able to walk tall. Without any fear in their hearts, assured of their inalienable right to human dignity, a rainbow nation in peace with itself and the world . . . Never, never, and never again shall it be that this beautiful land will again experience the oppression of one by another . . . the sun shall never set on so glorious as human achievement. Let freedom reign.' These words would form the benchmark of our analysis as we put the story of the South African people together.

We ask, could South Africa—with its history of racial intolerance—really buck the global trend and become a truly nonracial, multiparty democracy? Is democracy not something that exists in only a handful of developed countries with a high degree of homogeneity and high social balance? Could the change brought about not by a Damascus Road experience but by ordinary, fallible human beings who ultimately recognised that they had been cast together by forces of history that could not be undone, and recognised too that in the final analysis they were dependent on one another to a degree where they could either live or perish together? Could it be that this change they brought along would hold for as long as it did up to this point two decades later? The impasse rested on the need to modernize the processes of capital accumulation, It also rested on the apartheid's inability to manage vast expansive forms of restructuring that were required, and on the other hand the liberation block was unable to force the capitulation of the apartheid regime.

In South Africa, blacks and whites did not trust each other. Their emotions were far more raw. Whites despised blacks, and blacks hated the white imposed system that oppressed them and feared the white-man's power over their lives. But raw and obscene prejudices, being so obvious, have certain integrity, and can be dealt with, once they are acknowledged. Outright hatred lends itself to an antidote; lingering dislike does not. Nevertheless, a history marked by brutally enforced inequalities appeared to have been erupted, enabling the black majority to pass through portals beyond which lay equality, dignity and freedom. A progressive path appeared to have been cleared. Along it, the devastation wrought under apartheid could be redressed.

The South African story is far from being a finished story, however, our assessment is that the story was not extraordinarily different in the geopolitical setting except that its special circumstances was made more so by the fact that it was not an international public relations hoo ha, but a uniquely home-brewed initiative (this partly explains why the world regarded it as a rainbow miracle because they found it hard to imagine how). Not only was it achieved without the apocalyptic conflagration many had feared, but also it seemed to spur a newfound sense of common purposes in a society that had become synonymous with terminal divisions. Little wonder then the bemused admiration of the world was matched by a sense of triumphant pride and hope among the majority of South Africans.

The period ended in the year 2002 was a dramatic epoch characterised by major global events. Several of these events were of historical significance that had transformed the global political landscape to a point of no return. Reagan, then the USA president, once told Gorbachev of the USSR that, 'If you seek peace, if you seek prosperity of the Soviet Union and Eastern Europe, if you seek liberalization, Come here to this gate! Mr. Gobarchev, tear down this wall!' . . . And with those few words was the end of the cold war, as we knew it then. The cold war that had gripped the East and Western Super Powers for decades on end ended without a single intercontinental ballistic missile fired. Shortly thereafter, stalked by a *coupe de tart* the Soviet Socialist People's Republic imploded and disintegrated into smithereens, followed by the horrors of the Balkans civil wars and the indescribable Rwandan genocide. The fall of the Berlin Wall in East Germany, Europe that was in a state of menopause reinvented itself as a unified region. China, a hydra, isolated by tradition bound rulers that had lived in a pre modern era was quietly transforming into a giant monolith superpower. The 'Two States' dream of Israel and Palestine was finally buried in the Dead Sea caves and Israel ultimately poisoned Chairman Arafat and snuffed his life. Then the unthinkable happened, shattering the USA invincibility with the 2002 September 11th deadly attack in of America's pride the New York City and its heart the defense head quarters at the Pentagon, a calculated response to the ongoing Zionist oppression of the people of Palestine. From these dramatic events, the world had irrevocably changed never be the same again and dare we say South Africa would never be the same too.

This breeze down memory lane is a prelude to the discourse as we cast our eyes retrospectively and forward into the imagined future. We should like to turn attention to surveying the African National Congress and how it deployed its trusted senior cadres to run the affairs of the nation in government. We take a helicopter view of policy and implementation of programmes beginning with the Durban conference of 1991 up to including the 2012 Mangaung conference. This overview lacks depth and specificity for a simple reason that a fair number of books have been written in regard to the matters that needed detailed discussion of South Africa's developments. Ours is to shine the spotlight on the actors who shaped the new epoch of the South African politics.

CHAPTER 2

The Reconfiguration of The Political Landscape

It is the dramatic story of how a handful of rookie politicians came out of the bush to take over the running of a complex and deeply troubled country that they thought was richly endowed but in fact was almost bankrupt. Of how they struggled to come to terms with an often hostile bureaucracy; and how above all they found themselves struggling not only with the complexities of their own society but also with the bewildering and often destabilizing forces of the new globalized economy.

The African National Congress

The African National Congress is a century old organisation boasting membership of over a million. The period 1994 to 2014 marks two decades of the party in power running the country. It has a colourful history and tradition; based on this longevity there is a sense that it is fair to infer a number of things about the organisation's veritable rich history. The first being that over this period of time it has accumulated considerable wealth of experience, depth of insights and wisdom refined in the crucible. The ANC leadership in partnership with 51.7 million South Africans was capable of setting a new benchmark in transforming a good country into a democracy that would be admired by the world. ANC is the choice party for a significant score of people for twenty solid years running and a darling of the international community. Furthermore, at the commencement of this democracy journey the ANC was in a better position to govern the country well because South Africa is the last colony to assert its independence from foreign rule. Within these perspectives, we can already extrapolate that the party has gleaned insights and lessons from the frontline states that achieved independence ahead of South Africa. This conjecture is justified in view of the presenting historical precedent and therefore, it is a valid postulate because South Africa emerged from the crucible unscathed by the devastation normally brought on by ravages of civil war.

Given all this, our democratic project ought to have been a classic textbook success story enamored by such things as empathetic government, ethos of excellence in leadership, efficient administration, flourishing economy making South Africa a powerhouse leader of the continent yes, even as a frontline citadel for modernity. At this point, a lot of good emerged from the ANC making the future to look brighter for all including the doomsday skeptics. ANC the flag bearer of the fight against apartheid enjoyed the support of virtually the entire world. The existence of the ANC in our political landscape has helped our young democracy to become vibrant. These are reasons why so many believed in the good of the ANC and placed their total faith in its capability. After two decades in power, the ANC has failed and has left the people of South Africa unquestionably disappointed. Why? How hopelessly wrong can the party be to hemorrhage so profusely in less than two decades? With the benefit of hindsight, it is possible to answer this question in way that is more accurate, truthful and definitively. In addition, there exists sufficient body of evidence and data to support of observation without the need to be defensive or offensive and playing to the gallery. We will highlight some of the more obvious reasons and try to explain why we think the way we do.

Firstly, the party has changed substantially from what it represented 58 years ago. On 26 June 1955, 3 000 South Africans gathered in a dusty square in Kliptown Soweto. Members of the ANC congregated alongside their anti-apartheid confederates to proclaim a new vision of the future. The dream had already been declared. 'The people shall govern.' South Africa would belong to all of its people, no matter what their skin colour. There would be work, education and security for all. Everyone would be equal before the law. It was an extraordinary affirmation, full of hope for the future. Today the Kliptown square has been renamed Walter Sisulu Square. It boasts shops, offices, a conference hall and a pricey hotel. As the birthplace of the new, inclusive South Africa, it has become a stop on the tourist trail. But just across the railway track, rickety shacks huddle together. The roads are rutted and muddy. Communal toilets stand useless, their doors open and rubbish piled inside. Next to them on the uneven ground wobbles a portable toilet, its door padlocked against vandals. A sludgy stream trickles past, fouled by children unable to find the key in time. Walter Sisulu Square still exists, but the aspirations espoused by the founding fathers in the Freedom Charter are dead and buried.

The ANC dominates the political landscape, thanks to the alliances it built during the 1980s and thereafter. It involved organised workers, women's organisations, peasants, the youth and faith bodies. ANC influence was also evident among liberal communities. Since coming into office, it has also drawn conservative constituents, including traditionalists and the flotsam of the National Party into its orbit. It is a given that the ANC entered negotiations with the aim of attaining an objective of a non-racial, non-sexist South Africa. These principles were elaborated in what became known as the OAU Harare Declaration, with the understanding that negotiations were not about a compromise between democracy and apartheid, but about the process towards attaining universally accepted principles of human rights. Under the guise of so-called minority rights, federalism and orderly transition, it pursued an outcome in which whites would have the right of veto over both the content and the process of change. This is magnanimous by any stretch of imagination.

Writing on its 2004 newsletter publication The ANC said, 'Negotiations were therefore as much a platform to find a resolution to the conflict, as a terrain of struggle to shift the balance of forces. Negotiations however entailed compromises on the path to be followed to the final objective; the prevailing balance of forces influenced this. In the first instance, at the beginning of negotiations, neither the liberation movement nor the forces of apartheid had emerged as an outright victor. On the one hand, the liberation movement enjoyed the support of a vast majority of people, ready to sacrifice anything for the attainment of freedom.' While its mass base was somewhat divided, many of its supporters and particularly the direct beneficiaries of apartheid still had the capacity to resist to change and internationally, there were powerful elements prepared, at least secretly, to assist the regime in insurrectionary take-over.

Second, perennial divisions whose origin is greed, corruption, a deadly combination of predatory instincts and intellectual vacuity that has given rise to the loss of original vision of its founding fathers paralyses the ANC of today. The problems of division in the ANC did not start when Mbeki insisted on a third term as the president of the ANC but dates back to the 1940s when a split led to the formation of Sobukwe's Pan-Africanist Congress. With the subsequent banning of black resistance movements in the 1960s, ANC divisions simply made less headline news and receded but never ceased. Initially, the ANC expelled the president of the youth league and three others and subsequently disbanded the entire national executive committee, the provincial executive structures and subsequently dissolved all that was left of youth structures on the pretext that the youth league were sowing divisions in the ANC thus brought ANC into disrepute. Truth is the older folks grew progressively intolerant and wary of the ANCYL's criticism of its poor leadership rather than the behaviour displayed by the youth's *per se*. The present day culture of the party is contra-indicated to its political objectives and at times this appear plainly at odds. The chances of successfully achieving the desired transformation of the government to be an effective instrument of democracy is not even remotely close—much less the chances of transforming the society to modernity. Evidence points contrary to the fact that the negotiated settlement was ever a terrain of the struggle to shift balance of forces in favour of blacks, because the majority of black people in South Africa's post-apartheid era are worse off, with the exception of those who are in high level government jobs current and past.

The spectacle of chaos ahead of the 2012 Mangaung conference was nothing new the nation hadn't seen in 2007 or before, except that it was the scale of brutality that shocked many as well as the extent to which the courts became final arbiters of the bitter divisions rather than the NEC of the ANC. In the run-up to the 2012 conference, murders of ANC members rose to 26 mainly as a result of factional clashes. These murders were tactics used by one faction to silence the other and courts were actively relied upon to change the outcomes of their wrangling the PEC of both Free State and North West provinces were nullified as a consequence of court decisions. It was unfortunate that the ANC chose to clothe the language of change in the post-apartheid era with antiquated clichés such as 'national democratic revolution'.

'Because we carry a revolutionary obligation to provide political leadership to the whole society, particularly the working class.' Fascism emerges only in times of crisis. It is a form of socialism that is wrap up in hyper nationalism and organized through a political authoritarianism under a demagogue. It is able to exploit economic and social crises to offer a feeling of belonging and an illusory path to respect. The problem of dealing with fascism in the democratic context is that fascist are happy to use elections to come to power, they have nothing but contempt for democracy, and once in power they will never cede it to the popular will. Our synthesis is that apartheid made revolution into the precondition of reform; democracy on the other hand has advanced reform as an alternative to freedom. We ask what is revolutionary about the ANC and what they stand for? There was nothing revolutionary during the negotiations and certainly none at this time. We ask again, is there anything ordinary people of South Africans can do other than accept the outcome of the negotiated settlement? This staid rhetoric is out of kilter with the patterns of a modernising society. It is this kind of cliché that is not helpful.

Third, ANC is immature as a party in government; it remains extremely sensitive to criticisms from people who wants to make it strong. It continues to characterise all opposition to its programmes as acts of counter-revolution and unpatriotic in character. The Gauteng's eToll saga is a classic case study. Through its predatory posture not only has it significantly dimmed the lights of democracy but has served to constrict its rhythms and altered the granularity of its texture. In pure democratic speak an opposition to the ANC is not an opposition to the constitution *per se* which is the supreme law of the land and dissenting voices that seek to modify ANC programmes are legitimate voices of dissention and a very necessary contradiction in the transformative process of birthing a new order.

For all intents and purposes such dissenting voices should be treated as legitimate expressions that form part of our inalienable right to constitutional maturation as a society, to label these voices as counter revolutionary serves only to underscore ANC's own insecurities and a disturbing level of immaturity as a leader of the nation. It was ANC president Dr A. B. Xuma in 1955 who warned, 'ANC seems to fear . . . criticisms constructive and otherwise from its following and others. People who voice their reasonable and considered views on Congress policy and/or no policy . . . are referred to as sellers-out or agents or friends of the government instead of being shown where they are wrong . . . Many who dare to criticise the hierarchy have been expelled.'

Sadly, we know the political graves of many who dared to criticized the party the likes of Bantu Holomisa, Andrew Feinstein and many others are strewn all over the land due to this injurious psychosis. Jean-Jacques Rousseau made the point, 'that strongest is never strong enough to master forever unless he transforms his force into right and obedience into duty.' In our view, there has been a singular lack of open-mindedness about new perspectives that has translated in an intransigent government, which sometime opposes the people who brought it to power in the first place. As soon as Mandela the ANC's moral compass left center stage the party began to descent on a slippery slope. Mandela's administration was inclusive and represented the full spectrum of the country's demographics. In it, was a semblance of excellence and exemplary leadership. Broad shades of civil society activists and people in private sector came forward to voluntarily offer their expertise to his administration without expecting pay or accolades because people generally perceived Mandela to be well meaning and working for the good of the nation rather than pandering to the whims of the ANC big wigs. The occupation of positions of power by individuals deployed in his administration never created the social distance between those individuals and the people they represented.

Fourth, the concept of cadre deployment is pre-modern. The majority of people ANC deployed in government after the Mandela administration were for better part professionally incompetent, possessed neither the requisite knowledge nor proper work ethic commensurate with civil servants ethos. The deployed persons interpreted their deployment in government to mean payback time for serving in the struggle a mindset that would backfire later on as service delivery gaps became obvious. In the main, the air of arrogance with which cadres carried themselves gave rise to the mistaken belief that they were financially catching up on what they lost during the struggle days as well as rebuilding their career credentials.

At first when the ANC ascended to political power, it saw proper to promote only itself and its loyal card-carrying members—a fatal mistake in the bigger scheme of things. In progressive politics, democratic parties all over the world accept that the nature of the 21st century societies they govern is one characterized by crosscutting loyalties, influences and persuasions that are a fact of life, all brought more or less into balance by good laws, active civil society publics and responsive leadership and it is something that cannot be avoided. The ANC deployment policy continues to be a plan designed to advance naked personal self-enrichment at the express disadvantage of the people who voted the party into power and the compromise of quality in the process. It is a clear path to demodernisation of our society.

The practice of deploying cadres into strategic institutions needed a party leadership that knew its limits, and a government that knew the source of its legitimacy and authority, of which neither is present. It was because of this cadre deployment conundrum that the competition for the leadership of the ANC and by proxy leadership of South Africa, degenerated into a circus illuminated only occasionally by farce while the rest of the nation watched with utter contempt. The fact that appointment to public office was the quickest route to self-betterment continues to be a thorny issue for ordinary South Africans and this is especially pronounced at Ward Councilor level leading the 2014 general election year. A danger always lurks where cadre elements pursued enrichment from the vantage point of political office, the cadres who saw these opportunities as license for self-aggrandizement rendered themselves progressively lethargic to the conditions of the poor people from whence they came. This arrogance of power, bureaucratic indifference and corruption rose sharply to a point where this is no longer just an internal matter of the ANC but affects the society as a whole because it is the nation's trust that is being trampled. It is clear to many that under these circumstances, the constitutional assurances are hollow words of no effect to those left outside of the predator collusion circle.

Fifth, whites in South Africa take for granted that the ANC is an African party, an assessment that discounts its westernizing proclivities. ANC is upholding capitalism and instituting neoliberal economic policies and has elevated English into the language of prominence yet, the fulcrum of its politics swings on race. Democracies operate through consent and consent produces legitimating. Democracies, being considered to be self-legitimating rarely needs legitimating. But buried beneath the democratic syllogism is unstated premise, that is if the state is justified because the people chose it, something must account for whose consent produces the legitimacy; for what makes the choice of some relevant and the choice of others not relevant? This is where the seeds of the failure of the ANC germinated. For instance, the ANC disregarded the continued reproduction of the legacy of despotism in the rural areas through the traditional authorities, which still treat people in the countryside as subjects of their chiefs. It failed to acknowledge that the old state power structures and functions, which reproduce the very colonial economic relations it rhetorically seeks to change, are in fact still intact.

Sixth, dysfunctional constituent components back in 2007, when Zuma dramatically ousted Mbeki, Malema the young rabble-rouser had proclaimed himself 'ready to kill for Zuma' and no one thought it prudent to discipline him for this kind of inflammatory brinkmanship. Instead, he was hailed as a kingmaker and a good leader, boosting an already substantial ego. As long as the youth leader restricted himself to rants against 'imperialist' whites and calls to nationalise mines and expropriate farms, he was a cool dude. The ANC Youth League once a formidable force that Malema and his playmates always claimed the mantle of its founders Lembede, Mandela and Tambo as the inspiration of their new fight for economic freedom, no sooner had they taken leadership of this important liberation organ had they single handedly trashed what their elders had woven over 69 years. Between the ANCYL Mangaung conference of 2008 and the ANC conference in 2012, the league would degenerate so much that in this period of time it literary turned into a kindergarten playroom (the reader would remember the fist fighting, 'drop pants and kiss my ass' spectacles, and the world youth congress 'kissing bash'). When the Sunday school circus finally came to an end, all that was left of it was an empty shell littered with broken toys and R21million mountain of debt. The final nail to the coffin was made by the Gauteng South High Court placing the League on provisional liquidation for its failure to pay money it owed others. Subsequently, Gwede Mantashe's sad task was to mop out the remains on the floor and reconfigure it anew might be this time they would think long and hard before a crowd sourcing strategy is implemented.

Lastly, ANC has never transformed itself to function like a modern party in a changed sociopolitical milieu. The party has failed to grasp the essential dilemma of post-apartheid South Africa, largely because White and Indian intellectuals, who are disproportionally influential in policy making as expert advisors to the government, are hundred times worse off in their familiarity with patterns of African civilisation. Their perspectives brought serious distortions and errors into policy formulation in all the spheres of government including education. The party continues to talk glibly about organisational renewal. Organisational renewal demands a re-examination of the basic assumptions, beliefs and behaviours that serve as antecedents of the organizational culture. Old thinking characterising the liberation milieu cannot support the new paradigms emerging from a new society. The ability to respond effectively to paradigm shifts, such as the shift from apartheid colonialism to an open shared society, depended greatly on the capacity of the ANC to learn afresh. Learning is characterised by the willingness of the leadership to question what has worked and what may not be working in the new environment a skill to develop new alternatives within the context of a changed sociopolitical landscape. There were three levels of learning the ANC leadership should have integrated in their new repertoire of skills in order to grasp these alternatives, namely methods fix, systems fix and behaviour fix. The resultant learning could have produced two corrective actions, the first being existing beliefs about a change could be revamped and second, this would have caused new values and new assumptions on the part of leaders emerging thus the ability to lead differently in transformation-type circumstances.

When new assumptions are made, it alters categories of unconscious thoughts, unquestioned biases and unchallenged frameworks of understanding that relates to presenting social dynamics of society. The party's collective beliefs, behaviours and assumptions inevitably affect the daily behaviours of its government officials on two levels. First, at the overt level represented by observable and direct actions and, at the covert level characterised by hidden motives. It is the absence of the latter that has immensely affected the ANC body polity to the extent that it has altered the core of its soul. In the wake of its failure to transform itself, the government or the society, the party leaders turned to their favourite past time demonising white people for everything that is going wrong in South Africa today, calling them contrarians, agents of Western imperialist and counter revolutionaries. The dominant cultural traits that make up liberation movements to succeed in liberation wars are often the very factors that contribute to their failure as governing parties. For example, open debates versus towing the party line at all costs, tolerance to differences of the various strains within the party versus the unity of the party, respect for the fundamental rule of law versus the protection of comrades and so on remain the dominant norm well into the postmodern era. The transference of this culture into democratic space creates problems of the relationships between party political actors and their external environment of the citizens.

The political settlement of the 1990s was a pact in which the oppressor and the oppressed found a compromise to prevent a scorched earth. The outcome of the multiparty negotiation process delivered a package of democracy of sorts, but not FREEDOM, which is what people have always wanted to assert for themselves. Negotiation leaders settled for terms that were suboptimal only later to fan the embers of anger in their supporters to ensure retention of loyalty to their respective organisations and so justify their continued existence in office. If political change did not deliver social and economic freedom for the masses of people, this raises the question: was democracy the reason so many sacrificed their lives in the cause of South Africa's liberation struggle?

We argue that freedom was the principal reason we went to war and many sacrificed their lives for; in any case, the political democracy would have been the natural outcome of this freedom. The liberation struggle in South Africa was never a struggle against apartheid, but a struggle for true freedom aimed at bringing forth total emancipation of human soul from all kinds of shackles including political, economic, social and psychological afflictions freeing black people to chart their own destiny. Freedom is yet to be realized by the masses of the people. ANC would like many to believe that it won South Africans their freedom at the negotiation table in 1994 after it prosecuted a successful armed struggle; of course, this is plain nonsense. ANC was dealt a bad hand and it has played that hand badly, all we are witnessing at this time is a desperate act of historical revisionism.

The task given to the ANC government by the electorate in four successive elections was to eliminate the basic causes of the national grievance wherever and in whatever form they had manifested themselves, and to work towards substantially removing the multitude of contradictions in communities in the interest of forestalling a shared open society. What is evidently clear now is that rather than deep social transformation, South Africa has undergone an elite transition. Elite transition is evidenced by a lot of talk about the expletives of democracy rather than the substance of freedom. White people want to become part of this nation and are ready to make an honest contribution under conditions that are favourable, are acknowledged as compatriots rather than treated as hostile outsiders. They too are tired of being demonized for the ills created by a black government.

Nation building as articulated through national reconciliation and national unity and social cohesion has become the first casualties in this democratic project. When the ANC failed to change the basic structure of social relations in the society it failed to lead the nation to modernity and that is the bane the ANC must shoulder collectively. The analysis of South African society where race and class interact is complex. It is our belief that there never were many races only one human race. The non-racialism myth peddled by the ANC has been tested and found wanting. The national question that remains to be resolved, is that the poor masses must secure self-determination that would bring bout real freedom from the oppression of the poor by the rich elite class, while liberating the former oppressors from their fearsome domination and guilt. We now shift attention to look at the three administrations the ANC charged with leading the government.

The Mandela Years

Sparks, the author of *Beyond The Miracle* wrote, 'It is the story of singular triumphs and some distressing failures. For this is a country not only of white and black, but one where the impoverished meet the rich every day, where Christians and Jews and Muslims and Hindus, sophisticated urbanites and tribal traditionalists, must all surmount their historical conflicts and summon the will to find a common national identity. The white minority government had used its exclusive access to political and economic power to promote the whites' narrow interests at the express disadvantage of the Africans. Gender discrimination had excluded women and exploited them to a point equivalent to slavery. The extreme levels of poverty and diseases, the urban ghettos, lack of waterborne sewage, absence of tarred roads, no access to electricity or recreational amenities, decent homes, low wage jobs, a health system that neglected the wellbeing of Africans, the social maginalisation of the communities of South Africa by whites is the history we emerge from.'

Although Mandela spent 27 years incarcerated, he was hardly out of national and international limelight. There was the Release Mandela Campaign and the Anti Apartheid Movement linked permanently to his name just to keep top of the mind presence. And so, when he reentered the political space, it was brinkmanship with regal authority. His public stage command was equal to if not exceeding that of the Hollywood A-list celebrity saints. Mandela was faced with the task of immediately forming a transitional Government of National Unity and a caretaker cabinet made up of former enemies. This GNU coalition comprised of those who ran the apartheid government, Bantustan leaders, former prisoners and freedom fighters. At the time of assuming office, Mandela was already 75 years old and he made clear that his was a single-term office with no ambitions to stay on beyond this time. Even though he was president, his role in government was more of elderly statesman supervising the affairs of cabinet. More than anything else, his role was not to play politics but to become a unifying statesman that rearranged the political stage and nudged the players into get accustomed to the new configuration.

FW De Klerk and Thabo Mbeki became Mandela's first deputies respectively. Somewhat surprisingly, camaraderie characterised the early cabinet meetings while all sides were trying to settle down, with the Nationalist Party expressing an earnest desire to cooperate. The GNU was not expected nor did it deliver anything of substance in the 5-year term it was allowed to function, other than keep the former enemies in one room talking together for as long as it was necessary to cool the outside temperature in other words, the emotions of the people sufficiently. Mbeki had to increasingly shoulder the responsibility of daily management during the transitional phase. In the years following his election into office, Mandela gradually withdrew from national duties and devoted his energy on international affairs where his iconic status was well regarded.

Although Mandela's administration failed to keep both the IFP and NP inside the GNU to the end of the legal mandate term, one of its achievements was the establishment of the Truth and Reconciliation Commission (TRC) that was the basis on which national dialogue for nation building could be forged—intended, as it was, to build a new society without retribution. In 1996, the TRC was established to lay bare some of the wounds of the past. The commission chaired by His Grace The Most Reverend Desmond Tutu took two years to start and finish its work. The TRC brief was to look into human rights atrocities committed during the apartheid era with the premise that any individual was eligible for amnesty if they were prepared to come forward fully disclose their crimes and bare it all, then they would receive full absolution. To do its work the TRC ran round-robin public hearings around the country and listened to rather well choreographed confessions by the apartheid soldiers. Between 1998 and 2001, public hearings were held in many small towns and townships of South Africa. While many stories were told, the real stories have yet to surface. A mere 1 146 individuals were given general amnesty from future prosecutions out of possible 71 000 people who sought indemnity. Victims of abuse were promised reparation under the TRC Act but due to filibustering by politicians with a direct interest in the TRC ritual, this delayed the final compensation and in the end black people were neither offered an apology by the offending whites nor offered compensation for their loss by the black government and hence double jeopardy presented.

This meant that abusers, many of those involved in other wrongdoing have remained unrepentant and have walked away without absolution. Our hearts are warmed when we read stories of men and women who from the depths of their hearts rather than legal obligation, went out of their way and sought absolution from those they wronged. On the giving side was Adrian Vlok, former Minister of Police, who washed Pastor Frank Chikane's feet as a gesture of penitence. On the receiving side were two Apla fighters who received forgiveness from the parents of Emmy Biel the exchange student they murdered. There were thousand more that reached out to black folks who were not headlines material but made an indelible mark in our hearts all the same, they will received their just reward from our Father in heaven grace and peace be upon them. In the final analysis, the usefulness of the TRC was merely that it provided an avenue to reopen wounds of hurt and loss for the victims without providing the much-needed catharsis to heal those wounds that resulted from the 57 years of brutal oppression and vestiges of English colonialism. Black people were left to deal with the residual effects on their own and many never could heal and so the scars of this trauma remain to date.

It is true that there were many residual issues that the negotiation process would not resolve, if they succeeded to surface them they failed to resolve them the fragility of the GNU is a case in point. Despite the polished public relations rhetoric on reconciliation and nation building by Mandela, it was a well-known 'secret' within the inner sanctum on both sides that there existed bad blood between Mandela and De Klerk; even with the best intention on earth that tenuous relationship could not be sustained and fall-out was inevitable. One day during a Cabinet session at the provocation by Mbeki, De Klerk lost his cool and snapped he later resigned and pulled the NP out of the GNU, effectively handing power to the ANC and remnants of other parties to govern the country on their own.

ANC conferences are highest decision-making forums, they instruct the incoming leadership to give effect to resolutions passed by conference and to create the necessary framework for government programmes. At the 1991 conference in Durban, the much-hyped slogan *Ready to Govern* became the ANC's mantra for the next five years. The preamble to the policy position stated fourfold objective:

- To strive for the achievement of the right of all South Africans, as a whole, to political and economic self-determination in a united South Africa;
- To overcome the legacy of inequality and injustice created by colonialism and apartheid, in a swift, progressive and principled way;
- To develop a sustainable economy and state infrastructure that will progressively improve the quality of life of all South Africans; and
- To encourage the flourishing of the feeling that South Africa belongs to all who live in it, to promote a common loyalty to and pride in the country and to create a universal sense of freedom and security within its borders.

These are not mutually exclusive goals. On the contrary, the future of our country depends on the harmonious and simultaneous realisation of all four. The advancement of the majority of people will, in the medium—and long-term, release hitherto untapped and suppressed talents and energies that will both boost and diversify the economy. Developing the economy will, in turn, provide the basis for overcoming the divisions of the past without creating new ones. Finally, the achievement of a genuine sense of national unity depends on all of us working together to overcome the inequalities created by apartheid. The beacons guiding these advances are equal rights, non-racialism, non-sexism, and democracy and mutual respect. A broad, inclusive approach, free of arrogance or complexes of superiority or inferiority, is fundamental. We have to develop a truly South African vision of our country, one that is not distorted by the prejudices and sectarianism that has guided viewpoints on race and gender in the past. We have to rely on the wisdom, life experiences, talents and know-how of all South Africans, women and men. There can be no 'apartheid' in finding solutions to the problems created by apartheid.

This document does not present a rigid ANC blueprint for the future of South Africa, to which our supporters will be expected to rally and our opponents required to submit. Rather, the document represents a set of basic guidelines to policies we intend to pursue. These ideas will be developed through discussion within the ANC, and through consultation with the broadest spectrum of South African public opinion. The policies will be adapted according to these processes and on the basis of experience. It is necessary to dwell on the problems, which will be faced by the first government, which is elected under a new democratic constitution.

This will help create an understanding of the magnitude of the tasks involved in transforming our country into one where everyone can enjoy a basic standard of living combined with peace and security. It will underline the fact that there are choices to be made and priorities to be established. Past minority governments and the current apartheid regime have pursued active political and social policies which, among other things, have led to: extreme levels of poverty and disease in the rural areas; the creation of urban ghettos where people have been denied even the most basic means of survival as a result of severely limited access to decent homes, electricity, water-borne sewerage, tarred roads, and recreational facilities; an education system preparing the majority of South Africans for lives of subordination and low wage jobs; a social security system geared almost entirely to fulfilling the needs of the white minority; a health system that has seriously neglected the well-being of most South Africans; the social and political marginalisation of the majority of people, the African community in particular, through their exclusion from public life and decision making as well as the denial of their culture.

These problems have led to rapidly increasing unemployment and a serious decline in living standards. Furthermore, they have deprived the black youth of opportunities to realise their talents. Our people remain divided. We do not know each other. We live apart, physically separated, spiritually alienated, frightened of getting too close, knowing that we have different life opportunities and different views of what change means. We are ruled by a multiplicity of fragmented departments, boards, councils and ministries. Apartheid has left us apart. It is critical, however, that we honestly face up to the extent of the problems confronting our country. The problems run deep and resources are limited. Accordingly, the policies proposed here represent our broad vision. These policies highlight our ultimate goals, which will need to be transformed into effective and realisable programmes in the short-term. In other words, we will need to establish priorities both within each of the different policy areas and between these broad areas. These priorities must be arrived at through democratic discussions and decision-making processes. Progress will also depend on involving as many sections of our society as possible.

What does readiness mean? Readiness in the broadest sense of the word presupposes the existence of a number of variables, including that the ANC was a cohesive organisation able to hold together disparate interests from within itself on the far right and the far left of the ideological spectrum—the liberation heroes from exile would drink from the same cup of the youthful leaders of the mass democratic movement heritage, the ability to bring the country to conditions of relative political stability and social cohesion, the ability to create a stable environment that would attract direct foreign investment, crafting social policies that were congruent with the expectations of freedom for the people of South Africa were also assumed as part of this readiness slogan. Readiness also suggested that the ANC would abandon both its small-mindedness to a big picture of South Africa, from myopic and antediluvian, to far-sighted and mould breaking—simultaneously embracing both opponents and adversaries. In a nutshell, political readiness meant the party had the capacity to bridge the chasm created by decades of separateness forced upon the nation by the white regime. That bridge would be in the form of ready to use skilled human capital, introduction of programmes with wider social appeal, working with the widest stakeholder community possible on the journey thus creating the desired impact for development to a country of our dreams.

The period 1994 to 2004 was a time when the ANC got to appreciate the magnitude of the problem its government had inherited from the nationalist party. It needed, in the first instance to figure out what would be the best way possible to craft appropriate policy instruments and knit together workable programmes to enable it to lay a firm ground to govern South Africa. It ought to have been clear that the ANC government was translating conference policy resolutions that were no more than rhetoric and wishful thinking, into a programme of action, for results to be measured on the ground. The government needed this time to create the necessary legal framework necessary for bedding down the infrastructure, to deploy fresh pairs of hands that were in alignment with the ANC's way thinking, taking into account that unhappy civil servants would vacate public service, needed to put in place adequate new systems to run the administration consistent with the new policies, a bigger fiscus to fund its ambitious programmes. On the face of it, this is what readiness is. Let us examine it closely. In the first 10 years the ANC government succeeded in many things, least of which was the scrapping of all old race laws, guaranteed freedom of press, abolished the death penalty, legalised abortion on demand, protected the rights of children and gay people, and advanced women in many spheres of life. The patchwork of sub national government structures developed under apartheid was consolidated into nine provincial governments, nine Metro Districts, and 683 Municipalities from 800.

Successes also included clean water to many rural communities, connecting electricity to more than 2 million people, integrated schools that previously were racially segregated and include almost all age cohort—thus granting free access to primary education. Furthermore, the ANC government also introduced free health care to millions of children, expanded access to electricity, water and sanitation, ended diplomatic isolation and rejoined the community of nations. It took on an influential role on the international stage and was later rewarded with a membership of the influential BRICKS economic community this marked a big diplomatic kudos for the government. In 1994 the government found itself crowded by 'bad neighbourhood' syndrome, particularly highlighted by political and economic state of Zimbabwe and the Sub-Saharan region that grew only at 2.4% real GDP.

The government took over a country that was political pariah, an economy that was in dire state due to the heavy load of sanctions. In terms of sovereign ratings, South Africa was on junk status credit ratings. The Net open forward position was minus $25billion. The government kick-started an economy that was on its death-bed and initially growing the economy by between 1.4 and 3.3 per cent a year between 1995 to 2006, restructured public finance and restored fiscal discipline—cutting budget deficit, reducing the national debt, bringing the inflation down from double digit 14.6% to within 6.3 per cent, reducing interest rates from 24 per cent to 14 per cent prime lending, lifting trade barriers, reducing a maze of tariffs and import duties, and instituted a somewhat effective tax collection system. Government borrowings as a % of GDP fell from 50% to 28%. Gross foreign reserves were sitting at $3billion and rose to $50billion. At one stage, Net Direct Foreign Investments exceeded $10 billion mark after accounting for outflows. South Africa's total equity market capitalization stood out at twice the GDP, the highest ratio of all BRICKS member countries. On the one hand, South Africa's performance was more correlated to China due to the commodities factor. Shortly after this, there was a steady rise of the African middle class with annual disposable income by some 40%.

Services delivered between 1994 and 2004

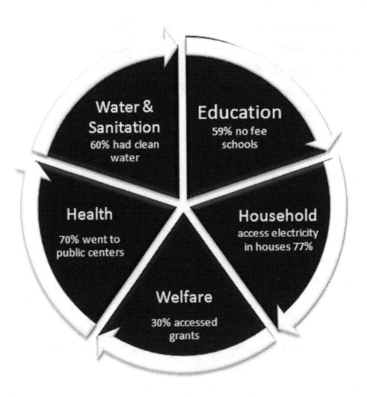

Source Social Barometer Journal 2005

Probably the greatest achievement by far was an end to the internecine violence between the ANC and IFP—a conflict that if it wasn't stopped, contained the seeds of counter-revolution—a real and immediate danger at the formative stage of a nascent democracy. Ethnic politics were largely eschewed. In place were several constitutional institutions such as the Constitutional Court, Chapter 9 institutions, namely, The Public Protector, Electoral Commission, Gender Commission, Human Rights Commission,

Competitions Commission, Consumer Protection Commission and the Auditor General's office. Many civic oriented forums were established to engage citizens so that they could hold politicians to public accountability, such as Community Policing Forums, School Governing Bodies, NEDLAC and Ward Committees to mention but some.

Programmes to transform social relations were also established and ran successfully for the first five years under Mandela's leadership, until bureaucrats under Mbeki administration subtly undermined them and in Zuma years, these programmes were effectively killed because much was at stake to hide the corrupt activities from the scrutiny of the civil society. In short, this was a 'golden period' of economic performance and a peace dividend for South Africa. Importantly, this impressive performance should have through the period transformed South Africa from and R80 billion to a staggering R1.3 trillion economy accompanied by prudent and fiscal policy. In total, there were 10 key economic areas that needed structural advances namely the macro fiscal and monetary balances, lower government debt cost, the overall cost of capital, improved corporate valuations, real asset returns, rising disposable incomes, rise of the black middle class, lower wage inflation and per unit labour productivity.

Sifting through what was contained in tomes of policy documents and a plethora of government programmes for the next 10 years, we looked for correlation between policy and the presenting results. It became difficult to find corroborating data for evidence for the claims made about success. However, at least in the first seven years, there was direct relationship between programmes implemented and results on the ground but after this period not so easy. In fact, we found that as the inheritor of levers of power, government went in and took advantage of power conferred on it by the previous regime and bureaucrats found new comfort. The liberation cadres became overnight bureaucrats so comfortable in the seat of power that they simply continued from where the white regime ended with glee. Readiness to govern the country at the time the government assumed office was not even close. It would have been more than acceptable that the ANC government had honestly admitted the road they embarked upon had never been traversed before; and on the basis of the information available to it at that stage their assessment should have been that they needed a better understanding of how to run a government in practical terms.

To be persuasive the government needed to be believable, to be credible its intent and observable actions needed to be transparent, yet these attributes were supplanted by political Machiavelli. We don't understand why they chose the option of populism so early on in the starting blocks but then again politics is a game of brinkmanship where everybody is a star. The cost of hubris is high. To have the humility of character accepting the that in fact the government was not as nearly ready to govern South Africa as they had initially estimated, would have bought government much more credit with the electorate. This would have given it the option to pick the 'size of density packets' with which to orbit at the new levels and allow itself the luxury of maturing into the job. Projecting hauteur and superciliousness is not always the smartest way of taking on a new job description. It is better to be vulnerable at the beginning yet remain authentic because people can identify with that and are readily enamored by one's authenticity. Trust is an essential element of nation building, and is also necessary to construct the long-term social contracts required to deal with the underlying causes of inequality and exclusion. Arrogance by government bureaucracy has impeded the formation of social compact with the people of South Africa, a necessary partnership feature for the long-term success of the nation.

A meaningful consensus between the state and its citizens was embedded in the constitution, and anchored on mutual sacrifice and mutual benefit between the government and citizens in order to realise the aspirations of the people—sadly, this is absent. Healing the divisions of the past and establishing a society based on democratic values, social justice and accountable government, have become elusive and we reckon according to their own prophecy the ANC must chase this ideal until the second coming of Jesus Christ. South Africans are a patient society, very forgiving and extremely tolerant people. South Africans understood as well as appreciated the enormity of the task at hand well before the government took office at Mahlamba Ndlopfu.

The masses knew that it would take considerable time and effort to right the wrongs the apartheid government had visited upon black South Africans. That the unemployment crisis created through systematic economic exclusion of black people over years of white rule would need a growing economy and corresponding skills to match the demands of the economy and a long lead time for the absorption of labour. That a *better life for all* was not mere billboard slogan or a magic wand—better life had to be realised through sweat and toil. Collectively, the nation somehow knew it was a long road to freedom; and Mandela aptly made a point in reminding himself and all of us who cared to listen with his book *Long Walk to Freedom*.

As he began to scale back his involvement in government to assume a mediating and ambassadorial role focusing on solving world's problems, it became clear and that patience was going to be a virtue the nation would have to embrace. Internationally, Mandela became an elixir of fresh breath resolving the intractable UK/Libya Lockerbie bombing problem that had stalemated for many years; he was instrumental in laying the basis for political solutions in the DRC, Angola and Indonesia. He became Bill Clinton mentor and a friend during his second term. Domestically he began laying a foundation for his Children's Fund and Mandela Foundation legacy. In his Political Report at the 1997 Mahikeng Conference,

Mandela would observe insightfully 'ours was not a planned entry into government. Except for the highest echelons, we did not have a plan for the deployment of cadres. We were very disorganised, and behaved in a manner that could have endangered the revolution.' South Africa's bright future that beckoned post 1994 has been disintegrating since the departure of Mandela from leadership.

Noble aristocrat

Mandela managed to shape a new reality in South Africa by doing things thought to be impossible by many. Talking with such characters like PW Botha, working tirelessly against violence which he had come to espouse at an earlier time, listening with observable respect to everyone—even to those he knew in his heart were wrong was admirable. These qualities became possible as functions—not just of having led two previous lives, but also from having found these previous experiences useful. Conventional theory on wisdom suggests that we learn from experience. Mandela has demonstrated that experience does not in and of itself teach anything. Rather, experience presents us with an opportunity for learning. No two people having a similar experience would necessarily come away having learned the same things from it though.

It is generally taken for granted that all leaders—more so those who are elected to public office—are sufficiently matured individuals and that they possess wisdom. We measure wisdom using five criteria, namely: willingness to seek opportunities to resolve problems, willingness to search for compromise, recognition of the limits of personal knowledge, awareness that more than one perspective on a problem does exist, and appreciation that things may get worse before they can get better. In addition to the virtues of wisdom, there is *intent* as a phenomenon of leadership dimension. Wisdom and intent are two attributes we use to assess whether or not Mandela rose to meet the demands of this highest office in the land and lead South Africa to a better place than the one he found it in. In seeking answers to the dimension of wisdom a person of credibility, who knew Mandela well enough to be as truthful as he could without the inherent bias to sell Mandela's enigma had to be identified. Ahmed Kathrada is one among many people who worked very closely with Mandela politically and personally as well as having known him the longest from the formative stages of the ANC Youth League, through prison life and in the period following freedom. On willingness to seek opportunities to resolve conflicts and search for compromises, we asked Kathrada about his experience of Mandela and he provided this rare insight:

I am often asked if the many years Nelson Mandela, Walter Sisulu, our comrades and I spent in jail changed our thinking about the way to bring democracy to South Africa and if so we had any regrets about the activities and offences that led to our lengthy imprisonment. It seems surprising to people that we could emerge such hardship and humiliations and talk of forgiveness and reconciliation with the enemies who caused our suffering. But the principle of negotiated settlement did not originate from Robben Island. I have worked with Nelson since the mid 1940s and although not formally expressed, the concept of nonracial and democratic South Africa has been the ANC policy since from its inception in 1912.

For many years, the ANC attempted and failed to achieve these goals through petitions and deputations. In 1949 these were replaced by boycotts and peaceful passive resistance, but this met only greater repression culminating in the 1960 Sharpeville shootings. It was under these conditions that Mandela founded uMkhonto weSizwe. He never envisaged military victory; MK was launched as part of the overall political struggle. When in the 1970s some overenthusiastic MK cadres arrived on Robben Island making wild assertions about imminent victory over the army, Mandela calmly brought them down to earth, pointing out that in the armoury of legitimate weapons of the struggle each had its place and that its use should be governed by time and circumstances.

Mandela himself has always been committed to the principle of reconciliation, nation building and non-racialism. He played a key part in drafting the Freedom Charter, which reflected these principles; he and other congress leaders invited all organisations including the ruling Nationalist Party, to take part. Thus, when Mandela emerged from prison, he did so with commitment to negotiation that remained unchanged from the day we first met. In stretching out the hand of forgiveness and reconciliation, he and those who were in prison and those who returned from exile, were basically continuing a policy that runs like a thread from the earliest days of the organisation. It is this consistency of purpose, coupled with his refusal both personally and politically to harbour feelings of bitterness towards those responsible for his suffering that the seeds of his greatness lay.

Where Mandela's greatness was shown was in the way he handled the issue of PW Botha's refusal to go to court. Mandela pleaded with him and eventually they forced him to appear before the court, but there was a technical mistake in the way they made the application and he was released. Everyone demanded he be brought back, but it was Mandela who said, just let him go. We have made our point. His handling of PW Botha was extraordinary. He could see that the path to reconciliation was by just ignoring him, and letting him stew in his juice. That is greatness.

Mandela learned new ways to think and reason and new ways to facilitate change by taking on a seemingly trans-human calm and long view. Given the same circumstances, another man might have become visibly angry more often. It is not that Madiba was not angered, but he had learned not to show it; and also the value of self-control and of acting appropriately as a means towards a valuable end. The current nation of South Africa, imperfect as every nation is, is a far better nation than it would have been without the ministrations of this progressive leader. Mandela was an astute politician and he sustained this through the humility of spirit. The willingness to seek opportunities and resolve conflicts and search for compromise would appear to have been Mandela's mainstay.

On the third element of recognising the limits of personal knowledge, the author believes that many people assume that if someone can succeed in an area, he possesses knowledge that may be valuable to them in their own endeavours. If you possess a high level of ability in an area, others may desire to connect with you because of it and if your success is in the same area as theirs, the potential for connection increases exponentially. If you have an area of expertise and generously share it with others, you give people reasons to respect you and develop a sense of connection with you. Some of Mandela's cabinet colleagues thought he did this best. If you are successful, in what you do there will be people who will want to listen to you. Mandela became Clinton's de facto mentor by virtue of this trait alone. Clinton paid more attention to him than he did to his White House Aides. This is where humility becomes an asset to a leader. Humility means two things a capacity for self-criticism while the second element speaks to the willingness to allow others to shine—affirming and enabling them. Mandela distinguished himself by the display of extraordinary humility and reached out to even the nondescript person, because he knew he could learn from any person thereby increase his own repertoire of knowledge he did not hesitate to show it. 'It is possible that if I had not gone to jail and been able to read and listen to the stories of many people. I might not have learned these things,' Mandela said that prison gave him time to think about the times when he had failed to acknowledge people who had been kind to him.

In this regard, we are particularly reminded of a public spat incident involving Mandela and one Zimbabwe Minister over a domestic matter of MDC and how graceful he was in handling that rather brutal public bruising. Anytime a leader is willing to listen to others and figure out how the thing he is offering fills their needs, it becomes easy for that person to reach common ground with others. Humility alone does not tell us whether or not Mandela knew the limits of his personal knowledge; humility had to be supported by a skill of communicating with others. Leadership and communications expert, John Maxwell says effective communication requires a leader to say I will be interested enough in others to ask the question; I will think of others and look for ways to thank them, I will let people into my life, I will care about people, I will think of myself less so I can think of others more and, I will move from my world to theirs. If communicators have a high need for security their intent is ill disposed towards helping others and they are unable to give of themselves.

On the fourth element, we asked the question: was Mandela better at accepting that there can be more than one perspective on a problem? Cyril Ramaphosa recalls one incident with his many encounter with the man and shares this view:

> Madiba has the ability to listen to his colleagues, to his adversaries and in listening; he is able to take in new ideas and new thoughts. Many leaders don't listen; they think they know it all. Where Madiba doesn't know anything, he concedes it. He also admits when he is wrong. There are not many leaders who admit to making mistakes either. And he is forthright. I can tell you with certainty in all the years that I worked with him, I have never for one moment found him devious. Honesty, integrity, forthrightness and truthfulness have been foremost hallmarks of Madiba's makeup and it is a joy to deal with a person like him.

Neville Alexander, then a young prisoner on Robben Island in the 1970s and a leader of New Unity Movement corroborates this view:

> Mandela made a central contribution to Robben Island not only through the impact of his personality and his general approach to people, but because he in particular was able through rigorous and sometimes exhaustive debate to bring people to understand that in trying simply to get the best conditions for everybody he was not being collaborationist. And generally speaking, we all came to accept that that strategy was correct.
>
> Mandela supported our youthful rebellious attitudes towards prison conditions and towards the warders, but they made us understand that we were going to accept that we would be there for a very long time and that tactically we were going to run ourselves to the ground by continuing rebellion and getting punished and beaten

up. And therefore it was better to have a strategy of slowly getting the conditions improved, getting the warders to understand that we weren't criminals, and to make use of the political period there to study, to teach others, and prepare for the continuation of the revolution once we got out. The humility of the man has always been extremely obvious, even though sometimes he could come across as very authoritative, rigid even, there is no doubt that on issues where he wasn't clear as he thought he should be, he was always willing to learn even from young people like myself at the time. Mandela is not just an icon. It is important to highlight those things that show how really a humble person, with tremendous vision and insight, was able to and still is able to inspire millions of people to go the extra mile, to go beyond themselves, to bring about a change, regardless of whether they accept what he stands for or not. I think that side of Mandela, is what is most attractive to people.

The one difficult element of wisdom though is accepting that things may get worse before they get better. He knew the importance of views that were contrary to his and accepted that a different perspective than his own may well exist and shed more light, the need to avoid frenetic reactions to situations that may take a longer term to resolve and to adopt a detached approach to certain situations. Mandela accepted that he could not fix something the very minute, month, or even a year he was presented with the demand. He would build solutions bit by bit, painstakingly ensuring that each piece was the right piece and in the right place. Although it runs contrary to human instincts, it nevertheless remains an eminently essential leadership trait. Tutu shared the following words about the spirit of the man:

> Suffering can of course embitter the one who suffers. But in many other circumstances, it can ennoble the sufferer. We were richly blessed that the latter happened with Mandela. The crucible of excruciating suffering through the rigours and tribulations of incarceration, the forced separation from his beloved Winnie and their young children purified the dross and deepened his spiritual resources. He began to be one who could understand the fears of his adversary and he grew in that time in magnanimity and generosity of spirit. He had an extraordinary knack of pulling off gestures that could, done by somebody else without his panache, have been awkward embarrassments. Mandela's many conciliatory gestures had the longed-for results of making all kinds of people feel they belonged, he was an inclusive man. During his presidency, this feel good factor was at its peak.

We also used the criterion of intent to understand Mandela's leadership impact on the people he led. New research has demonstrated this trait to be absolutely essential rather than incidental to successful leadership and thus personal intent, as a dimension of leadership has become central to leadership. Intent is the least understood and most under-estimated dimension of leadership, just as consciousness it is the most intricate of human properties to explicate, because it is hidden away from the realm of public space. However, intent undergirds and affects every effort in which the leader engages and consequently on which human experiences are built. Mzolo, an expert on this subject has demonstrated that intent is primal— that is, it is both the ORIGINAL and the most important ACT of the leader. An authentic intent makes the leader credible in the eyes of the people s/he leads while the opposite is that intent can be toxic resulting in the person of the leaders being experienced as destructive.

The force of intent is so real, so much so that it determines whether everything the leader does will work as well as it should in the immediate to long-term. Its effects extend beyond ensuring that a job is done. Intent changes the quality of every present moment and alters the trajectory and outcome of every future moment. All persons in leadership positions are hard-wired with a trait of either pure i.e. authentic or toxic intent the secret lies in how it is demonstrated in relation to others. If intent is toxic, it destroys even the most talented of leaders and irreversibly impacts those led. Here is an example: two leaders work together running a business both interact in two different settings with the same team of people. The first leader requests an added discretionary effort from the team he manages, to the point of self inconvenience, the team responds positively and does so willingly above and beyond. When the second leader makes the same request, team members make different excuses for why they are unwilling to help him. What's the difference? It boils down to the nature of intent.

People respond to others based not on the words used to communicate but to a greater extent on how they experience the person's intent about them. The human spirit readily senses a positive and a negative intent. People can receive all day long from a giver and reciprocate in equal measure, while they tire quickly of a taker. Intent communicates the inherent motives and thus speaks clearly about the presenting gravitas of the leader or lack thereof. In probing a leader's intent, we go beyond the directly observable actions, by paying attention to the presenting internal dynamics, the invisible processes beneath the surface to discern unconscious fears and motives that influence the behaviour of the person of the leader. Intent is more than just a thin veneer of exterior posture expressed in social gestures. Intent is more than human energy as it reveals something core to the human soul that is impossible to hide. To assess intent we look at those traits that point to causality, in other words those that are revealed directly by the person's actions towards others and indirectly by his hidden motives. Friendliness or magnanimity is not necessarily a measure of intent by a byproduct of something woven inside the intent. For example, showing compassion towards others not because one feels it was a duty to do so, is an indicator of the presence of pure intent where the unconditional nature of the caring act itself is even more significant when the beneficiary of the generosity bestowed cannot return the gesture, i.e. the giving is not reciprocated in a way that gratifies the giver. Mandela came close to revealing the core of his soul when writing to Winnie reflected thusly:

> In judging our progress as individuals, we tend to concentrate on external factors such as one's social position, influence and popularity, wealth and standard of education . . . but internal factors may be even more crucial in assessing one development as a human being, sincerity, generosity, absence of vanity, readiness to serve your fellow men are qualities within the reach of every soul.

To begin the survey in relation to Mandela's intent we asked the question: did the relationships Mandela had with his cabinet colleagues including officials in his administration and generally the people of South Africa, enrich them? To answer this question we looked to those who knew him well or had interacted with him in a more extended time than a casual chat along the corridor. The summary expressions provided by people are encapsulated in one word *selfless*. We found that he connected with people and he wished them well more than he wished it for himself. If you sincerely want to help people, connecting stems not from something that you merely do as part of who you are, but it is something that becomes more natural and less mechanical. Two people who had interacted closely with him summarised his intent rather aptly. Christo Brand, a Prison Warder in charge of Mandela in the last stages of his imprisonment in Victor Verster recalls his personal experience as such:

> You know when I started working on Robben Island in 1975 my uncle visited me, and he asked if I had seen Mandela. And my father asked who is Mandela? And then he said he remembered something about the trial, but if the man has been so long in prison, they should release him, because he is now worth nothing outside. And my uncle said, "No, they should have hanged him." One said he was worthless and the other said he should die. Mandela was always very concerned about our

families, even inside the prison. The first year I arrived on Robben Island we were not allowed to talk to the prisoners, but he and I would get an opportunity talk a little when I was taking him to the visiting booth. I would talk about his family, and he always asked me, 'how is your family, and what is your father doing?" After 1986 when my father passed away, I became very close to Mr. Mandela. When I had a motorcycle accident, I received a letter from a lawyer saying he wanted to sue me, and Mandela put his studies aside to write a letter back. I took the letter home for my wife to type. Today I can say that Mandela is still the same person and treats me with the same respect as the first day I met him. I would like to thank him for his friendship, helpfulness and kindness, for always giving me a chance and for listening to me and I want to thank him for having such faith in me, I feel very sorry that I didn't always have the same for him. I didn't believe when I saw him in prison that things would change like that.

Zelda Le Grange, Madiba's Personal Secretary since 1994 revealed something many South Africans could have never guessed about the man.

Madiba is not a difficult person at all. There is a beautiful Afrikaans word for it 'gematigd'. He is not impulsive. If you have been working with him for a long time, you know exactly how he is going to react to something. Deep inside he is an authentic human being. Often he would surprise us by requesting to meet very simple people to whom others would pay little attention. In the early days, he would go through the newspapers and notice people who had achieved something and ask us to arrange a meeting so he could congratulate them. And on another day, he would open a newspaper and we would predict whom he would want to speak to next just from reading about them from newspapers. Madiba would notice a poor man that he used to know years back, and he would ask us to do something for him and I would arrange donations of clothes, food and so on. To see that man's life enriched, to know that it's within your power to do something for someone is really the sort of thing that made his job worthwhile. After you see someone like him behave in a particular way for a long time you come to the conclusion that this is actually the way things should be done and it enriches you in a way no formal education could.

Because of Mandela, the nation had a newfound mood of optimism; a sense of nationhood had begun to emerge. Spontaneously the nation reciprocated Mandela's greatness with a campaign called *67 Minutes for Mandela* [although token in its form its symbolism is a profound one—67 minutes of inconsequential acts of charity in random places, do not change the face of poverty and neglect]. South Africans volunteered their time to help other South Africans in whatever manner they deemed necessary as a tribute to the spirit of selflessness. Before the sectarian interests hijacked the initiative [hijacked because it was glamorised by corporate fanfare and TV cameras on the 18th of July every year]. Sectarian interests managed to shift the emphasis from ordinary people unconditional caring for the others to brands riding on this campaign earning ad mileage in public relations rhetoric. The 67 minutes gesture nevertheless reflected a deep appreciation by the nation for the selfless spirit shown by Mandela in his living years. Similarly, the United Nations declared an international Mandela Day to be observed globally—the only of its kind in the world as far as we can tell. Mandela had fortitude and strength of mind because of lack of bitterness in his heart, the acceptance of his destiny and the courage to face the consequences attests to this. His love for children so deep—so much so that he has left South Africans a lasting legacy through the Children's Fund.

Generations of young people around the world looked to Mandela because they see him as the only president who symbolised the possibility of bringing morality to the arena of politics and that's why he remained a hope to this world. It was particularly gratifying when in the course of writing this book we listened to a news clip in July 2012 of young men and women from around the world gathered at a Johannesburg country club, discussing the lessons leant from the Mandela legacy and how best to present those lessons to inspire their own generation. It was perfectly forgivable that government failed to live up to conference resolution expectations. Frankly, we don't really care that it did because the nation building efforts more than made up for the shortfall. South Africans forgave the ANC government for many errors committed in its maiden years; that forgiveness was due to the credibility of Mandela's personality. According to evidence on the ground, there is a positive correlation between Mandela the brand and the nation that stopped tearing itself apart. People started to reach out to one another as humans and the nation's consciousness as one human race suddenly was within realms of possibility.

Subsequent to his departure from the political center stage people were not talking to one another as often as Mandela would have hoped for following his nation building campaign but the climate created by his magnanimity opened the possibilities for such social dialogue to find a place in their hearts. The overwhelming sentiment that was observed soon after the Mandela administration took office, was that whites gradually began to accept ANC's bona fides and as a consequence of that began lifting their veil of ignorance about black people in general. Small communities in rural towns reached accords in the 1990s that were unthinkable just a decade earlier. Mandela represented the very best of what is possible to expect of a political leader. No one else could have shown that scale of imagination and compassion for the people who oppressed him. As a leader, he set himself a task of humanising and depolarising a nation that has been racially divided for centuries. His catalytic influence has softened the hardened stance of the Afrikaner and aligned them in pursuit of common purpose. Not only have whites not lashed out in fear, but also the vast multitude of Africans have been prepared to wait and trust. Africans have shown preparedness to listen to what their former oppressors had to say about their part in seeking absolution and once they had done so, Africans showed an extraordinary spirit of forgiveness and readily offered the olive branch of peace.

Of all events in the last hundred years, Mandela's seminal efforts of nation building will go down in the annals of history as enduring legacy. Dag Hammarskjöld agrees when he said, 'Only he who keeps his eyes fixed on the far horizon will find his right road.' Good leaders keep an open mind but great leaders open the minds of others in the most intense circumstances, even against the odds of prejudice and politics. Leadership is practiced not so much in words as in attitude and in action. Mandela has truly become humankind's hope for the future at the time when politics has become a dirty word, stripped of all morality and Machiavellian to its roots.

South Africa is a better place to live in and one we are all proud to call our home because of a life that symbolized much of what is exemplary in humankind. Our inheritance is bountiful, rich and splendid. Johann Von Schiller once said, 'He who has done his best for his own time has lived for all times.' Mandela will be remembered as a man who showed that people are essentially good; the good in people is a flame that can be hidden but never extinguished. We believe that essence of Mandela's greatness was to change himself fundamentally during his period in jail and emerged as a potent leader and example for all humanity. Mandela's intent was pure and its impact at personal and corporately at government and community level was both veritable as well as it was enduring. His intent because it was devoid of self-aggrandizement spoke directly to the hearts of many people in South Africa and around the world. His legacy speaks of tenacity, courage, commitment and a relentless striving for justice. As our hearts quieted with sorrow from his departure, we know he has rested in the knowledge that he has replicated himself many times over in some of us and we pledge to honour his life and legacy by teaching our young and they too shall tell posterity, the sun will never set on so glorious human achievement! Ah Dalibhunga 'nto kaMandela, enkosi Bawo Madiba siyabulela!

The Mbeki Years

True to his word, when it was Mandela's time to step down at the end of his 5-year term in office, he handed over the presidency to Thabo Mbeki after the 1999 elections, took a bow and exited the stage with humility and grace. Mbeki made a flamboyant entry to the theatre of power and took the commanding position of the ANC with a gong and a swagger but a greater burden on his shoulders to surpass that which Mandela had begun loomed large. If Mandela was the father of the nation-building ideal, then Mbeki was cast into the role of championing transformation and changing the structure of the society. In 1997, at the ANC 50th conference in Mahikeng Mbeki was elected as its president and committed to pursue the following objectives:

Our strategy is the creation of a united, non-racial, non-sexist and democratic society. In pursuit of this objective, we shall, at each given moment, creatively adopt tactics that advance that objective. Our fundamental point of departure is that South Africans have it in their power, as a people and as part of progressive humankind, to continually change the environment in which we operate in the interest of a better future. In this phase of transformation, we seek to expand and deepen the power of democratic forces in all centers critical to the NDR, at the same time as we improve the people's quality of life. Our efforts, which are people-centered, people-driven and gender-sensitive, are founded on five basic pillars:

- to build and strengthen the ANC as a movement that organises and leads the people in the task of social transformation;
- to deepen our democracy and culture of human rights and mobilise the people to take active part in changing their lives for the better;
- to strengthen the hold of the democratic movement on state power, and transform the state machinery to serve the cause of social change;
- to pursue economic growth, development and redistribution in such a way as to improve the people's quality of life; and
- to work with progressive forces throughout the world to promote and defend our transformation, advance Africa's renaissance and build a new world order.

Shifting Domestic Balance Of Forces

A mere decade-and-a-few years after the democratic transition in 1994, the liberation movement can claim great progress towards a democratic and prosperous society. South Africa enjoys a system of vibrant multi-party democracy, with a progressive Bill of Rights that recognises political, socio-economic and environmental rights and obligations, and with separation of powers among the executive, the judiciary and the legislatures. Beyond the formal processes of regular elections and legislatures, various forms of legislated and other forums ensure popular participation. The Constitution enjoys the respect of the overwhelming majority of the population, and it is seen as the canvass upon which South Africans' freedom of spirit can find expression. While some within the ranks of those who were privileged under apartheid may harbour ill feelings towards the process of change and evince racist attitudes, virtually all of them accept that their aims and views should be pursued within the constitutional and legal framework. While pockets of ethnic chauvinism and regionalism still manifest themselves and may take new forms under the new conditions, our society has made massive progress in ensuring a common national identity. We have started to transform state institutions through policy frameworks and practices that guide them as well as improvements in their racial and gender profiles. A state entity has emerged that enjoys such allegiance that only the most fanatical can dare frontally to challenge it. Yet, much more still needs to be done to transform state institutions, and consolidate their legitimacy in the eyes of society.

The period since 1994 has also seen other macro social trends that include: rapid rates of migration to areas with better economic potential, with resultant sprawls of informal settlements in the major cities and towns; greater self-assertion by the youth in taking advantage of professions now opened up and opportunities in the arts and other areas; but also marginalisation of millions of young people who do not have the skills required by the economy; better gender representation in the legislatures and other organs of state; but also slow progress in the private sector and serious manifestations of poverty and women abuse; better advocacy and access in relation to the rights of people with disability, but a huge legacy of marginalisation; and greater focus on the rights of children, but still unacceptable levels of child poverty and abuse. The state has massively expanded access to welfare grants;

and the social wage includes such elements for the poor as free and compulsory education, free health care, free basic services, and asset provision through the housing and land reform programmes. Steady progress has been made in the battle against crime. However, the reach of such programmes is still constrained by access to information, availability of resources and capacity of the state.

But the majority of South Africans still remain separated by a wide chasm of income, skills, assets, spatial settlement patterns and access to opportunities. The majority of the poor are disproportionately black and female. Combined with this chasm and high levels of inequality is a value system within society that encourages greed, crass materialism and conspicuous consumption. These are tendencies that go beyond the necessary spirit of entrepreneurship, ambition, daring, competition and material reward that are inherent to a market-based system and perhaps to human development in general.

Overall, since 1994, the balance of forces has shifted in favour of the forces of change. It provides the basis for speedier implementation of programmes to build a truly democratic and prosperous society. The legal and policy scaffolding for this is essentially in place. The majority of society wants this to happen. At least in public discourse, except for a tiny minority, those apprehensive about change express their concerns more in terms of pace and scale rather than substance. The critical questions therefore are: is society mobilised for faster progress? Does the liberation movement have the cadreship able not only to withstand the pull of negative values but also to lead society along the road towards a caring nation that a national democratic society should be?

Under Mbeki's administration, the government programmes were obfuscated and it was unclear which policies—passed by the Mahikeng conference—formed the basis of government programmes and which were parachuted from Mbeki's presidency his inner sanctum think tank. Be that as it may, government programmes were fast tracked in a number of areas but the speed with which the implementation carried out often betrayed fault lines; where programmes showed promise those were not sufficiently deep to the extent that results were sustainable. The legal and policy scaffolding used to ramp up the pace for change did not have the desired on-the-ground impact. Evidence points to the fact that many erstwhile socio-economic conditions remained largely unaltered although in some instances deteriorated rapidly. Amilcar Cabral's advice is 'tell no lies and claim no easy victories' had Mbeki heeded this admonition his legacy would have been better off in the end. The Human Sciences Research Council report of 2005 tells us why Mbeki's administration struggled to make a ripple—much less a wave in South Africa.

By this time, South Africa was as unequal as it has ever been; the Gini coefficient was 0.62, very high by international standards.

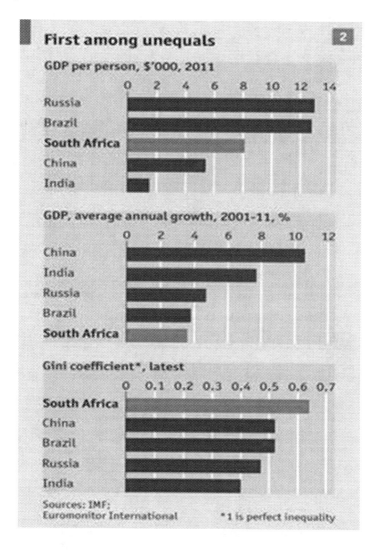

First among unequals　2

GDP per person, $'000, 2011

GDP, average annual growth, 2001-11, %

Gini coefficient*, latest

Sources: IMF;
Euromonitor International　　*1 is perfect inequality

Inequality compounds the societal division. Poor quality of education and high youth unemployment inhibited a broadening of opportunity necessary to reduce inequality and heal the divisions of the past. This was so for the past century and it had remained so for the period under review. The distribution of income to the poorest and richest sections of the society did not change significantly between 1995 and 2004 and worsened between

2006 and 2008. The majority of low-income households are black people where the median per capita expenditure among blacks was R333 a month compared to whites at R3 443 a month. For a number of years, growth in the labour force outstripped employment creation. Demographic shifts contributed to this development, as large numbers of women and young people entered the labour market. The sheer scale of inactivity, the long pre-existing queue of unemployed, and the growing cohort of entrants meant that it would take longer to get to full employment and to make major impact to household incomes nationally.

Increase in middle class between 1994 and 2008

		On Poverty Datum Line R650 to R1,399	Middle Class R4000 to R10,499	Upper Class >R1500
African	1994	22%	7%	7%
	2000	22%	12%	7%
	2008	24%	14%	9%
White	1994	7%	81%	18%
	2000	7%	75%	18%
	2008	11%	67%	20%

African entrants into middle class rose sharply so was white entrants into upper class BUT 85% of Africans remain poor

Source National Income Study Dynamics 2008

A high unemployment rate anchors widespread poverty. Different methods were used to raise the quality of education for poor children but have largely failed. Apart from a minority of black children who attended former white schools, the quality of education has regressed badly. Literacy and numeracy test scores are low by global standards. Learners in previously white schools perform better in comparison and their test scores improve with successive years of schooling. Skills acquisition is out of line with the needs of modernising economy. Universities continue to produce high numbers of graduates with BA degrees mostly not terribly useful to the economy.

The South African economy generates small numbers of low and semi skilled jobs. Even these do require a basic set of capabilities such as reading comprehension. Employers were turning away those who have left school early or failed, and were accessing only the top end elite group of recent commercial graduates. The cost of preparing young people is therefore high relative to the output in the economy, because the basic competence upon which further skills would be developed is often absent. The lack of work readiness continues to be a strong disincentive to recruiting these young people, and when they do not find employment before they turn 24, the chance of them being employed progressively diminishes.

Economically, South Africa diversified its mining exports and imports profile more generally from the late 1990s but mining and related products still accounted for a large percentage of total exports; however only make a small contribution to total employment pool. There have been major foreign investments in South African companies such as Barclays in ABSA, HSCB in Standard Bank and Edcon. Successful countries generally invest at high rates and are continually modernising public infrastructure to suit their economic, settlement and trade patterns. South Africa had missed a generation of infrastructure modernisation. The net results were that it could not meet 21st century needs of the economy. South Africa, if it wished to stimulate the economy needed in the first 10 years, an even more efficient logistic infrastructure than would have been the case under apartheid. This would have meant high levels of investment on infrastructure with institutional arrangements that would bring in private money. Public sector capital formation as a proportion of GDP fell until 2004.

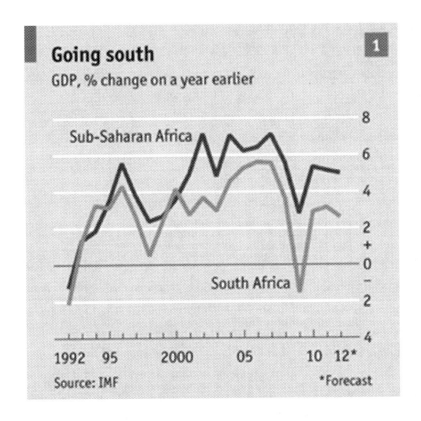

Going south
GDP, % change on a year earlier

Sub-Saharan Africa

South Africa

1992 95   2000   05   10 12*
Source: IMF   *Forecast

Similarly, reliable and affordable public transport was acutely needed to enable poor black people to participate meaningfully in the life of their surrounding cities, given the existing distances the spatial legacies apartheid created. We witnessed for example that Mbeki administration attempted to recapitalize and restructure the taxi industry in order to streamline it in line with the overall transformation agenda driving the economy but its efforts were thwarted by the often self-centered interests of taxi industry bosses and eventually the recapitalisation programme had to be prematurely truncated due to lack of industry and government consensus, to the extreme disadvantage of 7.5 million taxi users mainly black commuters. Between 1994 and 2009, there was considerable rural urban migration; contemporaneously a new phenomenon of mobility within the rural areas along major transport arterial routes was emerging, creating 'transport corridor densification' of the rural settlements. Linked to the logistic infrastructure problem was the challenge of ICT that carried great promise of keeping South Africa the continental leader in Internet and voice connectivity. According to DBSA South Africa was ranked at that time on the same level as Malaysia, Turkey and Korea but had since slipped from 72nd to 92nd on the ITU ICT Development Index.

While ICT is driven primarily by private investment, it is guided by national regulatory frameworks which, judged on the basis of their outcomes, have proven to be neither effective nor foresighted. Infrastructure is not just about bricks and mortar, it is about people and the systems involved to plan, design and build, maintain and operate complicated systems over a long period of time. Providing effective guidance through policy and regulation to support the finance, delivery and maintenance required sound institutional leadership, which were, all absent. The challenges for South Africa's public service post 1994 to 2009 were immense. The system of national government needed to be restructured into a coherent whole that could purse national rather than sectarian interests serving powerful cliques in the ANC.

However, 15 years after the end of apartheid, the public sector remained chronically unstable with highly visible instances of gross under performance that created a temptation to look for short-term fixes by setting up new institutional structures with multiple initiatives that sought to reform public service to no avail. In most cases, no time was given to testing the effectiveness of these changes before fresh changes were introduced. Public service policies have been implemented in unsolicited ways as successive new political appointees sought to make their mark in the administration. A multitude of initiatives were implemented which never improved the efficiency of operations or ensured adequate infrastructure, or managed human capital and financial management systems as well as technical expertise to the greatest benefit of the country.

The hugely expanded remit of public service, raft of new laws and regulations, consolidation of structures, lack of supporting infrastructure and the international skills crisis all played a part in the problems facing public service institutions. The public service was battling with the problem of service culture; it also was struggling with skills crisis. It was critical for public servants to forge a collective professional identity and loyalty to the values of the constitution rather than the sitting ANC leaders because politicians and Executive Mayors often had a short tenure in office and therefore were disruptive to the continuity necessary in these institutions. Local government was supposed to play a key role in delivering health care, education and housing services that are vital both for human wellbeing as well as the local economic activity. There were enormous variations in the ability of the municipalities to deliver these if at all. A review report by Department of Cooperative Governance and Traditional Affairs concluded that 'much of the local government was in distress, noting that urban municipalities tend to perform relatively better than those in rural areas. Provincial and Local government are therefore least able to deliver services in the poorest areas where those services are most needed. This high level of variation in service delivery leads to a strong sense of injustice in society', it concluded. Outside the metros, the 2-tier structure of local government simply did not work. In an effort to improve performance across departments and encourage collaboration and accountability of Ministers to the President, the administration first introduced a system of clusters where interministerial cooperation was imposed upon line functions with similar objectives for increased impact. Years later the cluster system changed into a corporate scorecard methodology of '12 Outcomes' that became the core business delivery focus of government that could be evaluated by the civil society. However, in the absence of the political will to hold the ministers to account publicly for lack of results the scorecard became just another political charade.

The centralisation versus decentralisation conundrum is an obvious manifestation of the lack of planning ability as well as the capacity of government to align infrastructural initiatives. In theory, the national government was responsible for delivering policing services, bulk water and electricity and transport, while the provinces were responsible for the delivery of houses, schools and clinics, and municipalities were delivering services related to electricity, sanitation and waste removal. Because of government's inability to coordinate centrally, the concept of three spheres of government was a total failure for South Africa it resulted in too much fragmentation between the national, provincial and municipal spheres of government resulting in extreme inefficiencies across all three spheres and thus caused the symptoms of failure of the government as we are witnessing today.

A concern was the failure to coordinate service delivery of household services and the ensuing revolts throughout the country that marked the sporadic sometime sustained service delivery grievances. These protests later resulted in a clear vote of no confidence on the government. In the wake of mounting evidence that things were not working as well as they were anticipated, the Mbeki administration wouldn't scrap unworkable ideas for something better but they had hoped that if they changed few management functionaries such as a Director General in this department and few other Chief Directors over there, the plan would eventually gather steam and finally work, lazy thinking at best.

At one meeting, Mbeki quoted a UNDP report findings which had observed that South Africa was a state of two nations: one black and poor, and the other white and rich. This report was published after a study that revealed a shocking story. It reported that if white South Africa were a country on its own, its per capita income would be ranked 24th in the world, alongside Spain. If black South Africa were a separate country, its per capita income would rank 123rd globally, just below DRCongo. What this showed was that a world where democracy was racialised as an exclusive privilege of minority group, giving rise to the vexing moral dilemma that apartheid was democratically sanctioned by a racial minority who voted for it in greater numbers with each passing election. These practices resulted in dualities in the South African economy: On the one hand, the country developed a political economy in which the distribution of wealth is skewed in favour of the white minority. This means that the economy is divided along racial lines, with the country's wealth benefiting mainly the white population.

This inequality is nowhere more visible than the income distribution. The other duality in the economy is one typical of a developing country—the rural/urban divide. South Africa also struggles with the problem of high unemployment. Of the formally unemployed, approximately 50% are engaged in the informal sector. These are quite often marginal economic activities, like hawking fruit, which does not necessarily eliminate material poverty. The history of the South African political economy has created deep inequalities in terms of the distribution of wealth. Moreover, the inequalities were brought about by people's participation in the economy: whites had open access to economic opportunities whereas black people were restricted. Numerous laws and practices in the previous period benefited the white population. Stereotype notwithstanding there is a kernel of empirical evidence supporting this.

Attempts of the Jobs Summit in 1998 and Growth and Development Summit in 2003 and Summit on corruption in 2004 produced interesting accords, but these soon floundered because each sector had entered those engagements to pursue their narrow interest. The outcome was the lowest common denominator rather than a measure to blaze out along a new road. A critical precondition for change to occur was a strategic leadership that appreciated the common interest, at the same time pursuing benefits for various sectors. Above all, it is a required appreciation that each sector will need to put shoulder to the wheel and, where necessary, make sacrifices, to realise the common good for all South Africans. Despite improved growth, the economy remained one of the most inequitable in the world. In the mid-2000s, some 40% of the national income went to the richest 10% of households. Deep inequalities were associated with extraordinarily high levels of joblessness. Inequalities and joblessness were also associated with the legacy of apartheid geography. By 2000, a third of the population lived in the former rural areas. Less than one in every three adults was employed. Over half of all households in the former rural areas depended mostly on remittances or grants, compared to under a quarter in the rest of the country.

The position was worse for young people, largely because too few jobs were created to absorb the large numbers of new entrants to the labour market. In the first quarter of 2010, the unemployment rate for young people aged 16 to 30 was 40%, compared to 16% for those aged 30 to 65. Among the employed, many workers had poorly paid, insecure and dead-end jobs. In the third quarter of 2008, half of all employed people earned less than R2 500 a month and over a third earned under R1 000 a month, according to Statistics SA (2009). The informal sector, agriculture and domestic work contributed a third of all employment, but two-thirds of working people earning under R1 000 a month. Moreover, one in five employed African women was a domestic worker. The share of wages in the national income dropped from 50% in 1994 to just over 45% in 2009, while the share of profits climbed from 40% to 45%. In the intervening period, there was the Millennium Development Goals, (MDG) AsgiSA and now the New Growth Path all of which are macro policy instruments aimed at taking the country to a higher growth trajectory.

To shift the country to a higher growth path the government claimed it would not be scared to make difficult political choices, be better than average at effective implementation, realign key areas of government policy and reprioritise the economic policy. The main indicators of success would be: jobs—i.e. the number and quality of jobs created; growth—i.e. the rate of labour intensity and composition of economic growth; and equity—i.e. lower income inequality and poverty. At that stage of pronouncement, the government did not have the ability to coordinate its efforts on core priority areas owing to the three spheres conundrum; instead, it was dispersing them across numerous efforts that did not contribute to expansion in economic opportunities. To achieve that step towards change in transforming economic conditions required a different mindset in leadership. To raise employment in South Africa needs improved education, a population of healthier young people, better-maintained economic infrastructure, a capable government and zero levels of corruption.

Again, Mbeki would have faired better had he heeded Peter Ducker's admonition, 'Decisions of the kind the executive had to make were not made well by acclamation. They were made only if based on the clash of conflicting views, dialogue between different points of view, and the choice between different judgements is necessary. The first rule in decision-making is that one does not make a decision unless there is disagreement.' The government had many noble intentions and it would appear that 20 years later they still had lots of energy to write about some of those noble intentions in their *Umrabollo* mag. Below we reproduce an excerpt of some of them.

Given the vision of a national democratic society and the motive forces of change, what should be the character of the movement to lead social transformation? In order for it to exercise its vanguard role, the ANC puts a high premium on the involvement of its cadres in all centers of power. This includes the presence of ANC members and supporters in state institutions. It includes activism in the mass terrain of which structures of civil society are part. It includes the involvement of cadres in the intellectual and ideological terrain to help shape the value systems of society. This requires a cadre policy that encourages creativity in thought and in practice and eschews rigid dogma. In this regard, the ANC has a responsibility to promote progressive traditions within the intellectual community, including institutions such as universities and the media. Playing a vanguard role also means the presence of members and supporters of the ANC in business, the better to reshape production relations in line with the outlook of a democratic society. Many leaders and cadres of the movement are found in positions of massive influence in the executive, the legislatures and state institutions. By breaking the glass ceiling of apartheid, the liberation movement opened up enticing opportunities for its cadres in business and the professions. Even within the trade union movement and students', youth, women's and other mass democratic organisations, unprecedented opportunities for individual material gain have opened up. All this creates a problem of 'social distance' between these cadres of the movement and ordinary members and supporters, the majority of whom are working class and poor. Political incumbency also presents a myriad of problems in the management of relations within the organisation. Patronage, arrogance of power, bureaucratic indifference, corruption and other ills arise, undermining the lofty core values of the organisation: to serve the people!

How the ANC negotiates this minefield will determine its future survival as a principled leader of the process of fundamental change, an organisation respected and cherished by the mass of the people for what it represents and how it conducts itself in actual practice. A number of principles need to be observed in dealing with this challenge. Firstly, the critical importance of political power as an instrument to address the ills of colonialism needs to be fully appreciated. In this regard, politics and public service need to be treated as a calling with requisite moral status, in which any of the motive forces can take part, either as a profession or as time-bound service. Secondly, the ANC should give strategic leadership to those of its cadres in institutions of government, through Conferences, Councils and Branch General Meetings. In this respect, it needs to act as the ultimate strategic 'centre of power' for its members. Thirdly, in order to ensure that its strategic mandate is carried out, the ANC needs massively to strengthen its monitoring and evaluation capacity. This will ensure that cadres deployed in various capacities are able to improve their work in meeting set objectives. At the same time, these cadres should have sufficient space to exercise initiative within the strategic mandate rather than being subjected to micro-management. Fourthly, systems of information sharing within leadership structures and across the organisation should afford those outside of government sufficient data to make strategic interventions. In the same measure, all cadres should apply themselves seriously to governance issues, practically to add strategic value to the work of government.

To the question put whether it had the cadreship able to not only withstand the pull of negative forces but also lead society along the road towards a caring nation, the answer is no, the ANC did not have such people. If it had, they were not deployed to places where they would have the necessary impact in society. In retrospect, we know that the ANC was not in a position to develop this kind of talent and we know why it could not do so in the intervening period. The definition of cadreship was narrow and self-serving. Only ANC card-carrying members who by virtue of rank in the organisational pyramid and on the right cabal were offered roles that had decision-making powers in government, disallowing a great many individuals with good credentials and exceptional talents. This actively ignored the non card-carrying South African compatriots who were available, willing and highly skilled to make meaningful contribution in government—thus help speed the change of society.

The government said they came to appreciate the importance of political power as an instrument to redress colonialism and went on to tell us it would treat politics and public service as a calling, in which any of its cadres can take part either on a professional basis or as time-bound service contract. Secondly, the party would give strategic leadership to those of its cadres in institutions of government, through conferences, councils and branch general meetings. In this respect, it would act as the strategic 'centre of power' giving direction to its members. Thirdly, in order to ensure that its strategic mandate was carried out, the ANC would strengthen its monitoring and evaluation capacity on all three spheres of government. This will ensure that cadres deployed in various capacities were able to improve their work in meeting set government objectives.

In the course of our research we sat in branch meetings, we asked branch members to relate their experiences. There is no evidence to suggest that in the last five years public service became a place of a calling. Rather, it became a place for cushy jobs for many deployee cadres in an ever-comfortable way; we saw them in their X5s, Mercs, Jags, Jeeps and Evogue Rovers as ostentatious public display of their newfound status. We heard them bragging about their farms in Mpumalanga and elsewhere, we listened to them at sports stadia and in shebeens talk about how they spoil their trophy girlfriends with fancy apartments in Deinfern Randburg. We could find no evidence that the centre gave a strategic leadership through its structures mentioned above. However, there is evident indication that decay began to set in government as early as the last years of Mandela's administration, and the corruption index spiked significantly under Mbeki's watch; and it was during Zuma's years that the looting of taxpayers' money reached an unprecedented level. The R206 million spent on Zuma's security upgrade to his rondavel estate in Nkandla is proof of this scavenging behaviour.

Evidence also shows that those accidently found with their hands on the till were never criminally prosecuted, pursued in the courts of law, dismissed from the government and disbarred from public service as a consequence of their corrupt activities. Evidence does however point to the fact that with each whistle blowing between the contesting factions, the deployment committee walked the minefield carefully by simply recycling the folks back in the system by way of reassigning them to a different province. In less visible cases, shrewd cadres left government, set themselves up in private practice with ex-civil servant white males as partners and returned to the departments they had worked for previously as 'expect consultants' and made even more money without worrying about Scorpions or the Hawks snooping furtively into their bank accounts.

A careful study of the conferences and branch meetings revealed that the dominant issues taking up time at these meetings were grievances ANC members had with one another and with Luthuli House. We could not find data confirming that NEC members went to regions to conduct political education, in point of fact branch members couldn't care two hoots about Karl Marx's *Das Kapital* or *The Revolution of the Proletariat* theoretical nonsense; they knew precisely what they wanted—better life—and we suspect so did the leadership. When NEC people addressed PEC's and General Councils on invitation they were generally polite and comrade like in demeanour and showing great respect to branches after all, it is the branches that elected people to power.

Just as the removal of Zuma as deputy president to Mbeki was unprecedented, so too was the unprecedented nature of the removal of Mbeki from the presidency of South Africa. Chikane, author of *Eight Days in September, The Removal of Mbeki,* gave rare insights concerning the Esselen Park NEC decision that dismissed Mbeki. It was after midnight of Friday, 19 September 2008—to be precise, just before 1.00 a.m. on Saturday—when the first text messages began to come through: 'the NEC has decided to recall Mbeki as president of the country'. Another said that ANC officials had been appointed to visit Mbeki immediately, that night, to inform him of the NEC decision. If you monitored cyberspace during those early hours of that fateful day you could have written a prize-winning drama.

This cyberspace record would have given us the totality of what happened and the feelings of those involved.

Earlier on that critical Friday, reports emanated from the meeting telling of tough debates, lasting into the early hours of Saturday morning. The voices of reason which pleaded that Mbeki be allowed to complete his term, perhaps bringing the election date forward, were drowned out by the angry voices of the night; even the proposal that he should be allowed a month or so to complete some of his critical commitments of state, which included a United Nations (UN) meeting the following week to consider the Millennium Development Goals. Another was the African Diaspora Conference, scheduled for 7 to10 October 2008, which would bring together African leaders on the continent and those in the Diaspora, in line with an African Union (AU) resolution. The Permanent Representatives Committee (PRC) of the AU meeting scheduled for 24 September 2008 to prepare for the Africa Diaspora Conference was also postponed. At the forefront of our thinking was how to preserve Mbeki's legacy, particularly his African Renaissance programme. Nothing should be done to affect negatively this legacy, which no one could take away from Mbeki.

The newspaper headlines on the streets of Johannesburg and Pretoria: 'Mbeki recalled' . . . 'Mbeki removed' . . . 'Shocking decision by the ANC' . . . and so on. The questions in my mind were: 'how is the president likely to respond? How do we assist him as his support staff and advisers to manage this crisis? How did we come to this point? How did the ANC, as the ruling party, find itself in this situation? What were the mistakes made within the ANC? What mistakes could Mbeki have made both as president of the ANC and as president of the country? Could the situation have been managed differently?' Post-colonial countries where coups are part of the culture have learned that once such events are set in motion they are difficult to stop. Fortunately, no such culture has developed in either the old or the new South Africa.

With regard to Mbeki, his history and the fact that he had lived his whole life for the ANC and had no life outside the party, this action felt like 'feeling on your own' or ending his life. What would he be without or outside the ANC? What would become of his life outside the ANC? What would South Africa be like after his removal? As my brain went into overdrive on these matters, I could not but conclude that South Africa would never be the same again . . . and neither would the ANC. Mbeki repeated his view, expressed earlier in the week, that if his organisation asked him to leave office he would comply, since he saw his role as that of 'service to the people' rather than 'a position' that he needed 'to fight for'. He had not fought for positions in the ANC before and he was not about to do so now.

He re-emphasised his commitment to ensuring that the country was not destabilised by his problems with the ANC.

It was interesting for some that the party used the concept of a 'recall'. There were problems, though, about this concept in relation to a sitting president, since parliament and not the party elect the president. The concept of a 'recall' makes sense within the context of the 'deployment' policy of the ANC but could not be applied directly to a president who is elected by parliament. The language of 'recall' is usually used by presidents to 'recall' an ambassador who is appointed by the president, but could not legally be used to remove the president from office. Only parliament could remove the president, in terms of s 89 and s 102 of the Constitution. Constitutionally, the president could have ignored the 'recall', to force the party to use the constitutional mechanisms to remove him from office, if they could achieve the voting threshold required, which was unlikely at the time. On my return, I found the president's official residence full of comrades and some family members who had come either to express their support for Mbeki or just to sympathise with him. Some wept in disbelief at what had happened and others pondered why he could not be allowed to finish his term of office, as he was left with only seven months.

The plan unfolded as follows: firstly, once the delegation of the ANC had answered the two questions, details of how we would manage the process of the departure of the president would be formalised. Secondly, and whatever the responses of the party to the questions the president had asked, the president would meet his cabinet to inform them of his decision to resign in response to the 'recall' decision by the ANC. The cabinet secretariat was commanded to set the meeting up for 16:00 the following day, the Sunday afternoon, when it was expected that the NEC would have concluded its meeting, given that most members of the cabinet were also members of the NEC. Thirdly, the president would inform the country about his decision. We agreed that this should be done on the Sunday evening, after the cabinet briefing. The timing for the announcement was precipitated by the demand expressed later from Esselen Park, where the NEC of the ANC was meeting, that Mbeki deliver his letter of resignation before 19:00 on Sunday.

To ensure stability in the country, Mbeki would meet the command structures of the security forces (the South African National Defense Force [SANDF], the South African Police Services [SAPS] and the intelligence service), brief them about his decision to resign and impress upon them their professional responsibility and the imperative to ensure that there was stability, safety and security in the country. Not only did the president need to do this, he must also be seen by the nation to have done so, in order to assure the people that everything was under control and that there was no risk of instability.

The secretariat of the National Security Council (NSC) was instructed to arrange these meetings one after another on the Monday morning. An announcement would be made once the meetings were arranged, to ensure that there was no anxiety among the command structures of the security forces. It was agreed that the presidency would interact with parliament to determine the best way to handle the resignation. On the international front, the minister of foreign affairs, Nkosazana Dlamini-Zuma, was already in New York to participate in UN annual meetings, including preparations for the president, who was due to follow. In the midst of these discussions, a message came from the ANC NEC meeting in Esselen Park relaying that the president could not continue with any of his responsibilities, particularly his international commitments.

Indeed, the party 'foul mood' in Esselen Park, in Gauteng, was transferred to parliament in Cape Town, in the Western Cape the following day. The party determining what the president could do and not do while he was in office was a clear violation of the Constitution, including the oath of office of the president. This decision turned a party 'recall' of the president of the country, which in itself was problematic and a challenge constitutionally, to an act of stopping the president from executing his responsibilities. This act brought us close to the definition of a *coup d'état*. The act of forbidding the president from exercising his constitutional responsibilities and mandate was tantamount to 'an illegal change of the president' which meant that he was stopped immediately from continuing to act as president even before he resigned. As long as a president is in office, no one can forbid him or her from executing his or her constitutional responsibilities and duties.

Many people do not understand why the president gave in so easily. Some felt that, in doing so, he let them down. Others felt strongly that the president had not given the country an opportunity to test the constitutionality of a party 'recall' of the president of the country, who was elected by parliament. Yet, many others were ready to resist or campaign against his removal but were disarmed by the president's decision to comply with the decision of the party. If he had chosen not to resign, the country would have been plunged into a crisis of enormous proportions, as there was no constitutional provision for the party to do what it wanted to do except through parliament. The other option was the 'orange revolution' method used to unseat governments in certain Eastern European countries; an option that would have required the mobilisation of the masses and would have entailed considerable risk, as the people would have been deeply divided.

In addition, we had classified information that suggested refusal might have resulted in some resorting to desperate methods which, too, could have threatened the stability of the country. At this point, there were a considerable number of comrades, both within and outside government, who were engaged in activities that could have easily landed them in prison. However, the decision was that this was not the route we should go, as it would have deepened the crisis. Thank God that Mbeki, in his magnanimity had the letter delivered on time to Mbete at Esselen Park. The downside of this approach is that the country was denied the possibility and opportunity of testing the 'cadre deployment and recall' stance of the ANC and its constitutionality. But Mbeki would argue that it was the best way to save the country at that time. Additionally, he did not want to be the subject of such a debate. As the letter was delivered to Mbete, Mbeki addressed the nation saying:

'Fellow South Africans, I have no doubt that you are aware of the announcement made yesterday by the National Executive Committee of the ANC with regard to the position of the President of the Republic. Accordingly, I would like to take this opportunity to inform the nation that today I handed a letter to the Speaker of the National Assembly, the Honourable Baleka Mbete, to tender my resignation from the high position of President of the Republic of South Africa, *effective from the day that will be determined by the National Assembly* [my emphasis]. I have been a loyal member of the African National Congress for 52 years. I remain a member of the ANC and therefore respect its decisions. It is for this reason that I have taken the decision to resign as President of the Republic, following the decision of the National Executive Committee of the ANC . . . . wherever we are and whatever we do we should ensure that our actions contribute to the attainment of a free and just society, the upliftment of all our people, and the development of a South Africa that belongs to all who live in it.' He went on to say: 'Indeed, the work we have done in pursuit of the vision and principles of our liberation movement has at all times been based on the age-old values of Ubuntu, of selflessness, sacrifice and service in a manner that ensures that the interests of the people take precedence over our desires as individuals. I truly believe that the governments in which I have been privileged to serve have acted and worked in the true spirit of these important values.'

In the speech, he also alluded to Judge Nicholson's judgement, which had precipitated the decision to remove him from office, stating that 'since the attainment of our freedom' the government had 'acted consistently to respect and defend the independence of the judiciary' rather than 'act in a manner that would have had a negative impact on its work'. Even when government had to publicly express 'views contrary to that of the judiciary', it had done so 'mindful of the need to protect its integrity'. Consistent with this practice, I would like to restate the position of Cabinet on the inferences made by the Honourable Judge Chris Nicholson that the President and Cabinet have interfered in the work of the National Prosecuting Authority (NPA). Again I would like to state this categorically that we have never done this, and therefore never compromised the right of the National Prosecuting Authority to decide whom it wished to prosecute or not to prosecute. This applies equally to the painful matter relating to the court proceedings against the President of the ANC, Comrade Jacob Zuma. More generally, I would like to assure the nation that our successive governments since 1994 have never acted in any manner intended willfully to violate the Constitution and the law. We have always sought to respect the solemn Oath of Office each one of us made in front of the Chief Justice and other judges, and have always been conscious of the fact that the legal order that governs our country was achieved through the sacrifices made by countless numbers of our people, which include death. In this context it is most unfortunate that gratuitous suggestions have been made seeking to impugn the integrity of those of us who have been privileged to serve in our country's National Executive.'

Although I was a member of the team that had worked on the speech, as I listened to him speaking it struck me that the ANC seemed to have made no attempt to hear the president's side of the story; no attempt to apply the *Audi alteram partem* (hear the other side) the basic rules of justice. While the Supreme Court of Appeal would dismiss Judge Nicholson's inferences, the ANC's dismissal of the president was never reversed nor was there any intention to do so. In any case, the Nicholson judgement was simply an excuse for indulging in other interests. Although there were challenges and controversial issues such as the HIV and AIDS debate which, some believe, marred his presidency, the unprecedented 24 hours had nothing to do with that. Instead, they were a culmination of a vicious and debilitating internal strife within the ANC, centered on the removal of Zuma from his position as deputy president of the country and the charges of corruption inferred against him. Mbeki's illustrious service to the people of South Africa, the African continent and the rest of the world did not matter. Of all the commendable things Mbeki did during his presidency, what loomed highest was his African Renaissance vision, which had already taken root with programmes such as NEPAD and the APRM. No one—not even his worst enemies—could rob him of this. 'Effective from Thursday' meant that he ceased to be president at midnight on the Wednesday, creating a vacuum for the eleven hours until the new president was sworn in. The resignation of his cabinet was controversial. Some resigned as a matter of principle as they felt that the removal of the president was both unjust and unacceptable and they wished to express their solidarity with him. Others resigned because they believed they were serving at the pleasure of the president and could not remain in office if the president who appointed them was removed.

The ANC was concerned about the resignations and called on the ministers and deputy ministers not to resign, to ensure stability in government, and meetings were arranged to persuade them to stay in office. A few changed their minds but the rest, who had already submitted their resignations, remained adamant. Some of those who resigned felt it would be better for the new president to reappoint them rather than to inherit them from his predecessor. Not unexpectedly, the controversy escalated, with some within the ANC accusing Mbeki of encouraging resignations *en masse* in solidarity with him, an accusation denied by Mbeki and all those involved or affected.

Although Kgalema Motlanthe was already in the presidency, he could not assume the responsibilities of president until he was sworn in; and since Phumzile Mlambo-Ngcuka had resigned, she could not help us as her resignation took effect on the day Mbeki ceased to be president. Thus, we found ourselves in a situation where we had a president whose task was all but impossible because he had been informed that he could not continue with some of his presidential responsibilities—a violation of our constitution. On the other hand, we had a nominated president who was also not in a position to perform any presidential tasks until he was duly elected and sworn-in in terms of the constitution. Arrangements were made for the ministers to be enabled to act in terms of this section to designate one of their own to act as president from midnight on the Wednesday when Mbeki's resignation would take effect. The minister of communications, Ivy Matsepe-Cassaburi, was designated acting president at a meeting chaired by the outgoing president.

His departure had to be *ngoku!* As a result, he had no chance to go to Cape Town and clear his office or the official residence at Genadendal. Staff at Genadendal was instructed to pack his and Mrs. Mbeki's personal belongings and arrange for their transportation to Gauteng. Once his term of office ended Mbeki could not be flown by the air force without the permission of his successor, so one of the first issues I had to deal with when I met President Motlanthe after he had been sworn in was to get permission from him for the air force to fly the former president to Cape Town to deal with his personal belongings. Again, President Motlanthe was very gracious, saying he had not known the former president needed his permission. By the time permission was obtained Mrs. Mbeki had done everything possible to move out of Genadendal and, in the end, Mbeki never returned either to Genadendal or to his offices at Tuynhuys, feeling it inappropriate to do so once the new president was in office.

The NEC members who voted to halt Mbeki's leadership were incensed by grievances against him less so by facts of the party. So strong was the division in the NEC over the recall that the then Minister of Defense and his deputy as well as the Gauteng Premier, a handful members of the NEC, some Heads of departments and an assortment of rank and file that subsequently resigned their ANC membership and shortly announced the formation of the first post-apartheid break-away party. The Congress of the People (COPE) under the leadership of the erstwhile black consciousness firebrand Mosioa Terror Lekota was announced in Germiston Civic Hall. The existence of COPE merely confirmed a fractious ANC rather than a departure in policy.

Fours years after leaving politics Mbeki would observe soberly, 'Our beautiful land is drifting aimlessly because of the poor leadership that started with me, a confirmation of something that many had already known that the old struggle heroes did very little if anything at all to contribute to a new South Africa of our dreams. In its defense, the Mbeki's administration managed some advances towards the society of our dreams excerpt one thing that singularly damaged its reputation the spirit of impunity that prevailed under his watch both at official and party level. It became a culture in which hardly anybody was called to account for wrongdoing despite strong evidence showing such (the dismissal of Rutledge from a Cabinet position was an exception to the rule) Broadly speaking, the Mbeki stewardship of South Africa failed to produce a better society but it nevertheless laid the foundation for a possible good launch had a competent successor found.

Cultured gentleman

According to the profile on the ANC website Thabo Mvuyelwa Mbeki in his own words 'was born into the struggle', on 18 June 1942. He joined the Youth League at 14 and became active in student politics. After leaving the country in 1962 from Tanzania, he moved to Britain where he completed a Masters degree in economics at Sussex University in 1966. He played a prominent role in building the youth and student sections of the ANC in exile. Following his studies, he worked at the London office with the late Oliver Tambo and Yusuf Dadoo before being sent to the Soviet Union in 1970 for military training. Later that year he was appointed assistant secretary of the Revolutionary Council. Appointed to the NEC in 1975, he served as ANC representative to Nigeria until 1978.

Mbeki rose to head the department of information and publicity and coordinated diplomatic campaigns. From 1989, Mbeki headed the ANC Department of International Affairs, and was a key figure in the ANC's negotiations with the former government. Mbeki was handpicked by Mandela to be the Deputy President of the new Government of National Unity; was elected as the new President of the ANC in 1997, elected President of South Africa in 1999 and resigned as its President in 2008. He was extremely bright and an astute politician, no doubt. Yet in spite of his talents and 15 years of leadership in government he succeeded to show just what ego can do to destroy a man. What is it about ego that allows leaders to take their organisations from a good place but never allows them to move beyond that? We ask why is it that having an inflated ego interferes with the success people pursue?

Mbeki had a reputation of an intellectual scholar and possessed great transformational as well as transactional strength; he could maneuver with the greatest of ease between state protocols and managing his large contingency of presidential team as though it was walk in the park. He spent a great deal of his time developing ideas, most of which were original and very helpful to a wider audience beyond South Africa. He was not a populist and consequently his speeches did not contain rhetorical flourishes. They were firmly constructed and well argued, meant to be taken seriously and deserved critical scrutiny. People who have worked with Mbeki long enough to know the man found him an interestingly curious gentleman. A man of vision, hope and reason. Far from an idealist, Mbeki had a 'passion for the possible'. Because he had an inward personality, to outsiders Mbeki appeared to be a demagogue, aloof and distant unfair or not that's the perception people had of him. However smart Mbeki was, the need to showcase brilliance undid what was otherwise a sterling political career and significant contribution to the struggle for the liberation of South Africa that had qualified him for the highest office in the land. Mbeki made a fatal mistake many talented men and women who allow their rise to power to be defined by ego and blind determination to get what they want—he inadvertently confused his own identity with that of his ideas. In the end, this party-created man was done in by the need to see himself at the centre of every achievement of the ANC and its government. Mark Gevisser, author of *Dream Deferred* had this to say about Mbeki's interpretation of his mandate, ' . . . and his mandate was nothing less than the salvation of his people. Mbeki was haunted by the nightmare of a seething majority that would boil over into rebellion because its dream of liberation had been deferred rather than redeemed.' The saviour mandate would weigh heavily on the shoulders of anyone carrying such a mantle.

Soon after his ascent to the executive office, anyone with different views was treated as a dark cloud blocking the light of his vision. Disagreement and disloyalty became a similar concept. In his mind, position equaled omniscient. He created a climate where silence was taken for agreement. Regardless of what others had to say, a genuine exchange of ideas became progressively diminished until Mbeki was sure that what was being questioned was not his ideas. But as long as this element of security was missing, progress stalled as he closed his mind to questioning and the emergence of new ideas. He embraced his authoritative nature and began commanding the ANC according to his whims and predilections. In the process, he marginalized a sizeable portion of his cabinet, the NEC and the ANC. Overlaying his authoritarian approach to dissent within the party was an extension of a blanket intellectual intolerance, which for a period of time smothered debate within the broader academia, media and society. In many instances under Mbeki's leadership, we experienced a definite clamp-down on criticisms of the ANC, especially when such criticisms were directed at the chief himself. Unfortunately, power in the context of a dominant party in which there is no distinction between the will of the citizens and the interests of the party can breed intolerance and discomfort towards alternative views.

During his presidency, Mbeki showed little respect for opposition parties or, indeed the ANC dominated parliament, which he attended only when he presented his annual address or the budget vote speech. He had an unbridled hostility towards civil society formations; his view was that they were interfering with his mandate to govern the country and his people. Clinton warned, 'the road to tyranny, we must never forget, begins with the destruction of the truth. The truth is universal—look after it'. Truth is incontrovertible; panic may resent it, ignorance may deride it, malice may distort it, but there it is remaining absolute. We watched ANC people attempt debate, but instead they ended up spending fruitless time in differential diplomacy and political tiptoeing.

As the perceived brilliance separated him from others, it also led to a one-way mindset where everyone was a student, and he the teacher. The effects of showcasing steadily added up until it disabled a culture of meaningful dialogue within and outside the government ranks. Debates require a heavy investment of humility to keep intensity productive, to keep vigour from becoming violence, and, when necessary, to keep people from being lulled into courteous but meaningless exchanges that continues discussion, but don't advantage dialogue. When Mbeki moved from displaying leadership to showcasing his individual brilliance, the smartest people were actively marginalised, even ignored at times when they were needed the most. When others in the NEC stopped listening, Mbeki further isolated himself not only from their interest in his ideas but also from their brilliance in making his ideas even better. The irony of brilliance is that Mbeki had less influence, the opposite of what he should have achieved. In an organisation such as the ANC, even when the *one* outdoes *everyone*, one's relevance in the long run ceases; the result is a culture void of rich history. Ralph Stockman sounded this solemn warning, 'The larger the island of knowledge, the longer the shoreline of wonder,' Delusion of grandeur grew in the shoreline of wonderland and TM begun to drift to the distant yonder alone or perhaps with a handful of diehards.

As is the case with many retired politicians, once he left center stage Mbeki tended to be a monochromatic person who was not of particular use to society outside of politics. This partly explains why after his dismissal he immersed himself in mediation diplomacy in war-torn Africa away from the eye of the South African public. Looking closer at a deeper personal level Mbeki was a needy man. A needy person wants praise, something the audience must give. The needy person wants approval, something the audience must give. The egotistical person wants to be superior and a little better than everyone else, something the larger audience must acknowledge. Even a person motivated by a sense of responsibility wants to be recognised as the faithful one, which is something the audience must declare. Mbeki conjured up an image of ANC members' being mercenary in their conduct. Unfortunately, he would find himself surrounded by mercenary vultures ever circling to devour him. In the end, his legacy lay ruined in ashes. Why? His intent failed.

Mbeki's intent failed largely because he was more concerned about himself than others, this was demonstrated by the fact that he showed very little unconditional positive regard for others, in other words that everyone was worthy of respect and capable of contributing, even when not particularly acting that way. Unconditional positive regard for others had the effect that although he was not interested in changing their identity even as he was inviting them to change their minds and see things from his perspective they failed to see it that way. Pride is the most deceitful of all expressions of ego. The pride expressed in his behaviour undermined unity in the party and ultimately was the cause of its division into cabals and vengeful factions that weakened the party and further obscured his brilliance. We now know it was pride's peculiarly destructive power that ultimately brought Mbeki down in a manner seldom witnessed in modern politics. We are reminded of Proverbs 16:18 'Pride goes before destruction, and a haughty spirit before a fall.' Pride takes innumerable forms but has one end self-glorification, which is the ultimate purpose of pride. The proud Mbeki sought to glorify himself above the ANC that made him into what he ultimately became; the consummate statesman. So intolerable to God is the sacrilegious arrogance of those who, by praising themselves, obscure God's glory. In a sense by unmasking pride, God is laying out for Mbeki the path to his true greatness.

The Zuma Years

When Mbeki's light lost its glow, the Zumarites wasted no time to extinguish its flicker doing so with acrimony and personal vendetta of epic proportions. The ANC was not done with divisions. We remember very well the build-up to the 2007 conference was riddled with divisions that were immeasurably wide and the leadership contested fiercely and publicly. It produced a fray of factional zealots that were impossible to unite because there had to be winners and losers with one shared interest of hatred for one another. These divisions filtered through to the branch level and entrenched factionalism to the degree that they are its hallmarks today. The cracks are wide and deep; The Zuma election was an unanticipated event spawned by the Mbeki 3rd term plan accepted but in a narrow sense, it was a personal vendetta that was orchestrated much earlier when he dismissed Zuma as the Deputy President of South Africa. This push was meant to humiliate him personally. It was also in part, because the disparate alliances were competing to position themselves for power and money and he was their proxy. Zuma was catapulted to the number one job not because he had any special leadership qualities making him a cut above the rest in the ANC, but was understood to be a stopgap man until the ANC could raise a broadly acceptable leader among its younger generation. What appeared an inconsequential issue for the ANC carried large portents for the country.

Out went Mbeki the prince of glory, who had enjoyed the top spot since leading his party post apartheid. By general reckoning, none of the surviving generation cohort of the 1940s of the exile struggle heroes appeared fit to be a future king because too few of them had been prepared for such high-powered office outside of being struggle revolutionaries. This meant that the throne would be occupied by the next available name on the list—regardless of personal merits of the individual concerned. In other places of the world sand trickles through an hourglass at a steady rate. The ANC once had a lot going for itself, but it tended to become gummed up with internal strife or stuck in prickly personality politics. Yet, now and then, something jogs the glass, and those grains of sand briefly unclog. Just such a nudge came on 28 September, with the announcement of a sudden change at the top of pyramid.

A mere stripling at 68, Zuma's election stirred much speculation and disquiet. He had a reputation for incompetence that is rare among princes. Some human-rights watchers were sufficiently suspicious of the prince after the conviction of his financial sponsor that exposed him to direct criminal prosecution. While in exile he commanded an anti-terror squad that successfully thwarted both SANDF infiltrations as well as neutralised most of would-be opponents inside the MK ranks. He was defiant when he ascended the throne. Zuma does bring personality, simplicity and neat songs to a nation tired of quarrels and opacity from Mbeki or is it? Stuck between impatient masses disappointed by Mbeki and the greedy party bigwigs, Zuma drifted and dithered offering neither visible principle nor firm leadership. Accepted by his inner sanctum that neither his character nor his skill was adequate for the task at hand.

His personality would suffice short-term but not in the long run so the shuffling forward of Cyril Ramaphosa as credibility insurance was hatched. It is generally accepted both inside and outside the ANC that the fundamental implication of his deployment was a consequence of the internal ANC factionalism due to the absence of credible leadership rather than the outcome of democracy. Initially Zuma had to play to the gallery of the cabals that dictated the agenda while working to solidify the rear guard of the KZN stronghold. In dealing with the expectations from the ANC Zuma could not moralise about values or a culture of struggle under conditions of corruption he simply did what he had to do. Indebtedness from those in the ANC who were prepared to kill for him became for a time an albatross around his neck and effectively rendered him dead on arrival. The ANC Polokwane 2007 policy documents stated inter alia:

> To achieve this objective, the ANC government will continuously improve service to society, through enhanced public infrastructure, efficient systems and requisite personnel. The ANC will implement a comprehensive social security system which brings together initiatives such as free basic services for the poor, passenger transport subsidy, social grants, expansion of the asset base of the poor through housing, small business and land reform programmes as well as private retirement savings, unemployment and accident insurance and medical aids. Government will align and integrate the various programmes—economic and social—directed at eradicating poverty with the aim of ensuring effectiveness and better monitoring and evaluation. The ANC government will implement a comprehensive human development strategy which includes: improvement of the general education system; intensification of education in mathematics and natural sciences; promotion of social sciences that help build social cohesion; expansion of the nation's artisanship base; improving throughput and research in the universities; and an effective adult basic education programme.

> In dealing with issues of crime, the ANC proceeds from the premise that an improving quality of life also means improvement in the safety and security of

citizens in their homes and environments where they live work and engage in extramural activities. Three principles are critical in addressing the challenge of crime, especially its uniquely random and violent nature in our country. The first of these is that the battle against crime cannot be separated from the war on want. In the main, incidents of contact crime such as murder, grievous bodily harm and rape occur among acquaintances in poor communities where living and entertainment environments do not allow for decent family and social life. Secondly, specific mindsets and historical conditions drive elements of the crime problem. These are the proliferation of firearms in the hands of civilians, greed and conspicuous consumption, the psychology of patriarchal power relations and attitudes towards weaker members of society especially children. Thirdly, the networks of crime have grown in their reach and sophistication across national boundaries. These include syndicates that deal with money laundering, human smuggling as well as drug trafficking and abuse. The overall programme of national democratic transformation will gradually eliminate some of the conditions that breed social crime. So shall our contribution to creating an environment of peace, stability, economic growth and social development in Southern Africa and the rest of the continent. Critically, focus must be placed on mobilising society to make life difficult for criminals in our midst. This should include an overhaul of gender and family relations and intolerance of abuse within communities. The transformation of institutions dealing with crime, including integrated efficiency is also critical. This applies to management, expansion of personnel, utilisation of latest technology, enhanced intelligence capacity, commitment to work with the people and eradication of corruption within the 'criminal justice system'. It also applies to the efficient regulation of the private security industry to ensure that its various capacities, integrity of its recruitment practices and employees' conditions of service are in line with the requirements of what is otherwise an important part of our nation's security establishment.

In the period immediately following his election into office, there were major shifts of the global forces creating negative economic climate worldwide. The global financial meltdown of 2008 had direct impact on our economy—this posed an immediate challenge to his ability to lead the country. Added to this were new expressions of corruption and greed in government that had increased the wastage of public resources making it difficult to respond to the crisis for the benefit of the people. The results of the meltdown caused South Africa over a million job losses in less than two years thus escalating the unemployment rate significantly. The Reserve Bank predicted that South Africa's growth rate for 2012 and 2013 would be 2.6% but had to revise it downwards to 1.9%. Looking a little further ahead, to what is for us the fundamental challenge in South Africa there have been multitudinous complaints that the upswing in economic growth we have seen over the past decade under the government, has not produced the commensurate number of jobs. When you analyse it, you see why. Retail and wholesale trade, tourism, transport and communications, financial services and to a certain extent personal services and government have been the strongest growth sectors.

The top three laggards have been agriculture, mining and manufacturing. Construction has more or less fallen in between. It used to be a laggard, but it has recently been the big growth sector because of the residential building boom we experienced a few years ago. The problem is essentially that those sectors of the economy that are in decline are precisely those sectors that can absorb unskilled labour most easily. The economy has been moving progressively towards a services orientation in line with many other countries in the world; unfortunately, services require greater skills intensity, and that is where South Africa is lacking. We have acute shortage of skilled labour but an abundance of unskilled labour, yet the economy has been moving in the direction of activities that demand skilled labour proportionately more than unskilled labour. On the other hand, the rand has depreciated against major currencies, petrol price went to record highs and consumer spending dropped. Skills shortages are a brake on growth and are just one reason why the country's inclusion in the BRICS looked incongruous. Our economy is much smaller than that of the other BRICS countries, and is likely to be toppled from its spot as Africa's biggest economy by Nigeria's in the next decade. Nigeria and Angola although have started from a lower base have galloped ahead in recent years with growth pushing 10%.

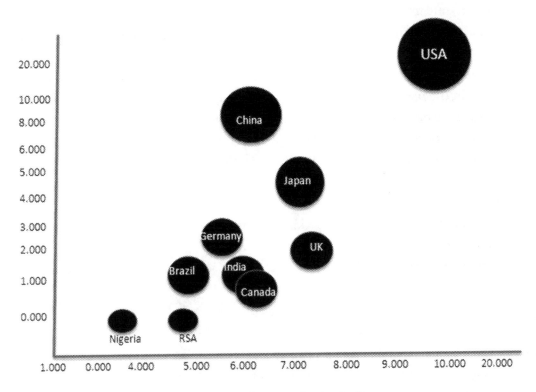

South African's position in relation to BRICS

Market Capitalization in $bn

Source Bloomberg, IMF Database

Developmental state by definition is a programme in which government mobilises society with a capacity to intervene in order to restructure the economy through public investments. The developmental state thrust dictates that the state undertakes intensive state-led interventions with a view to integrating the first and second economies, poverty alleviation, employment creation, effective delivery of services and sustained growth. To that end, government combines macroeconomic and microeconomic policy instruments to bear on the economy. 'Decisive action is required to thoroughly and urgently transform the economic patterns of the present in order to realise our vision for the future. Given the realities in our country, we opted for a mixed economy where public, private, cooperative and other forms of social ownership complement each other in an integrated way. Within this mixed economy, we re-affirm the active and interventionist role of the state in ensuring economic development. It must be a state that has the capacity to intervene in the economy to lead development,' read the January 2012 statement. The trouble is that the shift to a new growth path requires a different set of leadership skills and a new culture in governance; and also delivering the NDP plan requires that the government address key trade-offs that included:

- Present consumption and future growth, since that requires higher investment and saving in the present;
- Between the needs of different industries for infrastructure, skills and other interventions;
- Between policies that promise high benefits but also entail substantial risks, and policies that are less transformative and dynamic but are also less likely to have unintended consequences;
- Between a competitive currency that supports growth in production, employment and exports and a stronger rand that makes imports of capital and consumer goods cheaper; and
- Between the present costs and future benefits of a green economy.

At its high-level party workshop in 2007, the ANC concluded that the public service they have put in place was not ready for a major undertaking of the kind demanded by the national development plan. In the light of failed delivery on basic needs such as electricity and garbage removal, how was government going to deliver a mammoth national development plan? Did Zuma have the gumption to lead his party with a different energy to a new milieu? Was there a different culture in government, were there new people with better skills to undertake delivery of this work? Do we need another 20 years to see if this also would fail? Facts speak for themselves and you must be the judge.

Zuma's first term saw the flare-up attacks of foreign nationals by black South Africans and he failed to respond decisively to these developments. We don't feel persuaded that these were xenophobic clashes, this kind of violence although misguided and unfortunate it was an outlet of anger by black people, these clashes served to indict the government's lack of progress in many areas, including social cohesion. It is a testimony to the fact that rage is born out of despair a consequence of fractured hope of the post-liberation period. Could black people hate themselves that much that they would desperately vent their anger on others? The evidence uncovered however points to a different reason.

The economic downturn, devastating cascading effects of high interests rates, rampant food and fuel inflation, increasing corruption combined with clear lack of delivery of basic township services lead to the perception correctly or otherwise that Africans from outside South Africa appeared to have money to bribe officials for houses and licenses for taxi routes and *spaza shops*, while citizens 'had to stand in never-ending queues and stomach being treated like shit by government officials', explains a resident of 4th Avenue Alexander township in Gauteng a place where riots started. The effusion of South African's outrage had annealed into a quieter, but no less powerful, sense of grievance and the smoldering townsfolk remained determined to expose that corruption is very costly albeit in human lives as unintended as it was. According the National Planning Commission Diagnostic Report of 2011, it is reported that the Special Investigative Unit estimates 20 to 25% of state procurement expenditure, amounting to roughly R30 billion a year, went into the pockets of individuals mostly connected to the ANC. Corruption in the main arose from lack of accountability of political leaders and public institutions managers despite the competence of watchdog agencies such as Public Protector, Auditor General and Human Rights Commission.

Vehicles of self-gratification have become sophisticated today they include previously unheard of phenomenon called 'javelin' and 'warehousing.' Arrangements are made where incumbent government official would approach a *tenderprenuer*, (this is a comrade turned overnight business man and is within the ANC branch or provincial circles) facilitate the awarding of a tender(s) business from government on the understanding that this was [his] investment share that must warehoused by the consortium to be accessing at a later stage when his government contract ends, which at the end of the five-year term they would exercise. A second underhanded method is called javelin in that they would be careful to write the specifications of the tender contract to fit a specific contractor or consortium right down to the tee, and then manipulate members of the adjudication committee to vote in line with that specific criteria. They subsequently engineer his/her exit from their government day job so that they take up directorship and /or shareholding empowerment status in the consortia so awarded the tender. From the outside, it looks very clean and in accordance with tender rules, but in fact, the corrupt plan is hatched and sealed many months in advance.

Once the full extent of corruption become apparent, South Africans were appalled and could scarcely hide their umbrage in the manner in which those in government betrayed their trust. Public outcry has remained high. Many people felt compelled to take a stand in response to the assault to our national integrity causing activists to launch political organizations premised on challenging the ANC's economic mismanagement of the country head-on, including ex government managers forming civil society lobby groups to add a credible voices to the growing culture of endemic corruption. Whether this is a kneejerk reaction remains to be seen in the months ahead. Njabulo Ndebele once wrote an article for the *City Press*, 'these corruptive collusions become new foundations for solidarity. They effectively replace old solidarities of the struggle. The latter though can continue to be invoked as a necessary mantra of commitment, and far less as an objective to be pursued. Corruptive collusions offer group protection and will be hostile towards any regulatory means whatever their merits as long as they come from outside of that group. Even the constitution is regarded as an outside interference by these collusions.' Taking a stand former Chief Justice Arthur Chaskalson, would remark in his judgement, 'Corruption and misadministration are inconsistent with the rule of law and the fundamental values of our constitution. They undermine the constitutional commitment to human dignity, the achievement of equality and the advancement of human rights and freedoms. They are the antithesis of the open, accountable, democratic government required by the Constitution. If allowed to go unchecked and unpunished they will pose a serious threat to our democratic state.'

For all we care to know, corruption remains just a nebulous concept if its not attached to human face and Public Protector has put a face to corruption when she related a tragic story of a young lady from Qumbu in the Eastern Cape. The lady mother of two had been denied a child grant by SASSA. The explanation given to her by SASSA was that she already had two children in the system. Her insistence that she only had one child and that her child was not one of those in the system had fallen on deaf ears. She then brought the matter to us. When we investigated, we found that there was indeed somebody using her name, which was receiving a grant for two children. On further investigation, we found that she was a victim of a syndicate, a criminal syndicate that was cutting across three organs of state and a local supermarket. This is how the dots connected. Home Affairs would give out IDs based on identity theft, which result in something that Home Affairs calls a duplicate ID, where an ID is shared between one, two, or sometimes four people. A similar pattern occurred in the Department of Health, where a clinic would give health cards for fictitious children. Then SASSA would process the application and adjudicate favourably despite the limitations, and then a local supermarket would be used as a pay point. Not only does it rob people primarily the poor, but also corruption is increasingly associated with health risks and even deaths, which could happen to all of us'.

Mashiqi argues that single party dominance is a major component of the debate about the relationship between the party and the state. South Africa does not have a strong history of opposition. If we limit ourselves to the past 64 years, ours has been a political reality of single party dominance since 1948. In actual fact, it can be argued that, to the extent that we should be concerned about the reality or the perception of the disappearance of the line between party and state, this country has never had a strong tradition of separation of powers. Democratic values are the one side of the coin and public accountability is the other side—the one does not exist without the other. Accountability entails transparency in the governance of public institutions in which the activities and conduct of officials must pass public scrutiny.

Accountability and transparency are tools intended to enhance ethical behaviour, thereby remove the conditions under which corruption thrives. Under Zuma, the notion of public accountability became a fuzzy concept rather than a value ANC leader ought to live by. As the ANC tried to deal with this issue, among the questions it had to ask itself were: could it claim to have a legitimate president able to exercise accountability and disciplined management of government affairs? Second, could it clean up and improve its image under a leader so compromised? In the end, the party simply lamented the leadership deficit pointing to itself rather than Zuma saying, 'yet, as with all historical phenomena, to mark time is to move in reverse. The consequence is either gradual regression, with self-satisfied elite unsighted; or a rapid collapse of social cohesion under the weight of corruption, poverty and lawlessness.' Rare admission.

Lack of foresight and judgement were Zuma's Achilles heel. First, it was Mokotedi Mpshe, and then came Menzi Simelane followed by Bheki Cele and Richard Mdhluli; now it is Riah Phiyega. All of these men and women did not ask to be appointed, however they were placed in rather invidious position and would became an albatross around Zuma's neck. He succeeded to get rid of the more vulnerable individuals who did not have a strong political base to launch counter offensive measures such as Siphiwe Nyanda, Scelo Shiceka, Gwen Mahlangu, Jimmy Manye, Julius Malema and Dina Pule but he got stuck with equally vulnerable but protected lot in the likes of Angie Motshega, Mildred Oliphant and Lulu Xingwana. Such is the price when one is beholden to cabals. If we took, few steps back and looked at these shenanigans with a different eye we may be surprised at what we see.

It may very well be that Zuma has always been honest even though somewhat naïve with the nation about the things he does in private and in the public domain. Rather, this indictment is a reflection on the oligarchy that propped him up as their man, knowing full well that as a leader he was dead in water and could never act as moral authority over any one. This gave [them] tacit license to cash in because the door has been opened by this behavior. Consequently, high prevalence of predatory behaviour in government and the looting of taxpayer's money is no longer just a matter of casual conversation at dinner a table, nor is it a mismanagement of a budget of Ditlopo municipality in Mahikeng but a pervasive culture that is rotting the very soul of government.

The man JZ

Most people in the ANC initially believed that the answer to Mbeki's ego and Machiavelli was Zuma's humility. Zuma was born on 12 April 1942 in Inkandla, a remote part of KwaZulu-Natal. He spent his childhood moving between Zululand and the suburbs of Durban, and by age, 15 took on odd jobs to supplement his mother's income. Owing to his deprived childhood, Jacob Zuma did not receive any formal schooling. Heavily influenced by a trade unionist family member, he joined the ANC in 1959. He became a member of uMkhonto weSizwe in 1962. In 1963, he was convicted of conspiring to overthrow the government, sentenced to 10 years' imprisonment on Robben Island, left South Africa in 1975 and lived in several African countries working for the ANC, where he rose rapidly through the ranks to become a member of the ANC National Executive Committee in 1977.

He was appointed Head of Underground Structures and shortly thereafter Chief of the Intelligence Department. Following the unbanning of the ANC, he was one of the first ANC leaders to return to South Africa to begin the process of negotiations, and was instrumental in organising the Groote Schuur Minute that reached decisions about the return of exiles and the release of political prisoners. In 1991, he was elected the Deputy Secretary General of the ANC. In 1998 he was honoured with the Nelson Mandela Award for Outstanding Leadership in Washington DC, USA. In 1994, he was elected National Chairperson of the ANC and chairperson of the ANC in KZN, and Deputy President in 1997. He became the President of the ANC in 2007 and the President of South Africa in 2009.

Having given over five decades of his life to the cause of the ANC many who knew him well, said Zuma Msholozi kaNxamalala or, 'JZ' was a good cadre of the ANC, a good listener . . . to a fault and variously described as 'a man I can trust'; a person true to his convictions, always dedicated and honest in his dealings with the organisation. Zuma is someone who would never sell the organisation, never take a position unless he believes it protects the vision of the organisation and the future it has committed to. Our avuncular Zuma an effable father of 17 has personal charisma, including his laughing and singing abilities. If politics were religion, Zuma would be its god. Pony Tonybee, British commentator once argued that it is not frivolous to emphasise the nature of the man because no one can accurately say what leaders really stand for, or predict what they will do once in power. The ANC has shoehorned Zuma into ways of believing and speaking that is at odds with his real self. Our analysis of several interviews during his term in office, revealed serial discomfort with public such as the independence of the judiciary and its ability to up-end executive decisions when the need arose. There are many examples where a negative correlation between party and the man has been established. Zuma is human and humans have to a greater degree complex ego personalities layered, add to that complexity full-blooded politician then the enormity of difficulty increases manifold. Zuma is not a modernist.

The promotion to Mahlamba Ndlopfu could not have come at an inopportune moment in his political career. There is a tenuous tension between the man and the party's ideal. Similar to his predecessor, Zuma is an egotistical man and the element that revealed it most eloquently was the need for acceptance. The reason many people don't consider seeking acceptance as a rather devastating element of ego is because genuine acceptance is valuable and most humans thirst for it. When others in the ANC were shaping Zuma's self-confidence, he shaped his thoughts and actions to what he believed they would approve. He sought acceptance because he believed if he could constantly get approval of his backers, it would feed his ego what it lacked. Zuma's backers must have felt jaded at their misjudgment.

Zuma is the victim of many things but the need for acceptance screams the loudest. Members who voted for him on the basis that he would bring effective government are now concerned that his private conduct has undermined effective government throughout his first term and does not bode well for the remainder of the second term. He became a perpetual pleaser and never offered to be understood for his own thoughts nor evaluated on his own merits. Zuma was prone to say whatever he thought would afford him acceptance, which ironically increased the chances of caricature. Because of his desire for recognition and respect, he was often out of balance with reality. He could not draw a distinction between who he was and what he did in the cause of his role as the leader of the ANC and Head of State; consequently, he lacked authenticity. As it does, humility generates genuine confidence that protects a leader from confusing his identity. Even though he grew into the need to seek acceptance of others, Hartman asserts that our core motive drives our behaviour and these never change.

The core ambition of humility is a remarkable devotion to progress. That devotion requires a sequential focus on others first and *me* last—never any other way. As the broader masses of people in and outside of the ANC began to sense his intent, it altered their perceptions and interaction with him and they grew increasingly weary of what he said. Their trust in him progressively diminished. Devotion to progress often requires sacrifice for causes greater than oneself, with no immediate return. Humility is not a dichotomy—it is a duality. As much as humility has the capacity to say, 'I am deserving of respect, and no more deserving than another, I am accomplished', and at the same time, it says, 'I am unfinished'. Duality, as a unique property of humility leads a man to an appropriate sense that he is unfinished on his journey. Duality doesn't force a leader to become something the leader is not. Humility is not the architect of plain personality; rather, it is the engineer of stronger ones. When a leader embraces humility's confident, dual nature, the signs of ego are eradicated.

Once in power Zuma settled down to strengthen the rear guard of his home province and his true self gradually revealed. He showed scant regard for public institutions. Under his aegis, he has sought to undermine the independence of the courts at every available turn, the prosecution authority and the press. We have seen the dropping of the arms deal charges on the most spurious of grounds and substitute it with a fact-finding commission of enquiry that would take years to reveal the truth this was aimed at protecting himself. We have seen him introduce spies as his personal protectors to shield him from the law. We have seen him refusing to obey court orders to comply with the rule of law and protect the integrity of the constitution, especially the Glenister judgement, which directed his government to create a corruption-fighting unit that was independent of him and his administration.

We have seen him spending a quarter of billion rands of public money on a vast new luxury complex for himself and his family while he has access to three official residences around the country. We have seen him brazenly refuse to give any account of his expenditure, all the more obscene because its ostentation is in the midst of one of the poorest regions of the country. We have seen him stand by impotently as the education of the nation and public service collapsed under his watch. For four successive years, most municipal entities in the country failed to meet the Auditor General's minimum standards of public accounting of finance and administration as required by the law, yet nothing was done to avert the collapse of these institutions, and this while and increasing number of young people remained unemployed because of this crass inefficiency. We have seen him conflating the interests of the party and state, dishing out contracts for public works as rewards for loyalty to him personally.

Zuma presents a unique kind of a problem to South Africa. How exactly might citizens engage with a leader who is convinced that the ANC has history, tradition, and popular support and that it would rule South Africa until the 'Second Coming of Jesus Christ'? A leader who takes broad swipe on fellow black South Africans that criticise his deficient leadership skills and crass materialism, calling them 'clever blacks' that imbibe white culture when what they care for are their pets—cats, birds and dogs. A leader who tells citizens who object to being treated like government cash cows and exercise their economic right by boycotting the e-tolling of Gauteng's super highways that they should stop thinking like Africans in Africa because Johannesburg is world class city that cannot be equated with a national road in Malawi or to an under developed town like Rustenburg.

This is the problem with the e-toll system. Black citizens domiciled in Gauteng are getting punished twice. First, they got punished by the apartheid government, which dumped them as far away from the city center as possible so that to get to work they were forced to travel long distances. Now the ANC government is punishing them again by taxing black people heavily, because of the greater the distance they will have to travel to work from outlying townships, they must pay more. In comparison, to whites that have lived within city limits will pay less even though they earn much more than most black people. E-tolling puts Gauteng citizens in a moral predicament. Should they abide by the law that victimizes the victims of the apartheid regime and become accomplices in this injustice, or should they defy this unjust law? Would a law that unfairly discriminates against poor segment of the community by penalizing them with higher costs not be in violation of their rights under the constitution? The constitution does not require citizens to abide by immoral and unjust laws, in this case a law that disproportionately taxes the poor more than it does the rich is an unjust law.

Zuma was unlikely to be a kind of leader of the open shared society of our dreams because he came from a culture in exile of secrecy, solidarity and vertical hierarchy. Right now, he lives in a new world with policy challenges that demands openness, accountability and horizontal networks. It could well be that he does not have original ideas of his own. When Zuma favoured popularity over candour, conversations often became artificial and reality escaped him. He carried this sense of popularity with him and whenever circumstances suited him, he'd exploit this to a full extent. In the national assembly, opposition parties called for a debate on his fitness to hold the office of the president in the wake of the Nkandla exposé his kneejerk reaction was it wouldn't happen. He paused, prevaricated and eventually relented although the opposition parties hesitated to bring the substantive motion to the house pending a court clarification on certain house rules. Nevertheless the point was made he was no longer welcome as the president of South Africa and the nation was united in this view.

Whether the ANC believe this is immaterial. Instructing parliament to respect that he is a leader of the country served only to highlight that he is pretty daft after all it is leaders with a God complex that behave in this manner. Throughout his presidency, Zuma has ensured his family and family associates were first in line to benefit from potential government and private sector business opportunities whenever these became apparent. It is not necessary to go into details about these facts as many books have already been published detailing how he acquired the wealth, he has. He would have faired better if he did not ignore Ziegler's advise, 'You can have everything in life you want, if you will just help other people to get what they want.'

Regardless of whether or not the upgrade for his security at his Nkandla rondavel estate was inflated increasing the value of this estate or it was for the Nxamalala clan's comfort, it was a subject of much public outcry. The R215 million of tax payer money spent on transforming a dusty rural structure into something that would impress a time-travelling member of the Borgia family is an affront to the people of South Africa especially in the face of the high levels of poverty the country is experiencing. DA's Mzibuko laid a complaint with the office of the Public Protector to investigate how this money was spent and whether it was for security reasons as alleged. The upgrade was reportedly to include a helipad, three underground living quarters with 10 air-conditioned rooms.

A medical clinic for the president and his family, houses for security staff, air force and police units, underground parking, playgrounds and a visitors' center. An Astroturf field that cost R100 000 a month just in maintenance alone. The Inter-Ministerial probe confirmed that spending was on the security upgrade and said it was necessary but preferred to declare the estate a National Key Point which meant that everything about the money spent on his private home was classified information. The security cluster ministers Cwele, Mthethwa and Radebe demanded to see the provisional report before it was published after seeing it they insisted they want to classify it and went to court to block the Pubic Protector from making it public but later abandoned their challenge.

The *Mail & Guardian* article of 29/11/2013 reported on the preliminary findings of the Public Protector investigation into Nkandla upgrade titled *Opulence on a Grand Scale*. The newspaper reported that 'Zuma has derived 'substantial' personal benefit from the works that excedded security needs at his Nkandla homestead and must repay the state an estimated R20million for non security feature extras that include a swimming pool, visitor's center, amphitheatre, cattle krall, a marque area, extensive paving and a new houses for relocated relatives.' The article further stated that Zuma must account to Parliament for violating the executive ethics code on two accounts of misleading Parliament for lying that he and his family had paid for all structures unrelated to security and secondly for failing to protect state resources. The cost escalted from an initial R27 million to R215 million with a further R31 million in works outstanding concluded the article.

Besides the questionable upgrade to his residence, there was the concern about Umlalazi-Nkandla Smart Growth Centre. A R2 billion multipurpose center investment near Nkandla homestead with world-class facilities that would include government offices, a library, theatre, a school with boarding facilities, a community safety center, a recreation centre with a swimming pool and tennis courts and light industrial units, including an agricultural market. What are the economic prospects in Nkandla that are so compelling to attract such big investments? Nkandla is a rural backwater of KZN and shares boundaries with poverty-stricken villages such as Babanango, Khathaza and Ebizimali that are without the most basic services such as clinics, hospitals, and proper classrooms for children and running water and electricity.

We can't be sure about all the entitlements accorded our heads of state. Let us assume therefore that Zuma was doing nothing new his predecessors hadn't done before and let us compare what has gone on before him. Public records would show that an Afrikaner businessman donated the Houghton estate as a reciprocal goodwill for his selfless dedication to nation building. At first, it he used it as a guesthouse then later made it his home. The money spent by government on the security upgrade at this house was R32 million. The Qunu village retirement homestead was refurbished by money from of his own wealth (it is worth noting that Mandela was a multimillionaire in his own right) Figures on security upgrades are unknown at this time. Mbeki leaves in a modest R22 million estate, in Lower Houghton. This mansion was built near end of his term in office from money he earned while employed in government. Government spent R12 million on the security upgrade to this residence. Monthlante leaves in a humble gated community inside a golf estate in Midrand bought through a loan that he is currently paying off. The money spent on the security upgrade to this residence is under R10million. FW de Klerk private home has security upgrades to the value of R236 000. From the available public records, there is nothing to suggest that any of the previous presidents have used taxpayer money to the extent that the upgrade of the Nkandla estate has caused waves. This clearly shows indiscretion on the part of Zuma. The money was spent. It was wrong, and hard to justify. Political commentators have excoriated the president for grossly mismanaging taxpayer money by saying the looting of the state is part of African culture.

Zuma's behaviour upends the very concept of social justice espoused in our constitution. When juxtaposing this preposterous extravagance with the material conditions on the ground, one is left thinking what on earth these politicians think they are doing. Take for example, Philippi in Cape Town, residents of this small community are still using chemical toilet system and not far from them, other Capetonians are using toilet without enclosures. In Limpopo and Eastern Cape, village children went to school and learn without textbooks for nearly a year. Lekoa, being one area worst affected by previous tragedies of South African; the Sharpeville and Boipatong massacres we thought, the government would at the very least put the people of these townships top on the priority list for reconstruction and development ahead of Soweto. In Sebokeng, Boipatong, Everton and Sharpeville few public facility have been built to improve the places in 20 years. In Tembisa, the second biggest township in South Africa after Soweto, residents has been called to settle debt dating back to the apartheid days of the 1980s despite the fact that unemployment in this community is the highest in many years. We can go on and count genuine grievances of poor communities that have not been attended to since the rule of ANC government several volumes would not contain them.

In 2012, he asked the country's industry executives to make sacrifices by postponing awarding themselves hefty bonuses in light of the pain highlighted by the miners' plight of Marikana, as well as the hard economic circumstances the country faced at this time. Between 2006 and 2009, executive pay in South Africa rose 200%, while average workers gained just 15.4%. The Access to State Information Bill giving government broad powers to classify anything as being in 'the interest of national security' is meant to protect him during his tenure and after he has served government. We understand that to rise to the highest office confers grave responsibility and that leadership essentially, is the loneliest summit of human endeavour, but South Africans must find it difficult to understand why Zuma sought the presidency to begin with. David Shapiro of Zappiro cartoonist, depicted Mandela in the most gut wrenching humour bordering on absurd; we loved it, Mandela loved it so much so that he encouraged it by making it a subject of most his jokes in public platforms. Eventually the satire became a series that is now a treasure for the nation at the Africana Museum in downtown Johannesburg. Not so, with Zuma, displaying an infuriating equanimity about the prospect of a further caricature on his person was prepared to go to war.

Zuma took umbrage with just about every cartoon depiction. In 2008, the 'Justice Lady' offended him so much that he sued for defamation of character but, on the eve of the high court hearing—embarrassed by his folly—withdrew the suit claiming that he was ill-advised to do so in the first instance. In 2010, his blue light convoy of bodyguards arrested and charged a UCT law student who raised a middle finger to the passing motorcade as a sign of his indifference to Zuma. In June 2013, on the morning of the court hearing Zuma's lawyers entered an out-of-court settlement with the student. In 2012, Goodman Gallery exhibited a series of 'Hail the Thief II' by Brett Murray. This body of satirical work continued Murray's acerbic attacks on abuses of power, corruption and political dumbness by the ruling clique. In the sequel show, Murray's work formed part of a vitriolic and succinct censure of bad governance and were his attempts to humorously expose the paucity of morals and greed within the ANC elite. 'The Spear' painting saga had Zumarites hopping mad, proclaiming the insult to the president is an insult to the nation. #Tag 'Yeah right dream on' trended tweets.

The nation disagreed with this view, stood firm in the belief that public figures are fair game and that humiliation is a feeling most often felt by those who harbor a god complex especially the type that lacked humility. The drama that ensued in protest form in the streets of Rosebank, in Johannesburg High courts, on television talk shows, on publications board was entertaining tragedy of comedy. In the end, the painting prevailed. Art will always honour its truth. The Book of Proverbs tells us, 'If you can't control your anger, you are as helpless as a city without walls waiting to be attacked.' In his quest for self-preservation, Zuma had changed from the warm, charming and effable person to a ruthless politician. Zuma is not the kind, benevolent, humble son of a domestic worker sold, but we came to know him as a full-blooded politician that we regard with deep repugnance. At the time of writing Zuma had completed his first term in office. A term of office best forgotten for the crises of confidence he suffered, specters of human tragedies and service delivery dramas too violent to describe, all of which simply overwhelmed the president. Whether or not Zuma had learned from these experiences and gained new insights that would shape his leadership for the second term will only know in the years ahead.

We have looked at the role played by the NEC in deploying cadres who ran the government and the respective performances of the three administrations. We now return to probe the question: did the ANC succeed to 'lift the trajectory of the national democratic revolution to a higher plane' making South Africa better place for all or, has it diminished the potential of South Africa to realize its status as a leader among Africa's emerging economies? We step up and look deeper at the impact the government's performance has had on our society by assessing the health of the nation. Promises are one thing, getting down to the nuts and bolts of fulfilling them are a different matter altogether.

CHAPTER 3

Diagnosing The Health of South Africa

Corruption and misadministration are inconsistent with the rule of law and the fundamental values of our constitution. They undermine the constitutional commitment to human dignity, the achievement of equality and the advancement of human rights and freedoms. They are the antithesis of the open, accountable, democratic government required by the Constitution. If allowed to go unchecked and unpunished they will pose a serious threat to our democratic state and its freedom

From a medical perspective, the identification of diseases is by the examination of the presenting symptoms and by various investigations, an informed clinical opinion proffered. Said assessment is conducted using a set of scientific diagnostic protocols and techniques and the examiner's opinion becomes the basis on which remedial intervention is proposed. A thorough grounding in empirical reality beyond anecdotal sound bites had informed our conclusions. Evidence supporting our conclusions comes from reports of the Auditor General, findings of the Public Protector, Special Investigative Unit and the Constitutional Court judgements. Routinely the president addresses the nation through parliament presenting his thoughts on the state in which the country is in and would share government's plans for the year ahead. Half of what he presents is regarded in political parlance 'official spin', official government line, facts are often exaggerated in order to make the government look impressive compared to its previous performance. The problem is that his ministers never do the other half that he promised would be done. Ours is an assessment of the impact of government programmes on the general health of the society as a whole on an extended time horizon and we do this by tracking four important markers, namely the health of economy, social cohesion, race relations and the quality of education. The hinge upon which these markers pivot is political leadership and we comment upon this pivotal point objectively as a matter of fact at the end. We should like to point out that the nation's health is not necessarily limited to these three markers for example, the vibrancy of sports and arts, on edge science and technology, the country's attractiveness to the global community through its tourism as a destination of choice, are critically important to the health of the nation. For the purpose of our analysis however, we will limit our review to the factors mentioned.

It is axiomatic that a healthy nation is a nation that holds free and fair elections at fixed regular intervals, democratically choosing its public representatives to run the nation's affairs, the public officials in turn appoint other organs of the state namely the judiciary and the executive. The state is the servant of its people—not its master that dispenses patronage in pursuit of self-aggrandizement. The vibrancy of the society is seen through its economically active populace who are gainfully employed in wealth-creating endeavours and shares their wealth with the nation in taxes, philanthropy and welfare. A communal spirit in the place of self-centeredness is the dominant character of the society. Citizens knitted together in high moral values, harmonious relations among diverse cultural groups characterised by the absence of ethnic tension, is the norm. Humanity expressed in moral rectitude is the heart and soul of the nation.

The government enables the economy by providing public infrastructure network to move goods and services, public health, good quality education, corruption—free and responsive public servants. The society founded on constitutional order and the rule of law is its pillar. The citizens enjoy total freedom to pursue unlimited human endeavours and have the freedom to live with dignity under crime-free social conditions; poverty in its spiritual or physical manifestation is an exception rather than the rule and social justice is its cornerstone. A healthy nation is an educated nation. Freedom of the press, choice and of movement taken for granted. Children are loved, nurtured and cared for by adults and are protected from family breakdown and anti-social crime such as rape. Citizens tended to live long enough to see their golden years. These are not lofty ideals but a reality of what a healthy nation should look like, because the Creator of life designed it to be lived this way on earth, we know this to be true for many societies in the world. Let us examine how our nation measures on this social barometer.

Economy

For the government's role to mean anything to the people of South Africa, it needed to address the economic legacy of the colonial past in a manner that was vastly different to how other African states have gone about their own eradication of colonial influences in their economies in the past 20th century. There were 10 key areas that required decisive action more along the lines of deep transformation namely, unemployment and inequality, current account deficit, stabilization of fiscal and currency volatility, increased savings rate and reduction in consumer indebtedness, manufacturing sector improvement, labour and wage stability, public sector productivity, new generation infrastructures, improve sovereign credit ratings and the development of the ICT industry. Throughout history, many countries have experienced dramatic decline rather than progress after attaining self-rule. The Hapsburg and Argentina and many African countries all bear witness to this reality.

Prior to assuming office, the ANC think-tank strategists appear to have done little due diligence on the internal dynamics of South Africa's economy and in some instances they appeared to have ignored the counsel of those holding better ideas e.g. The Washington Summit. We know that the government held numerous economic workshops as well as scenario planning up to and including the time of transition to figure out the best possible position the country's economy should follow. It came as a huge surprise to many that; the ANC would send delegations to study the economies of Cuba, Vietnam, Angola and Zimbabwe that had nothing fundamentally in common with the emerging economy of South Africa at that time. Economies that shared strong similarities with South Africa were Malaysia, Germany, Japan and the Singaporean economic systems. We believe these were better benchmarks, we know they would have learned far more and given better counsel to their principals.

When Mandela attended the World Economic Forum in Davos for the first time, up to that point he was solid on the proposition of nationalisation contained in the Freedom Charter. But after frank and sobering conversations with his counterparts from China, the Netherlands and Vietnam, it would appear that he had a moment of epiphany and effectively eschewed nationalisation as a principle for advancing South Africa's economic transformation agenda and a new possibility for South Africa's prosperity was within view. From the mountain of policy documents drawn up by ANC theoreticians, we studies each document refuting the preceding one, ultimately culminating into four-tracks-one-concept conundrum. First, it was the RDP in 1994, which was Mandela quick-fix delivery plan to the poor on social infrastructure; this plan was closely allied to the Freedom Charter. RDP was quickly replaced by GEAR in 1996, a centerpiece of the macroeconomic plan by Mbeki. Then came AsgiSA in 2006, a turbocharged plan aimed at eliminating the remaining constraining factors in the growth of economy and speeding the implementation of GEAR constituent parts. The integrated NDP plan superseded AsgiSA in 2011 as the official policy road map.

South African 1996 - 2012

Index	1996	2012
Population	40.6m	51.7m
GDP	143.7	402.2
Unemployment	4.7m	6.1m
Employment	9.0m	14.0m
Access to services		
Electricity	58.2%	84.7%
Clean water	60.4%	73.5%
Sanitation	50.3%	62.7%
Functional Illiteracy	33.6%	22.3%
Welfare	2.4m	15.5m

Source 1996 National Census

The NDP was conceived by the National Planning Commission and positioned as the centerpiece of the developmental state. Subsequently, it turned out that even this plan was not canvassed adequately with tripartite alliance people, much less with the nation as it was rushed to the ANC June 2012 policy conference that later embraced it as the game changer. Numsa a Cosatu proxy was upset that the ANC had adopted the plan and they denounced the NDP as a betrayal of the 'democratic revolution'. Numsa's argument stems from the fact that NDP and GEAR share the same theoretical underpinnings and therefore commit the same policy error as GEAR did. It would also appear that Numsa was upset at the language used since most of it appeared to be borrowed from the opposition Democratic Alliance. In March 2013, Numsa published a full—spread advert in the Business Day publicly rubbishing the ANC.

In light of this debate, we performed our own comparative analysis to arrive at the conclusion that NDP and GEAR were similar in intent and purport to fulfill the same economic end objective. Therefore, there is semblance of truth in the argument that the NDP does not address the economic fundamentals that are colonial in character and that when implemented it would perpetuate the two economies dichotomy. Congresses, workshops, policies and strategy workshops, white papers, yellow papers and green paper protocols flowed with rapidity of rivers yet little were achieved. Government repeated 'strategic constraints' and 'capacity problems' as if in it would solve the problem. Difficulty is one excuse though never accepted by history. We found the explanations for the strategic policy choices between these policy positions and difficult trade-offs made in order to launch the transformation agenda, purely conjectural masking a lack of a coherent vision.

The introduction of the GEAR policy somewhat marked a break with the colonial past but not far enough to alter the foundations created by that order. At first, Mbeki parachuted it into effect bypassing Parliament and the NEC and roping in Cabinet as its rubber stumper. His technocrats championed it as the pillar of government transformation agenda; discarding all conventional wisdom of debate prior to implementation gone ahead and implemented it under a cloud of bureaucratic secrecy. It is recorded that at one stage, Gavin Reilly—then Presidential Advisory Council Chairperson, he and his entourage went to see Mbeki about the Council's thoughts with regard to the direction the country should take on the economy. They discovered that Mbeki had already arrived at that conclusion independently [in his view] South Africa needed a different policy than what his party had been working on in the past seven years. Impressed by his strategic foresight and business astuteness, they congratulated him blessed his plans, asked him to shift it to top gear right away. Forced to choose between preserving racism and saving capitalism, white capital and the state opted to renegotiate a new paradigm.

By reorganising state power, making it democratic and nonracial, capitalism was regrounded by the old order and given a hold for sustainability by the neoliberal agenda and its emergent black middle class. In essence, the South African economy was never *de*racialised it was simply *multi*racialised. As the nation would learn subsequently that the two economies polarity argument was premised on the notion, that race is acceptable as a principle for distributing wealth and power—in light of the changing regime only the definition needed an upgrade. The goal was to raise blacks as one racial group to become equal with whites as another racial group. In the eyes of the government, there were compelling reasons for using state machinery to create blacks into hitherto white citadels of power. Unless blacks assume positions of ownership, talk of nonracial transformation is delusional. Just as before, whites remained subjects and blacks objects.

The principle of advancement on the basis of one being black served to sharpen expectations for some and deepened disillusionment for many. The economic re-engineering programme of employment equity, affirmative action, broad based black economic empowerment was a plan ostensibly drawn up to respond to the 'two nations' dichotomy where a large dispossessed and aggrieved black majority class must assert itself among the wealthy privileged white minority class, on the grounds that for whites to share their wealth now was necessary, prudent and right. If the white elite failed to share their wealth willingly the state, would on behalf of the masses appropriate their wealth at some point and redistribute it. And so what began as a widely embraced concept of perfectly legitimate economic redress policy descended in a very short period of time into a beneficiary scheme for the well-connected insiders and never trickled down to the masses of the poor who eventually became economic outsiders? In the case of the Mbeki administration, there was a subtext. Not all black beneficiaries were of the right kind; only those deemed so by him and his faction. It was at his discretion to decide whether a private benefit such as BBBEE was simultaneously a public good for the masses. The BBBEE aim was to be the driver of the economic redistributive programme for the poor; its empowerment tool consisted of deeding chunks of equity to various consortia of black shareholders, on the understanding that they would redeem the purchase price at a later stage through growth in the share valuations. Most of these were 100% leveraged. There in lay the problem.

Most of the empowerment projects launched at a time in history when there were extreme global volatility and languid stock market. As debt mounted and shares stagnated, many deals lost their promise, collapsed and were eschewed. It was hardly a formula for a long-term inroad into the market economy. So, the strategists had to hurriedly hatch a plan B. In this regard, the Empowerment Act was swiftly amended to strengthen it and give it more substance. Codes of Good Practice; Equity in the workplace, Scorecards and Enterprise Development categories were added to incentives compliance by reluctant players—yet the failure was glaring. Punitive measures to force rigorous compliance were tightened but met with quiet resistance. The country was looking at a mega billion rand investment in what was essentially a race-based ideological project without the punted broad economic trickle-down benefits in the medium term. This R500 billion-equity transfer faced severe financial challenges at that time and it was headed for the dustbin of history. Certainly, the first wave of the empowerment endevour has failed.

In the end, this project added little competitiveness to the South African industries, did not improve the life of consumers, had done nothing for the creation of the small business sector, did not improve the climate for job creation, nor that it has in and of itself, advanced the original objectives of the 2003 Empowerment Act of giving economic citizenship to the majority of South Africans. In the wake of the colossal failure of this national project, there was a new development rather chilling in its development. Quietly and unassumingly making no waves as it made its way into the heart of South Africa's economic engine. People from Pakistan came in the country as ordinary tourists, medical tourists, asylum seekers, refugees and anything in between that the official Customs Office ZA1 form at would allow for. Have entered the country set themselves up as small traders in the townships quietly negotiating a take over of unsustainable existing spaza shop businesses from black owners and starting new ones. Most of the 21 Gauteng townships are now reluctant hosts of the franchise network of Wal-Mart the Pakistani version conveniently operated on all corner gantries of the township marketplaces. Nearly half of prime land of the Western Cape is foreign owned along the up market holiday routes of South Africa, it is now a matter of time before Gauteng falls into the hands of foreigners including Pakistanis and Chinese with dire consequences of Islamic and other Eastern religious encroachment in the civic and cultural life of black people. This is a peculiarly interesting lesson in economic empowerment to a nation that is literally sitting and waiting for the arrival of a better life, and perhaps more profoundly, a sobering wake up call to a nation that has just emerged from 57 years of social and economic exclusion by a minority race.

The triple challenge of HIV, unemployment and poverty were not dented even in the slightest by this project. We must conclude that although clothed in sophisticated apparels with complex labyrinth, it remains a primitive attempt that wanted to take from the white wealth-owning class and give to the black wealth-seeking class. However, this kind of social engineering does not happen through laws or cajoling. The government policy of pushing for the rapid expansion of the black tycoon class has conversely led to a cult of crass individualism and conspicuous consumption while some 12 million people live below the absolute poverty datum line. Now black tycoons are society's new heroes, rather than honest entrepreneurs who have built up their business through hard work and ingenuity. The government has used its power to create black elites who sit increasingly comfortably alongside white elites.

The link between capitalism and oppression and the stupendous concentration of wealth in the hands of a few render trite the vainglorious declaration that oppression and its social consequences can be resolved by political democracy that is underpinned by market forces.

While democracy may present opportunities for some without a systematic effort led by the masses of people, to unravel the skewed distribution of wealth and income, the social reality of apartheid will remain firmly in place—only this time it will be under ANC management. This government remains beholden to a failing neoliberal economic strategy and has no discernable vision for dealing with inequality and poverty. The redistribution of economic assets and ownership, the democratisation of economic power, the empowerment of black people, women and youth, and the growth of job creating industries were great platitudes that did not meet the expectations of the poor.

A small section of South Africans are growing wealthier but inequality is still a large factor. The levels of inequality between black people has seen the divide between wealthy and poor growing faster than any other race, i.e. by more than 20 per cent. Some have opined that Mbeki needed a pliant and dependent political class that would support him in the showdown between the benefiting elite and the angry black masses, and big business believed it needed black middle class as a buffer against a restless poor working class. The promise of caring for the poor has proven itself a lie. The government through its conduct has perpetuated an anti-black reality. Politicians would typically talk about rising inequality and the sluggish recovery as separate phenomena, when they are in fact intertwined. Inequality stifles, and restrains growth. And yet, after four decades of widening inequality and the greatest economic downturn, nothing has been done about it.

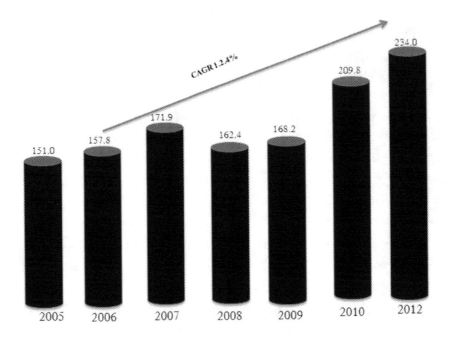

There are four major reasons inequality is squelching our prospects as a nation. The most immediate is that the created middle class is too weak to support the consumer spending that has historically driven our economic growth. Second, the hollowing out of the middle class since the 1990s, a phenomenon interrupted only briefly in the 2008, means that they are unable to invest in their own future, by educating themselves and their children and by starting new businesses. Third, the weakness of the current middle class is holding back tax revenues, especially because those at the top are so adroit in avoiding taxes. Fourth, even though inequality did not directly cause the crisis, inequality is associated with more frequent and more severe boom-and-bust cycles that make our economy more volatile and vulnerable.

The International Monetary Fund has noted the systematic relationship between economic instability and economic inequality, but the government leaders have not absorbed the lesson. Our skyrocketing inequality means that those who are born to parents of limited means are likely never to live up to their potential in their generation. By allowing inequality to remain this way, our society is squandering its most valuable resource: our young. The dream of a better life that attracted other people to our shores is being crushed by an ever-widening chasm of income and poverty.

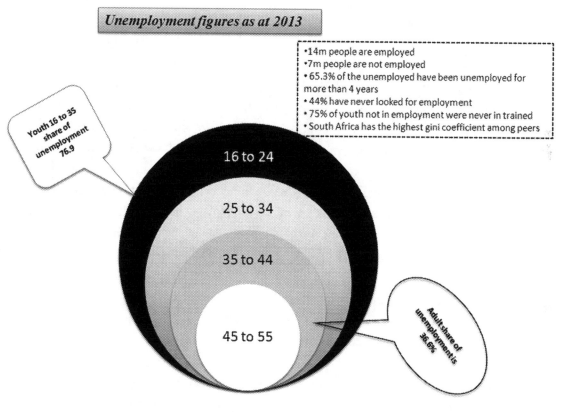

Unemployment figures as at 2013

- 14m people are employed
- 7m people are not employed
- 65.3% of the unemployed have been unemployed for more than 4 years
- 44% have never looked for employment
- 75% of youth not in employment were never in trained
- South Africa has the highest gini coefficient among peers

Youth 16 to 35 share of unemployment 76.9

16 to 24
25 to 34
35 to 44
45 to 55

Adult share of unemployment is 36.6%

Source Stats SA, Quarterly Labour Force Survey 2013

The central determinant of any successful society is the proportion of its young economic citizens retained in sustainable jobs. Unemployment of the youth is of grave concern to all. As measured by the employment ratio—the proportion of the working-age population with jobs—South Africa ranks far below emerging markets in 'BRICS' partners. Whereas gainful employment absorbs 71% of the working-age population in China, 65% in Brazil, 57% in Russia and 55% in India, in South Africa it is 40.8%. The average ratio across 19 emerging markets is 56%. Among the youth (15 to 24-yearolds), South Africa's employment ratio is 12.5%—only one in eight—compared with an emerging-market average of 36%. This is plain wrong. Employment represents the primary source of income for the overwhelming majority of the population. Gainful employment is also crucial to youth's sense of dignity, self-esteem, independence and social usefulness. The scale of South Africa's job-creation failure thus reflects a tragic loss of potential not only at the individual level, but—on account of the foregone contribution to national output—also at the wider societal level.

Given the evident social and political dangers attendant upon marginalisation of the country's youth, much policy discussion in South Africa over recent years has indeed been devoted to the possibilities of reversing the tide on youth unemployment. However, although the issue has clearly risen much higher up the rhetorical space, there is still no sign that government is seized with the urgency the challenge presents. While it has acknowledged the dangers imposed by unemployment, the government continues to dabble in sermons and expletives without offering practical solutions that remove conditions of unemployment. When it comes to talking about real solutions government officials are stumped for words.

Government talks about solutions in vague superlative terms such as tax credit incentivising employers, training subsidies and work seekers grant which are provisions aimed at bringing youth to the workplace without preparing these youths adequately before they enter the gates of the workplace in terms of real skills needed to benefit the industries. Party bigwigs take refuge in calls for poverty reduction and solidarity with the poor. These calls are at best ignorant and insulting at worst. In the longer term, resolution of the youth unemployment problem requires the meeting of two preconditions: on the supply side the elimination of the gap between real wages and productivity by improving the quality of the labour force through education and training, so that young people seeking work will be equipped with the skills that meet business requirements. On the demand side, providing the incentives for profitable private-sector job creation on a significantly larger scale.

The alignment of forces in the debate about a youth wage subsidy is indeed a strange one. On the one hand, government has put forward the proposal and, after some eight years of internal debate, resources have been allocated for its implementation. The Democratic Alliance, ironically, claims early successes after it has started implementing the scheme. The NYDA has expressed support for the wage subsidy but the ANC Youth League when it still existed rejected the proposal it defies logic. Debate around this issue has been raging for many months now at Nedlac involving government, business, workers and civil society. Indications are that we should not hold our breath, as a resolution will not come soon. This is the actual tragedy. For, try as government may to devise long-term strategies and plans, these will take years to impact on employment generally and on youth marginalisation in particular. What is needed is a raft of urgent interventions that will facilitate the school-to-work transition, which is the bane of our society's economic and social wellbeing. In the concluding chapter, we discuss this detail.

Naturally, a trade union movement has the responsibility to defend the interests of employed workers: its members. It should be expected to protest against measures it sees as having the potential to create a two-tier labour market, which ultimately would lower labour standards across the board. But why not accept this as a temporary intervention to absorb as many young people as possible into economic activity, expand the numbers of workers and potential union members, and from this beachhead sue for improved standards? The answer to these questions lies not only with Cosatu. It should also come from employers and all of society. This is because at the core of the wrangling on this issue is the fundamental question of trust, a crucial deficit in South Africa's macro social environment as we have argued in earlier chapters. Youth wage subsidies all over the world have been shown to facilitate young people's entry into the labour market. But this is if they are implemented in a manner that deals with the many negative consequences that they can otherwise spawn. Researchers on this issue have pointed to some of these challenges namely:

- Deadweight loss—employers will take advantage of the subsidy but employ older workforce
- Substitution effect—employers will absorb subsidised young people and get rid of unsubsidised older workers.
- Displacement effects—industries without subsidised workers will be crowded out and general employment negatively affected.
- Destructive churning—companies will take a group of subsidised workers and when the subsidy period for these comes to an end, they will simply replace them with new ones.
- Corruption—the system does lend itself to graft on a mass scale.

And so, cogent arguments and effective measures to obviate these challenges need to be put on the table. In this regard, the NYDA may have a point in arguing that there needs to be a system of effective check and balance, which itself could also absorb young people. To the extent that these issues are addressed, generic slogans about a two-tier labour market system and poverty wages will not pass muster in the court of public opinion. These are the issues that organised labour and organised business wrangle about but have to resolve urgently.

The 11million jobs to benefit the youth that the South African economy must generate by 2030 at growth averages of around 5.4% is predicated upon creating a growth focused small entrepreneurial business sector. When we examined policy conference resolutions and pronouncements in the recent past we found that the party had not only neglected to shed light on how they envisage achieving this outside the parameters of policy framework, in fact it transpired that they did not have a policy position on SME as a vehicle for economic change. Small business development issues have received no attention from the party; and what attention it receives from DTI is wishy-washy or woefully inadequate. Recently, the presidency presented the Development Indicator Report in which it stated the country was on course and is doing well to half the unemployment and poverty, but without the development of the SME sector, this is an absurdity. The role played by SME as a major job-multiplier is important for the flourishing of our emergent economy. Small business could be helping to create tens of thousands of new jobs, but a highly concentrated economy, poorly skilled workforce, stringent red tape, high failure rate and a lack of an entrepreneurship culture are all stymieing the sector' performance. Small enterprises contribute between 27% and 34% of the country's gross domestic product, this is about the same size contribution as that of Malaysia but higher than Chile and Brazil at 20% of GDP.

Yet, South African small businesses are faced with one of the highest failure rates in the world at 70% in the first year. The economy is dominated by large companies, which made it difficult for entrepreneurs to enter any business sector and also contributed to the low number of perceived business opportunities among South Africans. Compared to India at 10.4, Peru at 4.2, Philippines at 16.2, Thailand at 15.2—South Africa sits at 5.3 on the SME measurement index. The reason for this is that South Africa does not have the ability to produce wealth and distribute it among its citizens; the ability to spark entrepreneurial activity is weakening and declining rapidly because a lot of it is driven by public sector rather than by the private sector. GEM and Finscope (2012) study estimated that South Africa has approximately 5.9 million active SME businesses. There can be no doubt that, compared to big business small businesses face a wider range of constraints and are less able to address the problems on their own, even in efficiently functioning market economies of the Western countries. Exemptions from regulations were often aimed at micro than small businesses. The SME sector could play an important part in creating the millions of jobs, but instead it remains hobbled by these numerous challenges denying the country the chance to fight unemployment.

In 2012, government thought it prudent to respond to the SME vicarious problem by restructuring two finance agencies into a single development funding institution (DFI). The Small Enterprise Finance Agency (Sefa) was established to address specifically the intractable problem of financing the emerging SME sector. However, no matter how good an idea may be the moment it is left in the hands of party demagogues it very quickly dies down because of contamination by politics or get compromised through incompetence. Although Sefa inherited competent human capital base from legacy institutions, it was hugely constrained by inexperienced management who had dubious record of accomplishment. This management team was hand picked by a dysfunctional Board made up of a bunch of individuals without any credible SME business experience and the few that are were junior directors under the shadow of the IDC.

A further constraining factor was the red tape in internal business processes, which were both cumbersome as well as unattractive to the SME applicants due to high rates charged upon obtaining the loan. This simply made it impossible for the government to rise to the challenges of the day. In 2012 government accepted recommendations by the presidential review committee to unbundle many state-owned companies and reconfigure others to enable a much deeper penetrative impact on the 'second economy' but in the absence of the repeal of many laws constraining it this is unlikely to make much headway in opening the way for the SMME space to flourish.

A recent survey commissioned by Omidyar Network (2013) found that South Africa, with the exception of financing, underperforms in the entrepreneurial landscape relative to its peers in five countries in sub-Saharan Africa. It found that the complexity of legislation coupled with harsh penalties for non-compliance, limited availability of appropriate skills and talent is a significant constraint for new and growing business ventures. Dr Neil Rankin says the route the government has taken is some sort of a Nash-equilibrium path. The story of John Nash in the book *A Beautiful Mind*, he is drinking in a bar with his graduate school colleagues and he sees a beautiful woman, and they say let us go and chat her up. John Nash says no, hang on, if we all go and chat her up we are all going to be interfering and no-one is going to end up impressing her. That is the Nash equilibrium: we all act out our best intentions but somehow it ends up that things are not as good as they could have been. The author believes that this is where we are as a nation at this time. There are other potentially more optimal growth paths we could be on, but because of the unique historic and political economic situation we find ourselves in, we are on this Nash-equilibrium growth path.

The economy at one point was ticking along at 5% and now it is ticking along at 3%. And it is going to be very difficult, especially in the next five years, for us to shift to a path that is different. The path needed is labour-intensive, potentially export-driven industries that will empower us to grow. People are rarely ever naturally poor; they are mostly poor because they have been shoved aside by the apartheid machinations, by war, by having their health trashed by environmental conditions and being prevented from having access to the means of wealth creation by themselves. As the political economy begins to wobble, as long as the economic elite remains predominantly white and blacks remain mostly poor, political competition limited by the dialectics of race and economic competition muffled by colluding, cross-owned conglomerates the government invincibility is shattered. Its shortcomings are traceable to the moral corruption brought on by its political hegemony of the country. There is truism in the statement that a conflict between political equality and economic inequality was irresolvable within the framework of the current democratic order. The relationship is also dialectical with two elements of equality promised by citizenship in the state and inequality in society begotten by absence of freedom for human endeavour at an individual level.

One of the ironies of democracy is that while it is the majority of the poor who elects government leaders, the leaders find themselves paying more attention to the whims of the rich. The employers and government are not listening and responding to the voice of the poor, which started as a hopeful plea but now has reached a deafening crescendo. The much-hyped promises of wealth redistribution are nowhere to be seen. Black people are asking where is the promise that the wealth of the country shall be shared when the redistribution of income gap has worsened? The miners, factory and farm workers' strikes and the township protests should all be seen within the context of a country whose poor are hurting, workers and the poor are experiencing direct deprivation while the new black elite continue to enjoy a better life. What levels of desperation would drive people to destroy their workplaces, which are their only source of livelihoods if this is not an early indication of the start of a revolution?

An astounding R69 billion rising to 86 billion by 2016 has been spent on land reform since 1994, with only 8% of land redistributed where the initial target was 30% by 2014. In 1996 there were 60 000 farming units—this number has shrunk to 35 000 by 2007 simply because there has been a reduction in financial resources for conservation and soil rehabilitation programmes. The recently adopted NDP offers a model to avert the problems seen inter alia in current land reform policies of land market willing—seller-willing-buyer to a 'just and equitable' principle. This roadmap suggests every municipal district with commercial farming land should form a committee comprising farmers and key stakeholders (whatever that means). Each of those committees would need to identify 20% of commercial farming land to transfer to black farmers.

They would look for 'land already in the market; land where the farmer is under financial pressure; land held by an absentee landlord; and land in a deceased estate.' The state would pay 50% of market value, and farmers would chip in to make up the other 50%. As compensation, they would receive black economic empowerment status and be assured their land will not be expropriated by the state. The plan envisages new ways of financing black farmers so they are not burdened by debt and the budget is not overly strained. Yet, this plan ignores the real danger attendant to landless black people cramped in squatter camps and in state created RDP dumping grounds. The government's imperviousness to the national question of the land that goes back to pre-colonial era and made worse by the 1913 Land Act cannot be resolved by piecemeal acts of handouts. We know from studies conducted by World Bank that extreme wealth of the few does in fact reduce the potential of the majority to better themselves, unless a direct state intervention rescues them.

A recent development in South Africa's political scene has been the emergence of a mass African working-class constituency that is openly hostile to the government. The wildcat labour strikes that started in the platinum mining sector of Marikana in Rustenburg by what many thought were illiterate rock drillers, became rolling mass action with a self-sustaining momentum affecting nearly the entire mining industry in the months that followed. In the end, the miners not only realised significant gains for their struggle but also made a big statement about the failure of the ruling class to look after their working class interests. These mining strikes were followed closely by whirlwind strikes and protests from nectarine picking farm workers in the wine estates of De Doorns, Wolseley and Ceres in the Overberg region of Western Cape. Thereafter, the truck and bus drivers went on a three weeklong strike of their own. Zuma's response to all these labour unrest developments in general remained nonchalant and insensitive at best. These developments emphasised the point that the ANC and its alliance had long ceased to be the vanguard of the poor working class but has become its antithesis. This emerging constituency has finally debunked the myth that the ANC alliance was pro poor. Those workers questioned the docility and obsequious servitude of modern-day system of patriarchal benevolence. In responding to these developments, posture among grandstanding politicians and business leaders were at best self-serving and dismissive at worse. The specter of these events has dented investor confidence in Zuma's leadership of South Africa and has led to downgrades of country's sovereign credit ratings.

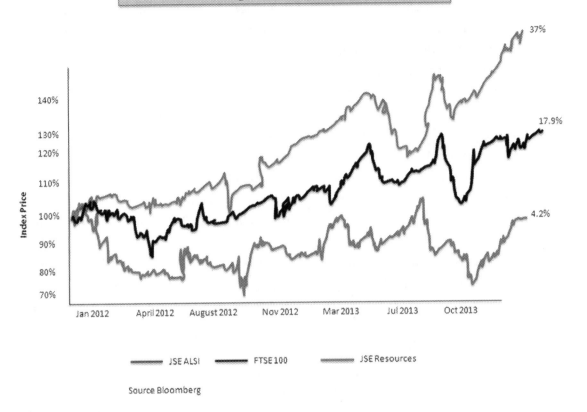

JSE Resources impacted by strikes in 2012

Source Bloomberg

On 21st March 1960, police shot and killed 69 black antipass law protesters in an internationally condemned act. Today 21 March, the day of the massacre in 1960, is a national holiday to recognise and pay tribute to those who laid down their lives for the democracy many now experience. It was therefore shocking that on the 16th August 2012 at 'koppie three' Marikana in Rustenburg we are confronted with the massacre of striking mineworkers in the most macabre manner, killed by black police on instructions from a black government. The striking Lonmin mine workers eventually secured an increase of around 22%. The cost was the life 34 miners, 10 others including two police officers, two security guards and as many as 78 others seriously injured.

There was international disbelief when the NPA in the immediate aftermath, 270 miners were arrested and charged with the murders of their fellow comrades, under the now defunct 'doctrine of common purpose'. It was widely reported in the media that police created an illusion of tribal weapons had been used by one group of protestors on Mgcineni Noki's *green blanket* men by positioning weapons next to the prostrate and lifeless bodies strewn across the koppie fileds. It was eyewitness account that alerted the nation of the police intent when in some instances police were seen firing at point blank range injured miners found alive. Light always triumph over darkness and truth is the strangest when it refuses to be hidden in a box and shows up in the most inconvenient time when others deny its existence. A year after the Commission of Enquiry had started, commission evidence leaders through an act of serendipity stumbled across a hard drive disk from a police laptop containing a crucial piece of footage that starkly exposed a lie police lived on throughout the inquiry, the footage revealed that police top management issued instruction to 'shoot to kill rather disperse the miners' a day before the massacre took place needless to say that this instruction was a direct violation of police standing order 262 which details crowd management strategies during gatherings and demonstrations.

Zuma quickly came under suspicion of political interference in affairs of state prosecution. He also stood accused of gross insensitivity about the loss of life, and lack of solidarity with poor black workers. His subsequent announcement of a week of national mourning was correctly regarded as a cynical gesture to placate the restless international community. His lamentable actions led to noticeable dissent within the ANC ranks. An emergence of anxiety about the exclusion of the voices of the ordinary miners from the Marikana inquiry prompted sociologist Professor Peter Alexander, in collaboration with researchers Thapelo Lekowa, Botsang Mmope, Luke Sinwell and Bongani Xeswi, to write a book and tell how the killings were orchestrated by police in order to preserve the truth independent of the Farlam Commission of Inquiry probing culpability.

Under the palm trees, we asked umaMkhize operating a public phone kiosk near a Pietermaritzburg shopping plaza what difference 20 years of democracy had made to her life. 'No difference', was her immediate response. It took some prompting before she started to number the things that have not changed: new houses in her neighbourhood, with no running water and electricity were a common complaint. 'Politicians come and make promises, then we won't see them for another five years' 'musani ukuganga ngathi nina we zingane sizihluphekela lapha' is a common lament from people like maMkhize. In a community that was once highly politicised, the heart land of Harry Gwala SACP's roaring lion politics seems to have become divorced from the world people see around them. Surely there has to be a way out of this morass. The Sowetan once carried headlines, 'The 2012 is likely to go down in history as the year the post Mandela revolution started.' In Zuma years, the ANC lost important by-elections that give an indication of the beginning of the end. It lost a by-election in Rustenburg after the Marikana massacre to the DA and in Nkandla to the IFP—a party that is practically dead, lost Tlokwe and Ngaka Modiri councils to the DA.

The 4th national policy conference of the ANC in 2012 document reads, 'Having agreed that the new phase in our transformation from apartheid colonialism to a national democratic society will be characterized by more radical policies and decisive action to effect thorough-going socioeconomic transformation, the national policy conference concluded that this will require a renewed ANC. The conference reviewed the experiences of the past 100 years in order to draw lessons for the future. In this regard, strengths and weaknesses and priorities for renewal were identified in order to reposition the ANC towards the second century.' It remains unclear how transformation would continue to be an agenda in the second century when the talk of developmental state is gaining currency in the ANC. It is our considered view that socioeconomic transformation agenda should have been the mainstay in the first 20 years of post-apartheid era so that going forward the next 20 years are devoted to advancing this society to modernity.

We ask why should a country that began a mere twenty years ago as the continent's most advanced and biggest economy (R400 billion). Real GDP growth of 3.3%, GDP per capita spend of 7.5, Net FDI of R11.9 billion, with international credibility. Good governance, strong capital markets, a bedrock of high-level skills, limitless commodities and an impeccable record of macroeconomic management. That it should suffer pedestrian growth rates, negative employment, falling international ratings and competitiveness, starvation is the new norm, government wage bill has ballooned at an average rate of 13.5% employing a majority of unskilled people, debt/GDP of 44 %, service levels have collapsed and in some rural parts of the country municipal doors have shut down? The loss of vision supplanted opportunistic action; the desirable outflanked the doable and delusion usurped reality would be our answer to the question.

Social cohesion

When we talk of social cohesion, we are referring to the interplay among the three spheres:

- Civic—seen through expressions of the public civic engagement
- Economic—seen through demonstrated willingness to distribute the country's resources to all sectors
- Social—seen through citizen's attitudes in mixing in sport teams and inter racial marriage.

A proxy for determining social cohesion and integration is the number of friendships across racial divide maintained by different cultural communities over an extended period of time—proceeding from the understanding that social transformation entails changing the material conditions of all South Africans for the better, creating a nation inspired by values of human solidarity and a nation united across cultural barriers. Social cohesion therefore must be the byproduct of healthy family structures and compassionate society.

Those who are excluded from belonging to the South African collective and marginalised from the benefits of citizenship are integral to the concept of the nation, since it is in opposition to their very exclusion that the nation and citizenship are defined. Through integration into social and economic systems, an individual becomes a social agent who is active in the processes of defining both the collective and the self. Inclusion in the collective is an integral part of the process of becoming. Poverty in this sense is the subjectification in place of social inclusion.

The combination of material and emotional conditions of poverty foment a people's lack of understanding of their rights, and the absence of a sense of belonging to their country. Furthermore, these effects of poverty can accumulate over generations. People deprived of their land in turn cannot make a living, educate their children, or contribute to the health of their community. The cycle continues as their children in turn are prevented from recognising their own potential. Understood from this perspective, the legacies of apartheid can be seen not just as a form of social exclusion, they represent forms of so-called structural violence, which is the institutionalisation of social processes that differentially cause suffering through organising unequal access to social resources, such as rights, security, capital and bodily and mental integrity, based on markers of difference.

This structural violence combines with symbolic violence that is exercised upon black people with their complicity. Blacks are aware and even knowing agents who have a role in structuring those outcomes; it comes as no surprise to us that to fight and be ready to die for an RDP house but not the land it is built on is regarded as a legitimate grievance. Symbolic violence combined with the moral ecology of townships shows how poverty is constructed mutually by the persistence of the ANC's promises and by the tacit acceptance of those promises by blacks engaging with their social environment in ways familiar to them.

Ramphele says, 'South Africans—black and white—are deeply wounded by the legacy of racism, sexism and engineered inequality over the last three centuries which the last 20 years of ANC rule failed to transform. The majority of black people suffer from an inferiority complex that is deep seated—both rich and poor are affected. The humiliation of being told in more ways than one that one is inferior is deeply wounding and infuriating. But the lack of self-respect engendered leads to inward directed anger—domestic violence, community vigilantism, public violence and other self-sabotaging behaviour, including looting of public resources and supporting failure of governance. Denial of mistakes and failure is a common feature of woundedness. Wounded people also tend to be subservient to authoritarian leaders and fail to hold them accountable'. Ramphele's use of 'wounded attachments' language is meant to help us understand the behaviours of township youth in the midst of persistent poverty that denies them hope of their future and their exclusion from the hope-filled South African nation. Their behaviour represents simultaneously the symptoms of South Africa's wounded racial history and present, and the yearning of the South African nation to unite a divided national.

The fact of the matter is that families have been destroyed firstly by apartheid, then by conditions of poverty under the present dispensation. Despite the repeal of apartheid laws, poverty and inequality persist in part because of the internalisation of inequalities, which still structure social relations under the present dispensation. The systematic exclusion of black people from employment, health care, education and land has resulted in the impoverishment of the majority of the population. Beyond these material effects are the emotional consequences of poverty and unemployment, including a loss of dignity and autonomy, of purpose and coherent structure to life of a sense of safety and the onset of feelings of hopelessness.

Many white people still suffer from the superiority complex that lead them to believe that they are entitled to more material benefits than their fellow black citizens by virtue of their superior qualities and hard work. There are also many who are paralysed by guilt about past racist practices and feel they have no right to exercise their rights and responsibilities as citizens, including criticising the majority black government. The tendency of deferring to authority is strong and deep-seated among white people too. Neither a superiority complex nor guilt is helpful to the transformation process that is sorely needed in this country. Lessons of history are very clear—if you think of yourselves as helpless and ineffectual, you sow the seeds of becoming victims of despotic governments that become your master.

Ramphele concludes by saying that South Africans need to complete the healing process that was never finished by the TRC process and focus on the psychosocial and economic wounds that beset our nation. We need to link hands black/white, men/women, young/old as well as rich/poor as citizens and start circles of healing amongst ourselves as a nation'. This highlights the muteness about poverty and structural injustice that was afflicting young people. The refusal by young people to recognise structural violence they face and their own acceptance of this violence indicate the crippling impact of symbolic violence in their lives. They may not make direct connections between poverty and structural injustice and may describe it in proximal and immediate contexts rather than the distal influence of apartheid-related injustices, because the immediate observable reality of poverty structured their experiences and is the frame through which they understand the present world. In contrast, the strength of their belief in their own ability to escape poverty reflects their youthful optimism.

Using a R18.50 a day income indicator, the country is poverty-stricken; the proportion of people living below the poverty datum line was about 53% in 1995 and 57% in 2014 meaning there are over 14 million people who live in poverty in South Africa today. The contribution of wage income and remittances to household fell, and was replaced by social grants, accounting for about 4.6% of the GDP. Nearly a third of households living primarily on handouts from the state were lapsing into a state of workless dependency. In 2001, there were 3.4 million people on grant; by 2012, this figure stood at 15 million. Average monthly payment rose from R462 per grant to R903. The main social grants that are on offer today are dependency, child support, disabled persons, foster care and elderly. The biggest spike is in child grant support. 36% of households receive social grants, 31% receive 2 grants per household. Without these grants, 94% of these households would fall below the poverty datum line. Grants were fostering rather than alleviating social ills. By any standards, this is a very high level of poverty for a middle-income country.

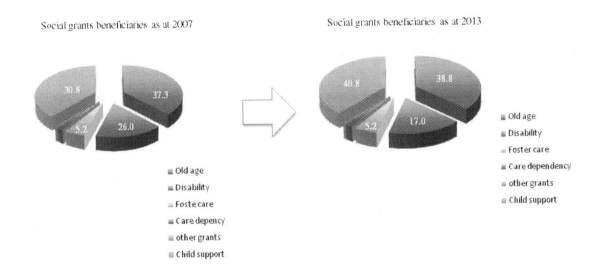

Social grant expenditure 2007 to 2013

Social grants beneficiaries as at 2007

Social grants beneficiaries as at 2013

- Old age
- Disability
- Fostecare
- Care depency
- other grants
- Child support

- Old age
- Disability
- Foster care
- Care dependency
- other grants
- Child support

Source National Treasury Budget Review 2013

Large migration streams to industrial areas—primarily from underdeveloped rural areas—continue, but are increasingly being diverted to local rural 'transport corridor' settlements that offer the promise of access to shack houses and services that would often follow in inadequate way. Deteriorating natural environments are increasingly limiting the socioeconomic prospects of rural populations, while rapid urbanisation is increasing the vulnerability of urban populations to disease, decay and social calamities of levels unseen before. South Africa is a host to over million refugees who are prevented from being value adders and instead they have to eke out an existence in ways that often create an impression of competition with already poverty-stricken citizens which leads to tensions among communities.

The social profile of a community in typical township today is a far cry from that of pre 1994 era and it is most depressing. Children—some as young as three years of age—are reportedly raped by people who ought to be their guardians with little protection from the social service with one exception namely, Diepsloot, a community north of Johannesburg perpetrators are killed by the mod when found, end of story and police have resigned themselves to this reality. Young girls, in some cases 15 years of age, intentionally fall pregnant in order to access the means to support themselves through the R285 child grant.

Boys from tender age of 16 years experiment with and stay on dangerously poisonous substances known either as *nyaope/woenga,* or a variation of sorts according to the latest mixture concocted together presumably in order to numb the pain of living permanently under conditions of crushing poverty where their father, mother, cousin, and siblings have not earned an income over five years. In 1997, young men between 20 and 39 years of age were 1.6 times more likely to die than women, by 2004 0.95 times were less likely to die compared with women. Total deaths in South Africa have increased sharply with numbers doubling between 1994 and 2004. Although knowledge and use of contraceptives remains consistently high, only a small proportion of women are protected against unwanted pregnancies and sexually transmitted infections (STIs).

HIV/AIDS (which are largely responsible for a decline in life expectancy and an increase in the maternal mortality rate) undermine the improved access to sexual and reproductive health services in the 10 years since 1998. The rise in total death, low life expectancy and high infant mortality are all evidence of a nation in severe distress. The overall picture is one of a country going through a devastating set of epidemics. The first epidemic is HIV/Aids, the second is that of injury, both accidental and non-accidental, the third epidemic consist of infectious diseases, the fourth epidemic is the growing epidemic of lifestyle disease. Many of these epidemics are not new but the nature of the evolution of HIV changed the nature of the disease burden in South Africa.

For a decade, there is a dramatic increase in Aids defined deaths among young adults, which is more marked for young women than men, although it is showing signs of abating now. Every second household must hawk either liquor or offal in order to eke out a meager existence. Garbage strewn along street corners not collected for months, burst sewage pipes form stagnant pools inside homes creating rats and snakes infestation due to advanced state of degradation and presenting hazard for epidemic outbreaks. Then surely, even the dull and the ignorant they too must know that things have fallen apart and it is about time that everyone stand up and pulls together in a collective effort to change the conditions in this country of their dreams. The graph below depicts the state of affairs in this country and their extent.

Social cohesion will materialise only after the conditions have improved substantially. Where things have changed for the better—where houses have been built, this is often still not taken for granted. Where things have not changed and where people remain unemployed or live under the terror of crime there is a deep skepticism. It is probably necessary at this stage to sound a word of caution the ground for a revolution is always fertile in the presence of absolute destitution. At some stage people will feel that they have nothing to live for. What happens at that stage depends on what happens in the intervening period the seeds of revolution are germinating.

Race relations

According the ideological position of the ANC, South Africans are not given by nature; they are a nomenclature of crude races. It was the ANC's mission to manufacture non-racialism citizenship in the state. Inherently, the idea of non-racialism intimates the practice of racialism. In denying the official status of race, a non-racialism stance acknowledges the unofficial role of the race, outside of the state. Cornel West once warned against the pitfalls of 'black authenticity' politics whereby every issue is reduced to racial reasoning. He argues that we must replace racial reasoning with moral reasoning, to understand the black freedom struggle, not as an affair of skin pigmentation and racial phenotype but rather as a matter of ethical principles.' Shouting 'racism' to silence rivals, for self-enrichment at the expense of public good, is unacceptable. South African identities are not 'gated communities' with fixed borders, more often than not they overlap, beyond the occasional shared value. We are plural and inclusive based on our 'interconnected differences'. Our common South African identity, and a shared future are built on a mosaic of the best elements of our diverse cultures and history.

On the question of prejudice Eusebius McKaiser argues states that there are two insights to be taken to heart when dealing with our own prejudices: one is that we should be on the lookout for sophisticated tactics we use, often subconsciously, to mask racism, such as seemingly innocent explanations for counter-productive choices; the more important conclusion is that we need to appreciate how racism is in part sustained by what we do or do not do in the privacy of our space. We therefore cannot make progress in the public space without rectifying what we do in private. If it does not begin in the heart, racialism cannot be defeated in the society and he offers the following social experiences:

Sketch one:
A couple of days ago I had a rather embarrassing experience. I was sitting at one of my favourite spots at the Rosebank Mall—popular coffee shop and restaurant

Ninos—overlooking the parking lot while waiting for my creative juices to kick in after a bout of writer's block. I got distracted by some noise, and looked up. Two women seemed to be having a fairly tense conversation. One of them seemed to have bumped the other's car. I didn't see the accident, so had no clue, which one of them might have been in the wrong. As they exchanged numbers, their conversation, judging by the increasingly wild gesticulation, seemed to be getting more heated.

I instinctively found myself silently egging on the black lady, as one might anxiously hold thumbs for your favourite boxer in the ring. The Indian lady seemed louder—I could certainly hear her voice more clearly—and this made me nervous about whether or not my player in the road rage match was going to win the verbal warfare. But alas, the black lady, though also talking a lot, seemed more timid, and so I feared that she might come out of it all worse for wear.

Why, you might wonder, did I instinctively side with her? Simply because she was black. I did not know her. I might never even meet her. For all I know, she could have been in the wrong, and hurled abuse at her Indian counterpart, thus deserving those loud protests. Yet, the fact that she was black was enough for her to get my sympathy and all my goodwill. There was no sympathy or goodwill, I'm afraid, for the person who looked less like me, the Indian lady.

Sketch two:

A good friend of mine, Seth, confessed to me many years after we first met that he had a rather horrible thought the first time he saw me. He walked into my philosophy tutorial at the beginning of his university career and when he realised that I was the tutor, he thought, 'Oh dear, my luck to be assigned the incompetent black tutor.' That is the sort of confession one can only trot out if your friendship is more solid than the skull of a politician. I chuckled, and we laughed it off over a pint of lager—or three. We didn't need to analyse the confession. It was obvious what was going on: my skin colour was assumed to be carrying information about me. And in this case, my black skin carried the warning, 'incompetent!' The onus was on me to disprove the assumption. Only white tutors could be assumed to be competent unless proven to be useless. It was the other way round for black tutors.

Sketch three:

Jessica dos Santos is a name we didn't really know until early May 2012, but now her story has been filed in the annals of Twitter infamy. She is a white model who had an unfortunate encounter with a black guy who reportedly made unwelcome and unacceptable sexual advances towards her. She was so angry that she tweeted about the 'kaffir'. Almost every South African on Twitter quickly, and ferociously, sanctioned her.

One magazine, *FHM*, almost instantly stripped her of some title she had won under their banner, and made it clear they would never work with her in future. She experienced the virtual equivalent of having a ton of rotten tomatoes thrown at her. Not even a breakfast function at which she attempted to reconcile with another thoughtless tweep, a black woman who retorted with unacceptable racism (suggesting that whites ought to have been killed) could salvage her bruised image.

She became the symbol of all unexpressed and latent racism that might exist in every nook and cranny in our country. And everyone wanted to prove their progressive credentials by venting more angrily than other tweeps. I encountered at least two responses that typified the engagement with Dos Santos's racism. One Facebook friend of mine gave me advice on my way to a recording for a television show on which I had been invited to appear to speak about the incident and its aftermath. My Facebook friend urged me to remind '*these* racists' [my emphasis] that their racism was disgusting and that 'they' had no place in our society.

At a friend's birthday braai, the incident, inevitably, also became a topic of discussion at some point in the afternoon. One guest lamented, 'you know, I almost feel sorry for that white girl. She must have been raised in an incredibly closed and insulated community.' The reactions of the online masses, and the reactions of my Facebook friend and my friend's braai guest, are intriguing: they suggest that racists are not us. Racists are alien. They are outliers in our society. They are not typical. They are a freak fact of our lives. If we could get rid of the three racists spoiling our rainbow image, we would be living in perfect racial harmony. (Cue: 'Ebony and Ivory' . . .) I find this lie fascinating. Racists, in reality, are among us. We *are* the racists. 'They' are not from another planet. But we dare not indict ourselves.

Sketch four:

I was an obsessive competitive debater throughout my university career. And so, when I arrived at Oxford University I was naturally drawn to the famous Oxford Debate Union. Probably the best part of my Oxford experience was the time spent growing as a debater, interacting with world famous politicians and newsmakers. The Union was a space that was so well respected that, frankly, it was a feather in the career cap of anyone—even a state president—to be asked to speak there. But make no mistake, you had to know your stuff, lest the ambitious young Oxford lions, donned invariably in black tie, would offer you a lethal point of information or, worse, deliver paper speeches from the floor that crushed your evidence. Fun stuff.

And so, in my first term at Oxford, I joined the Union and attended as many of the events as possible. During one of my first attendances, I found myself sitting in the main chamber of the Union. I do not recall the topic, but it was magnificent stuff with good opening speeches from both sides. Then it was the turn of a black guy who had been invited to the event. As the man got up and walked up to the podium, I found myself thinking, 'Please don't fuck this up! Please be the best speaker!' The basis of my mixture of fear and hope was simply that he was black. When the other speakers spoke, I had zero feelings about how they might perform.

Whether they excelled or sank was neither here nor there. I had no stake in how well they might do that night. And yet, this stranger induced in me—purely because he was black—fear that he might not be up to the task at hand, and a simultaneous desire that he should deliver a speech worthy of a two-minute standing ovation. Isn't it interesting that my racial affinity could do all this to me? Years later, I am not so sure if much has changed. I still, for example, find myself desperately wanting black debaters to beat white debaters in competition; not just, because I happen to coach some of them, but because black excellence is far closer to my heart than white excellence.

It is a reality that is found in every part of my psyche. It is, for example, more important to me that Pieter De Villiers, former Springbok rugby coach, should have a brilliant record as coach than it is important to me that one Jake White should have a brilliant record as national coach. What is the basis of my split loyalties? Pieter looks and sounds more like my dad and me than Jake White.

These four stories are variations on a theme: our racial baggage, as a nation recovering from a deeply racist past, is massive. Yet the way we deal with that past, in the present, is not very healthy. First, we are in denial about the fact that racial identities and racialism are very strong enclaves, and that they often form the basis of prejudices, and irrational racial affinities. We pretend the problem is small. Or we pretend that we never were, and never will be, part of the problem. The problem is out there. It is not in *my* home, in *my* heart. This is why the collective outrage against Jessica's racist tweet is less comforting than it might appear.

On the one hand, it is great that we collectively punish a racist in our midst. It means we do not tolerate racism rearing its divisive head. But there was, on the other hand, something disturbingly quick about the intense and voluminous reactions—something I am suspicious of. My fear is that much of the outrage was less about Jessica's racism than about deflecting attention from our selves. No one who came down hard on Jessica acknowledged their own racial baggage. The subtext of the criticism was clear, 'I am not Jessica. I am different.' And this is why my Facebook friend could so neatly distinguish between 'us' and 'them'. The 'us' refers to us innocent ones, and the 'them' refers to them racist bunch! But this is disingenuous. The real difference, frankly, between Jessica and us is that she got busted and we did not. It is easy to be outraged by a person's irresponsible behaviour. In reality, many thousands of South Africans drive over the legal limit every weekend and do not get stopped. Yet, with no hint of irony, these same offenders are often the first to throw stones in the direction of the busted one. It is a tactic that is aimed at drawing attention away from one's own behaviour. It is a lie we cannot afford to encourage in ourselves and in others. The problem with pretending that we are oh-so-different to Jessica is unless we acknowledge the scope of the problem; we cannot deal with racism and its baggage. That is why it is important that we examine our own lives, and not just preoccupy ourselves with spotting racism in others.

It is for the same reason that I introduced gentle disagreement into the braai conversation at my friend's house. I suggested that it was probably not true that Jessica grew up in a racist attic. But of course, it is a wonderful fantasy. Since you and I live in amazingly cosmopolitan places, we never could have done what Jessica did, nor would we ever. After the attic, Jessica cannot handle the pristine multiracial space in which her modeling career has landed her. This is the logic underlying the other braai guest's casual suggestion that Jessica grew up in a closed community. Again, we should be careful not to convince ourselves that racial baggage is a small problem out there. Jessica grew up in our communities. She is not one-of-a-kind. She is our friend, sister, daughter and colleague. She is not an alien, and her birthplace is not Mars—it is in fact South Africa. She was born in 1992; a Millennium kid and so cannot even be dismissed as a relic from Verwoerdian days. Rather, born into racial baggage like all of us. We dare not pretend our racial issues are over, or negligible. It is also evident that besides racial prejudice, racial identity runs deeper than we like to believe. This is not even necessarily a poisonous truth and yet we deny it.

There is no inherent harm in my quiet desire to see black debaters excel. In fact, given the historic educational inequities that partly explain why no black African has won the South African National Debate Championship (at the time of writing this book), one might even say that my passion for disproportionately focusing my coaching energy on black debaters is sensible. Yet how many of us would own up to be motivated by race in this fairly innocuous sense? Few of us, because we have closed the space in which we can be open about our racial identities. My experience of the two brawling women in the Rosebank Mall parking lot is not exceptional. When I tested my story with many friends less 'race-obsessed' than me, a familiar smile ran across their faces—they recognised the story instantly. I got the same reaction to my tale about the black speaker at Oxford. There seems to be a kind of trope here that is unsurprising. If I grew up in a community that was predominantly black, and had my first real interracial contact, socially, at my former whites-only high school, then it isn't surprising that I should have racial loyalties. It would be more surprising if I did not. Yet, we run away from these realities. We pretend it is only some people who see race everywhere—him and his handful of race-obsessed friends. But, how many South Africans reading this book do *not* have friends or lovers predominantly from the same racial group? How many people grew up in racially integrated neighbourhoods? How many of us, unlike the old white landlady in Sandton, could comfortably live with people who do not look like us? We have tighter social bonds with people of our own racial make-up than those who do not share the randomness of skin colour.

The story of rainbow nation bliss does not exist in the South African reality and pockets of places where it appears so are grossly exaggerated to give a taste of comfort to the bigotry of non-racialsm. We will take longer to get there if we convince ourselves that we have already arrived. We haven't. If someone like my friend Seth didn't own up to the fact that he took my skin colour as an indication of whether or not I was competent, then how could Seth ever have confronted his own racial stereotyping? How different we had once hoped it would be. Twenty years ago, our nation felt the hand of history on us as we attempted a new social contract—an experiment to move beyond racial lines as a source of division. It was a time when 'hope and history rhymed' for us, to borrow a phrase from Seamus Heaney.

And in the first few decades of our new democratic order, our society earnestly sought to move beyond the crude, racial classifications of apartheid. We were imbued with a hope of fostering a permanent sense of nationhood in a race-scarred country; to move beyond race as an ideology, which kept us apart. At several points in our journey thus far, the edifices of racial and cultural hostilities were proclaimed as steadily eroding, with a new dawn of racial tolerance and integration imminent. Yet two decades after apartheid, its racial nomenclature still persists and we seem to be as tormented by race as at many other times in our history. It is only by acknowledging in the first instance, that the racial challenges start with our individual selves, that we have a fighting chance of achieving that elusive race-free South Africa we chant about more often than we bother working at creating. And this is why the authors are grateful that Jessica put up her racist hand and demanded our attention. In the end, it is the Jessica's of this world who keep us brutally honest.

While racism is prevalent in every society to a greater or lesser extent, continued institutionalised racism in any form—whether designed to end the inequalities of the past—is problematic. The continuing tensions we suffer from in terms of racial cohesion underline how great the distance we still need to travel towards achieving reconciliation is. This is unsurprising given the experiences of other countries before South Africa. The lessons we can draw from Malaysia are that societies, which attempt to redress racial injustices through invasive legislation, often perpetuate racism rather than ending it. And the American dilemma demonstrates how long and tortuous the path to racial healing can be—and that it is not something that can be overcome in a single generation.

Armed with these insights, we may very possibly have *still* continued down the same legislative path we had chosen—but, at the very least, we might also have been imbued with a little more pragmatism about the setbacks we were likely to experience along the way. Malaysia is one of the Asia's shining economic successes but its official race relations have served only to bring race to the fore as a determinant. Instead of ending racism, its policies have perpetuated it. The ANC government should take leaf and learn from it. The truth is the ANC still struggles with the fact that there is only one human race—there never were many races. Non-racialism is a flawed ideological precept manufactured in order to give credence to a façade of correcting a societal ill called racism by self-appointed paragon who never understood the question of race to begin with.

The education

The Star newspaper headline proclaimed '1 Pass, 659 Fail' at a local high school a few years recently, 'Students with 25% marks are passed to the next grade' is another headline from same newspaper and '25 other schools fail to produce a single pass in matric examination in 2012', was Sowetan's headline referring to another absurdity, signaling that the notoriety of education under apartheid simply continued unabated. Education, although in theory sits at the apex of government priority watch list it is one thing the ANC government has succeeded to screw big time and this statement is not said in jest. Wendy Shilowa once observed, 'the quality of education had deteriorated, there was absolutely no doubt, and when I look back, the education then really seems much better than the education appears to be today.' It has been reported that the 2012 matric student cohort was the first 'born free' generation to graduate from high school. But with only half of the students who started Grade 1 in 2001 having made it to matric, it seems 'born frees' were also born with half a chance of being educated.

Thirteen years ago 1,7 million learners entered the public school system, the first post—Mandela school intake; 13 years later only 31% of those learners wrote grade 12. Of those who wrote, only 65% passed matric and a mere 15% got university exemption. Of those who originally started, school 13 years earlier, 5% gained university exemption. Worse still, only 1,5%, of those who began public schooling 13 years ago gained university exemption to study engineering, information technology, medicine, accountancy or the like, and of that proportion, a tiny proportion were black African. Why must we end up in this way? Over the decade the pass rate for school leaving exams declined from 73% in 2003 to 66% in 2006 and since then were artificially propped up into the 80% region. Nationally, fewer than half of all school leavers pass the school-leaving certificate, but more disturbing is the significant decline of the gateway subjects. Now the pass hurdle for a high school exit is set at 30% in three subjects and 40% in the other three, which means learners are not expected to demonstrate mastery over 70% and 60% respectively of knowledge base of the chosen subjects. How on earth do we expect students to become scholars at university level when the authorities make under—performance an institutional culture?

According to the Minister of Basic Education 80% of the 6 118 schools were dysfunctional. 414 schools in the top performing rank produced 66% of the higher-grade mathematics pass. 4 877 schools were poor performers. Only 32% of teachers had 6th grade qualification, 19% had senior secondary education. Only one in six gains university entrance. A third drop out within a year yet university standards are low. Approximately 1 million young people exit the schooling system annually, a largest percentage of those who exit do so at grade 11 or fail grade 12 of whom 65% exit without achieving a grade 12 certificate. Seven in ten have relevant qualifications at all. The annual campus protest by university students refused readmission because of serial failure in exams is symptomatic of systemic underachievement culture by black students. The ongoing amendments to curricula and the type of teacher training; in 2005 27% teachers had no mathematics background, 38% without science qualifications taught at black schools. Inadequate support to teacher training teaching time compared to other activities and the availability of teaching materials, language deficiency, the efficiency of bureaucracy, high levels of violence against children are some of the complex issues playing a role in the quality of education.

'Research from various communities, shows that in many places, teachers in blacks schools work an average of 3.5 hours, compared with 6.5 in the former white schools are not in school on Mondays or Fridays, they have other jobs simultaneously and the actual teaching going on in the classrooms is a fraction of what it should be.' 17000 schools are without running water and 15000 without libraries. The social environmental conditions outside the classroom for the poorest of the learners have as much impact as do those within the schooling system. Low literacy levels among parents; poor nutrition, violence and social fragmentation are factors that explain why the performance of school children from poor communities remained low in comparison to their wealthy peers—mostly in urban areas. A trend that is spreading across the country today is the growth of low-cost primary schools in the cities, in response to a lack of faith in state schools. Dr Salim Vally, head of the Education Policy at the Wits university, believes that South Africans deserve better. 'It is not difficult for any government to do better than apartheid governments,' Dr Vally argues it is not a secret that quality or meaningful education is only open to those who can afford to pay for it.

Passing or failing the senior certificate examination is no measure of the potential of learners but failure to complete secondary schooling and advance to further studies affects later productivity and prospects in life, while the lost earnings and lack of skill accumulation may make it difficult to escape poverty. Chronically poor education means that thousands of jobs go unfilled. Almost half the approximately 95000 of nursing jobs in the public sector are vacant, according to the SAIRR. Meanwhile, official unemployment is about 38% and the actual figure nearer 40%. Unequal education creates unequal employment. The unemployment rate among blacks is 36%, compared with 6% for whites. Youth unemployment is over 79%. Young people who fail to find work by the age of 24 will probably never have a full-time formal job. Excellence in education means children will take the initiative to seek deeper knowledge and information about the subject, beyond what could ever be presented to them, and critically engage with the knowledge with a view to turn that knowledge into better information useful for the wider society. The legacy of education goes beyond the opportunity cost of poor technical and professional skills at a personal level. The wider social impact is reflected in a weak science culture. Social capital built on trust relationship cements and enhances the development of foundations for stronger human capital and social institutions. Science and technology promote the generation, dissemination and application of knowledge that empowers citizens in daily lives. Science and technology have benefits that spill over to enhancing quality of life. It also calls to question how it is practically feasible to accommodate the requirements of employment equity and black economic empowerment goals, when so few black people are actually qualifying in the skills that are needed to fill the appropriate situation. The failure of the government to transform the apartheid education system into one that offers equity and excellence for all her children is a great travesty.

CHAPTER 4

Overall synthesis

Freedom and the transformation of our society were about the distribution not just capital but skills and opportunity. The transformation of this society was meant to give black people freedom to access the tools to overcome all forms of adversities in their path and freedom to do things for themselves and break free from government vagaries.

Judgement on the performance of the government is based on facts within the context of the period under review. It pains us deeply just as it does the rest of South Africa to admit tacitly that South Africa faces sunset. Its surreal feeling! As young compatriots, we sacrificed our youth in prison for the freedom of the people of South Africa; we had worked very hard for the government to succeed because if it did our sacrifices are vindicated. We also wished for a government that had the needs of the people of South Africa as its overarching priority thus fit for the role of a leader of our nation. Diction in text may be coarse we are conscientious in the service of the truth and remain unwaveringly committed to the ideals of the open shared society of our dreams. That said, in the course of researching the material for this book we met disciplined members of the ANC, many of whom we admire as role models for their selfless commitment to making change in government. Our disappointment is not with the contributions of these dedicated sons and daughters of the soil, but like the rest of South Africa, we are impugned by the overall ineptitude of the ANC. Loathing oppression of the black people by the white apartheid government was in and of itself not enough young people took a stand and fought to end the system that oppressed them. Many went into exile to undergo military training, while others organised mass insurrection for people's power through trade union movement, civic formations and faith-based organisations. Essentially we believed that what was done to us was wrong and we were going to right it because we knew better. Today, when we cast our eyes back since democracy began, bemoaning what the ANC has done to this country and its people is not enough we have to take a stand and say 'not in our name'. A friend, Godfrey, after a long conversation about the state of affairs in our country, took a long pause and said 'Ntate, we must pray for the fall of the ANC government.' Paused and digested hectic stuff!

We are sure many would emphathise with his indignation but we also know that Scripture exhorts believers to pray for those in authority so that there may be in peace in the land.

We conclude our treatise by summarising the journey the nation has travelled so far. At the beginning it was a rollercoaster ride from apartheid to democracy, from the graceful perfect formation of the flamingo flight in perfect formation high up in the sky, to walking apart from each other; others would opine that we have indeed walked this journey from high to low road. The dream of the nation is beginning to unravel at the seams and maybe one day rather than it wilt in the sun it will explode. On the question, have we prospered or become impoverished under the ANC stewardship? Individual opinions vary as to the extent of the problem but there is no gainsaying of the facts including the presenting evidence that points to the inescapable conclusion that our country is in a progressive metastases phase, without immediate surgery South Africa will soon pronounced a failed state and that day is calibrated not in decades, rather in years. Below we summarise the nation's balance sheet in terms of assets, liabilities and the deficit it faces. We should like to restate for the benefit of the reader that at the outset we were interested in assessing the overall impact of the government's policies on the society as a whole over a longer time frame and evaluate whether 'A better life for all' standard has been met or not. This summary should be sufficient to enable the reader to reach a conclusion.

Carl Jung once said, 'Everything that irritates us about others can lead us to an understanding of ourselves.' Anatole France further reminded us that, 'If we don't change, we don't grow, we aren't even living.' Things do not change, humans do. Restlessness and discontent are the first necessities of progress. The government may have failed to master change, yet change is the only thing that has brought us this far and tomorrow's progress is predicated upon continued change in order to create the necessary conditions for our survival. Most adult folks hold the older ANC generation in high regard as the time-tested vanguard stalwarts of the glorious liberation era. These are heroes who have walked the path of the downtrodden, the harbingers of the South African revolution that in whose shadow of greatness we all stand in awe of. Bequeathed to them wisdom to navigate our new found path to democracy. In short, the ANC heroes sit next to God. By any stretch of imagination, these are pretty impressive credentials! But there is a fundamental flaw here in that this over generalisation; in the first instance, the ANC leadership is none of this, if anything the opposite. They are out of touch with the reality of a modernising society. They lost an opportunity to plug into the youthful energy thus propelling this country to modernity.

Nation—building leadership

Liberation leaders are not known to have transformative propensities. The militaristic culture of the post-exilic ANC was never a good context for nurturing leaders of an open society such as we have today. Probing beneath the surface, we observe that those who led the liberation struggle are now the crowd who preside over the apartheid legacy partaking of its spoils. Older struggle veterans are not driven by the same sense of urgency demanded of a nation in transition. Older folks love to cling to staid protocols and procedures, not to mention their incessant desire to settle nefarious old political scores between themselves. The trouble of course grinding the axe of old scores is the burden ordinary folks must bear, often at a premium human cost. The conflation of liberation movement politics with democratic practice is one of the limiting factors to the current leadership in government.

A better way of finding new talent is to spot it at grassroots level where it is easy to identify early enough to nurture and mentor that talent through the relevant stages of leader development life cycle. What gets in the way of new talent is the problem of experience. We get caught up in this experience warp. We ask how much experience people have, when they got it, and what difference it's made and why we should care. One thing experience can cost us is curiosity. People stop asking questions because they think they know enough. The people who work for the president get the clear message that experience is what counts, and so they would rather watch and observe to play it safe. Another way experience undermines performance is how effectively it blocks truth telling. When there are 'superiors and subordinates' on a team, you limit mutual effort and responsibility. The team gets sucked into a pattern of thinking that there is a 'them and us' and the 'us' is just there in case something bad happens. Another way experience has limitations is through something called 'mitigated speech'. Rather than say nothing when there is less experience, people often sugarcoat what they're saying or downplay the importance, so others will 'swallow' it. What's usually lost in the soft lob is the real meaning and importance of what is being said. Experience only counts when the experienced person can set that experience aside long enough to be a novice and learn. That's when curiosity and candour make the difference they're intended to do.

Each epoch in history needs its own leaders as well as institutions to promote cultural shifts that meet new demands rather than superimposing orthodox often sterile practices prevalent in the twentieth century to a modern milieu. The need for transformative leadership is all the more urgent given the increased loss of confidence in government and public institutions beyond the ANC membership. The transformation of our society was about the distribution, not just capital but opportunities, reducing the widening gap on all levels, and ultimately changing the attitudes of people way leveling the society in a fundamental. The transformation of society was about giving black people freedom to access for themselves tools to overcome all forms of adversities in their path. It was the challenge to cease available opportunities in the lifetime of those opportunities and the freedom to change the established ways and break free from government vagaries. Jack Vance captures the sentiment succinctly when he said; 'Freedom and options must be exercised, even at the risk of inconvenience.'

Mbeki was the first to point out that South Africa is a country of two nations, one white and rich, and one black and poor. Actually, this is a country of three nations. The first is the white section rich and poor which aspires to a form of life that exist in Europe and North America where the rule of law is the norm and governments change frequently. The second are political elite of the ruling class who has enacted legislation to make their lives opulent and excessive while decrying colonialism. The third is the masses of people who are duped by members of the second group to vote for a better life. This group is given promises of free education, water, electricity and jobs. Until the third group has the common sense to discern the mendacity and self-interests of the proposal by the second group the government is never going to be subjected to the demands of serving the best interests of the majority. As often as they have done in the past, when leaders make decisions that are not in accordance with organisational values, often the organisation enters self-betrayal which invariably leads to self-justification, rather than corrective action and members lose faith in having a shared vision, thus moved into a zero sum manipulation of one another.

After apartheid laws were repealed in 1994, one of the most inclusive constitutions was installed and South Africa was re-envisioned as the *Rainbow Nation* with eleven official languages, sophisticated affirmative action regimes and the extension of full citizenship to people of all backgrounds. Nearly 20 years later—despite the promises of a new South Africa and the public displays of nationhood at the 2010 FIFA World Cup event—inequality and the spatialisation of poverty continues to run full steam ahead. A study of the speeches by the government leaders over 20 years revealed that they loved to repeat our problems to us often, problems that we are all too familiar with, which makes them seem they are on top of their game.

We have to wonder what happened to the promises contained in powerful speeches of the earlier times between 1994 and 1998, in particular, a speech delivered by Mbeki in 1995 in which he said, 'Two of the most important principles which were part of our perspective were participatory democracy and open [honest] governance. We came to those perspective not because we were particularly bright or inventive, but because we wanted to address the specific circumstances of our country, in which a situation we had the possibility to draw on the accumulated wisdom of the rest of humanity, and because we emerged out of our own definitive past.' South Africans have a common experience having lived in this country under these conditions long enough and so being reminded by the government—whose job it is to resolve these problems is rather trite.

Yet, the government is all for change: public institutions name change, province name changes, street name changes, currency changes, freedom Friday Days, party changes on its promises, history books get changed according to who is in power, so we don't know where we're coming from. Newspapers are sanitised, so we don't know the truth. And the future is uncertain. It is perfectly understandable that the ANC would hold a positive view of its performance and indulge in self-congratulatory campaign, claim more kudos than can be proven and celebrate whatever they wish to celebrate. Who wouldn't? Despite its lofty claims about own achievements, the preponderance of evidence before us is compelling against any claim of openness in government or participatory democracy with full citizens engagement. On the contrary, economic malaise and social decay are evident everywhere. Facts on the economy, education, health, and the moral fibre of the nation tell an entirely different story than those told by the officials.

The good categories

2009	2010	2011	2012	2013
Securities exchange 2	Securities exchange 1	Securities exchange 1	Securities exchange 1	Securities exchange 1
Strength of reporting standards 2	Strength of reporting standards 1	Strength of reporting standards 1	Strength of reporting standards 1	Strength of reporting standards 1
Good corporate governance 2	Trustworthiness 2	Trustworthiness 2	Trustworthiness 2	Trustworthiness 2
Financing through equity market 4	Good corporate governance 2	Good corporate governance 2	Good corporate governance 1	Good corporate governance 1
Legal rights 5	Soundness of banks 6	Soundness of banks 6	Soundness of banks 6	Soundness of banks 6

The bad categories

2010	2011	2012	2013
HIV prevalence 136%	Employment relations 138	HIV prevalence 141%	Business Impact of HIV/AIDS
Business cost of crime + violence 137	Flexibility of wage settlements 139	Quality of maths + science 143	HIV prevalence 144%
Quality of maths + science 137	Employment practices	Employment practices	Quality of education 146
Business Impact of HIV/AIDS	Business Impact of HIV/AIDS	HIV prevalence 141%	TB Cases 147
TB Cases 147	TB Cases 147	Employment relations 138	Quality of maths + science 137

Most improved since 2005

1. Legal rights index 45 to 1
2. Total tax rate 70 to 48
3. Mobile phone penetration 56 to 35
4. Financial market development 42 to 3

Worst since 2005

1. Primary education 48 to 125
2. Government procurement 29 to 105
3. Burden of regulations 59 to 123
4. Government budget balance 42 to 105
5. Favouritism in decisions of government officials 56 to 110

Source WEF Global Competitiveness index

The party standing has declined in the eyes of the South African people and the international community. The credibility has been wearing thin in the face of increasing delivery deficits, broken promises and an inability to communicate the reasons behind its failure. Survey after survey in private and public research domains produced data telling us that the government has lost the 'ear of the people'. One of the major weaknesses of the citizens was to place confidence in the importance of individual political actors who became the guarantors of our democracy as it was the case with Mandela because of who he is rather than with the citizens. The government was elected by the broader population and in that sense it had to approximate as much as possible the maxim 'the people shall govern'. The re-election of Zuma and Ramaphosa by the conference in Mangaung represents neither a setback nor a breakthrough in the politics of democracy—if conditions have emerged that make progress more likely.

We agree with the view against the fallacy that often shapes political analyses that our problems are caused by 'bad leaders and will go away if good ones take their place'. None of the country's problems were caused by an individual, rather they emanate from a historical legacy and the failure of the government to find a workable way out of this intractable past. The indictment is that most of the government initiatives failed in the main because they lack the requisite popular support for people to see their relevance in their lives. What South Africans needed was a compact on socioeconomic issues which would facilitate the transition from oppression to freedom. Without economic and social freedom, political freedom remains a hollow pastime of those who can make ends meet.

The failure by government to free up the capacity of people to find their own truth when tackling the demons of ethnic chauvinism, authoritarianism, social exclusion and economic deprivation meant that government has condemned black people to oppression once again and white people to new forms of guilt. This coupled with the deliberate underdevelopment of the human, intellectual and social capital of the people left the society on a weak base. From the ANC speeches it would appear to us that the party is stuck in a 1994 mindset where they talk about future aspirations and continue to romanticise, the ideal while the nation is looking for tangible change directly impacting their lives. After two decades in power, the effects of the ruling party's economic programmes have not filtered through to the masses of people but benefited only a small number mainly connected to the decision makers of the ruling party. Citizens have grown increasingly anxious with the lack of progress. Sporadic service delivery complaints that initially related to water, sanitation, electricity and crime issues became more generalised and raised questions with political overtones, so much so that calls for the removal of Ward Councilors is common place in the protests ructions.

Economic health of the nation

South Africa currently rates as the eighth most unequal society in the world, with 21% of its population living on less than R18.50 a day and 47% of the population existing below the minimum living income level of R600 a month. Of those who are described as poor, 93.3% are black people, 6.3% are coloured, 0.4% is Indian, and 0.1% is white. Overcoming past racism and enduring present inequalities constitutes the experience of being South African for the majority of blacks. At the same time, this extreme inequality frustrates the actualisation of citizenship and prevents the development of a sense of belonging for most black people.

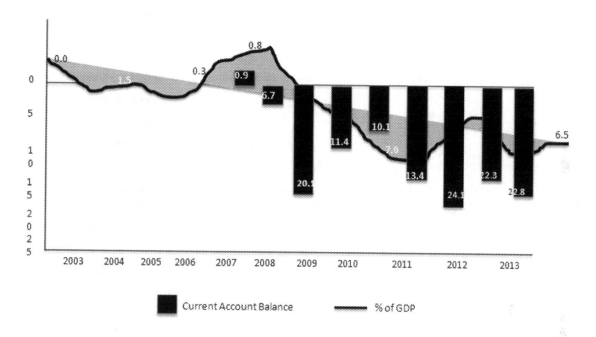

Current Account Deficit in ZAR bn

Source SARB Quarterly Bulletin Sept 2013

South African growth rate under current global and domestic economic climate constraints is sufficient to sustain a shrinking job market. In October 2012 the Governor of the Reserve Bank, said that the previous two months had hurt South Africa's reputation as a place to invest. She pointed to R5.6 billion in net equity-market outflows as evidence of a loss of confidence. 'The outlook at the moment is deteriorating rapidly,' she said. Mark Cutifani, Chief Executive of AngloGold Ashanti, the world's third-largest gold producer, says the strikes in the mining industry, which happened months earlier could lead his company to shrink sizably its operations in South Africa. Clusters of government departments have never worked together for a simple reason that individual departments lead by incredibly individualistic politicians have organic life of their own and don't know the meaning of collaboration let alone how to synergize for better outcomes. The much talked about monitoring and evaluation of the 12 Outcomes it seems was merely a PR affair rather than a key management tool for the president and confidence building measure for the citizens. Three years after they were first instituted government is still performing below the expected levels. These outcomes did not extend to lowest sphere of government—where the reality of politics mattered the most. Local government outcomes demand that Municipal Managers and Executive Mayors account for the management of these entities to the local communities but they continue to ignore this.

This paradox is best explained by the historian Giliomee, who notes in his book, *The Afrikaners*: 'In 1994, 75% of the white population earning over R500 000 per year were formally employed, receiving salaries and bonuses. 'By 2009, this figure had been completely reversed and 75% of whites in this income category were self-employed, either as owners of a business or as consultants or agents.' The point of whites turning to entrepreneurship can be further reinforced by data that suggests that, while a black university graduate is more likely than a white graduate to find a job within 12 months of graduation, white graduates are four times more likely to start and operate businesses. It is important to note, however, that only 10% of white adults fell into the R500 000-plus-and-above income bracket in 2009, while 50% were estimated to receive an income of less than R100 000 annually. With increasing levels of education, high levels of entrepreneurship, and low levels of unemployment, it must follow that white poverty levels are low. South Africa has no official poverty line. We therefore take a monthly household-income level of less than R5 000 as a benchmark of relative poverty. Using this benchmark, the proportion of white South Africans living in poverty declined from approximately 2% in 1994 to less than 1% in 2012. The figures for black South Africans were significantly higher, having declined from about 50% in 1994 to 45% by 2012.

The 1994 transition liberated black South Africans from oppression, but also liberated whites. Following the transition, 75% of whites in the country had a matric qualification and just 10% had any higher education. But by 2012, almost all white children were passing matric while 60% of those aged 20 to 24 were enrolled for higher education. The comparative figures are that fewer than 50% of black children are going on to pass matric and only 14% of those aged 20 to 24 are currently enrolled for higher education. This despite the fact that the white share of total tertiary enrolment has dropped from roughly 40% to 20% since 1994, while the black share has increased to 65%. Between 1994 and 2012, the rate of unemployment among white people increased from 3% to 5.7%. While this is a significant increase, the actual rate remains remarkably low by national standards.

For example, in 2012, 39% of black South Africans were unemployed. Black people were therefore five times more likely to be unemployed. The white unemployment rate was low, even when compared to a host of international benchmarks. At first glance, these low levels of white unemployment stand at odds with the white exodus from the civil service and the shifting employment equity profiles of large corporations.

This despite the fact that the roll-out of welfare grants to more than 15.5 million black South Africans saw the extent of poverty as measured at R18.50 a day, decline from a peak of 17% in 2002 to 5% in 2010 and now up again to around 15%. With such high education, employment and poverty differentials evident, high income differentials must be expected. The most striking way to point out such inequality is to measure how many cents a black South African is likely to receive in income for every rand received by his white compatriot. In 1994, on a per capita basis, black South Africans could expect to receive approximately 12 cents for every rand received by a white South African. In 2012, 19 years into our democracy, black South Africans were receiving only 13 cents for every rand received by white people. Here it must be explained that the key driver of such continued inequality is not white wealth but, rather, the non-existent education and labour market outcomes for black South Africans. We estimate that, on current trends, only 40% of black South African children are set to pass matric, and only 4% are set to pass maths in matric.

Likewise, the labour market absorption rate, which measures what share of the working-age population is employed, has fallen sharply for black South Africans since 1994 and now this number sits at just under 26%. The indicators force two new conclusions about the white experience since democracy. Firstly, whites have seen their education profile improve rapidly since apartheid ended and are today four times more likely to be in higher education than their black compatriots, who receive an appallingly poor standard of schooling. Second, employment equity and black empowerment policies have not driven whites into unemployment on a significant scale. Whites resident in South Africa are more likely to be employed than residents of the world's leading economies.

While history will record that the 1994 transition liberated blacks from oppression, it is an important footnote of history that whites were also liberated. They were liberated, first, from the guilt and pariah status that had been attached to their status as they supported and enforced apartheid. They were freed from the failing economy they had brought about in which low growth was ironically curtailing improvements in their own living standards. They were also unburdened from any sense that the state would look after their interests.

Herein lies one of the great paradoxes to emerge from the 1994 transition: as the focus of government policy turned to drive black economic advancement, so the whites were driven into entrepreneurship, which today best explains their continued economic prosperity even surpassing that of many black tycoons.

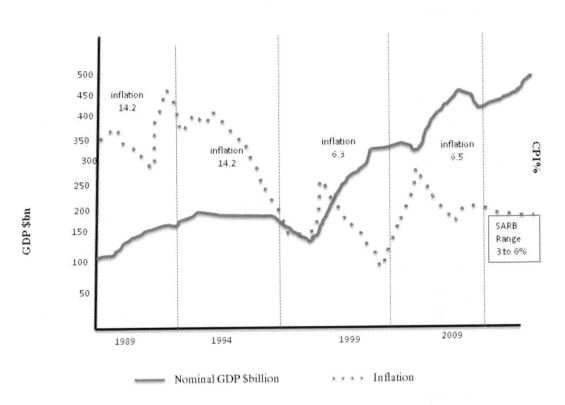

Macroeconomic fiscal position from 1994 to 2009

Source Euromonitor, IMF, WEO Database

Desirable indicators for the next 20 years

Economic indicator	Current figure	Target figure in 2034
Real GDP	3.3%	5%
GDP	800bn	2.0 tn
GDP per capita	7.5bn	16.5tn
Current account Deficit	6.5%	3.0%
Net FDI	11 bn	80 bn
Reserves	50bn	100 bn
Gini coefficient	61.2	50
Unemployment	42%	10%
Debt/GDP	42%	15%

In light of the above, we ask why the anger and rage, if most black people in South Africa today are doing better? We can confirm that poverty is not the defining problem here; rather the problem is that the rising prosperity of the nation is unequally shared among its people. The striking miners, farm workers, truck and bus drivers who are poorly educated workers in the main are stuck in lowly paid jobs with no prospects of advancing. Around them, they see better-educated workers who are rising to the middle class echelons and the tycoons of the BBZEE (Broad based Zuma Economic Empowerment a term widely used in mainstream press) type are stretching the gap vey fast. Many of the striking workers are young people who despaired because they perceived to be left behind, cheated and as a consequence humiliated. They are not enraged because they live in shacks and backrooms but because others were moving into better houses and driving cars and therefore it would appear they are losers in a society of their dreams. Nundera wrote that 'the swing from exhilaration to dejection creates a void in people's lives and a sense of themselves. If rejection and privilege, are one and the same . . . then human existence loses its dimensions and becomes unbearable light'.

For Gwede Mantashe to tell people of South Africa they are better off now than they would have been under apartheid is out rightly laughable if it were not ludicrous. Today, freedom in South Africa is measured by the acquisition of the material things; our society is scrambling to acquire these things because the government through the example set by its public officials measures our worth and assess the state of our self-esteem based on crass materialism. Our society today hands out dignity by a different measure and it has left many young black people feeling deficient; at a psychological level, they feel robbed of their self-worth. In short, we are witnessing the unraveling of a political culture that treats black people as consumers, not humans. Dehumanisation is dehumanisation whether it is at the hands of elites or those who profess to fight for others rights. The toilet wars that erupted in Cape Town in 2013 are the clearest example of this dehumanisation. People who have been treated inhumanly begin to act in dehumanizing ways and this is the heart of the problem today may be it is that the government don't seem to get it.

Khoza argues that we must abandon the notion that power came to us with the process of democracy when our former rulers 'gave us power'. That is a great fallacy. At the end of the day, the power was ours if we took possession of it. It soon emerged that many of our leaders stood naked, stripped of the power once enjoyed by former rulers without real power of their own because there were unsupported by the people. Mashiqi also argues, to the extent that there may be a confluence of interests between the state, the ANC and money, it should concern us quite deeply that corruption is an indication of the potential dangers of this confluence of interests. On the one hand, the country must grapple with the (Gramscian) reality of a class that wields political and economic influence without occupying the commanding heights of political power, and the impact of corruption in the state as a driver of internal ANC battles, as well as the impact of internal ANC instability on the state, on the other. The latter should probably concern us the most because internal ANC battles are about capturing the ruling party, en route to capturing the state in pursuit of narrow economic ends. As alluded to earlier, in provinces such as Limpopo, Mpumalanga, North West and the Eastern Cape, the state is the main creator of a middle class.

Because the middle class is constructed in this manner in these provinces, the parasitic and predatory elements are the link between political influence and state power. This has the potential to compromise our constitutional values because access to power has become the means towards ignoble ends of a nature that undermines the integrity of the state and that of our democratic society. It is this dimension of the conflation of the party with state, which should concern us greatly Mashiqi, concludes. The conflation of the state, government and the person of the leader emerged as the biggest threat yet. Mandela was acutely conscious of this weakness in politics and he positioned himself above its lure so that when the temptation arose he could not fall for it. Mbeki and Zuma were too eager to harvest 'low hanging fruits' and succumbed rather too gullibly to the trappings offered by state power and neglected the first and most important job description as heads of State that is transforming the state into a platform for democratic governance. And so, as a consequence of the single party dominance phenomenon we found that 'congressification' of South Africa's democracy is inevitable outcome. Single party dominance, especially where the state is the sole instrument of class formation, constitute a real threat to the interests of democracy and the state itself when the dominant party is riven by political internecine battles for money and control.

Movement for the national salvation

There is no democracy without democrats, that is, without people who in their daily social behaviour are committed to defending and promoting democratic values and so it is particularly important that citizens do not lose faith in the human project and should find ways to sustain themselves above the ephemeral disappointments. Sobukwe, Biko and Mandela's lives and actions have bequeathed to this generation a covenant that cannot be broken; 'That we shall, build a society in which all South Africans will be able to walk tall, without any fear in their hearts, assured of their inalienable right to human dignity, a nation in peace with itself and the world . . . Never, never, and never again shall it be that this beautiful land will again experience the oppression of one by another, and so it shall be.' Given this deep perversion the government seems more concerned with the personal advantages of the president, which generally bring them to focus their actions on resolving their internal conflicts around what the president wished. Rather than education their followers to become genuine cadres of the movement they have developed ethnic and regional clienstelism.

Naturally, the question becomes what have the opposition parties done differently to neutralise the threat? On the face of it, it would appear present day opposition parties do not have in them what it takes to change the body polity; because of fragmentation they are too weak to pose real and direct threat to the ANC's dominance of the political landscape. COPE has since spluttered amid infighting. IFP has withered away. As the DA morphs into a party for all South Africans, it is moving too slow to capture the imagination of the larger youth universe. There is of course a potpourri of inconsequential names such as PAC, AZAPO, FF, UDM, ACDP, Agang SA and EFF whose presence at this time does not matter much and would merit no further mention. If this is the case, then alternative thinking must emerge.

We would propose that challenge to the ANC hegemony must come from outside party politics. NGOs have a commendable history of holding the government to account and stepping in where it fails. Section 27, Rape Crisis, Right to Know, The Social Justice Coalition, Abahlali base Mjondolo, Freedom Under Law, Citizens Movement for Social Change are some of the voices that speak truth to power but in and of themselves are not adequate to create a counter force to change course. The salvation of the national integrity should proceed not through the ANC but should be advanced by the citizens through active civic engagements.

To bring political change outside the ANC is a monumental task this we acknowledge especially in the face of compelling ties of history, nostalgia, and the patronage dispensed by the party to the poor (there are currently 15.5 million South Africans receiving government grants of one kind or another) these ties will ensure the party is returned to power after the 2014 elections. The question is not what will replace the ANC, rather what *kind* of ANC will South Africa inherit post 2014. South Africa has attained freedom what is missing is the wisdom in people to provide a better life for themselves. 'For the Lord your God is bringing you to a good land, a land with streams and pools of water, with springs flowing in the valleys and hills, land with wheat and barley, vines and fig trees, olive oil and honey, land where bread will not be scarce and you will lack nothing, a land where the rocks are iron and you can dig copper out of the hills' (Deuteronomy 8.7). Yes, when God set people free God ensures they are sustained throughout, but God trust people to rid themselves of the acquired slave mentality and they must on their own break free of psychological shackles. Far from being a basket case, this country has wealth lying dormant waiting for industrious people to work on it. In the absence of such industry from people of the land, others from outside will enter the land exploit its wealth and redirect the exploits to their own land and leave citizens in poverty once again despite their political freedom.

The goal of salvaging the national integrity of South Africa is to rise to the challenge and lift the country back from the brink of abyss. It is not to say people must worship politics, but South Africans must begin to appreciate that to bask in past glory entombed in nostalgia, eulogizing geriatric liberation heroes and a blind loyalty to the liberation politics is an expensive luxury they can ill afford right now. It is time black people access their collective strength and effect the change they would want to see. The destiny of this nation is too important to leave it to the whims of the few in political parties but also complaining about the ANC and how it has failed them is simply not good enough as an excuse. Under the present conditions, the opportunity to make things happen is available to all of us. Society advances only by the extra achievements of the individual; we are the sum of all those individuals. Young people must not fear the winds of adversity because a kite rises against the wind rather than with it.

To change the system that perpetuate inequality and strips people of their dignity people should assert themselves more vocally than they have so far rejecting the culture of ostentatious opulence from the party political leaders stand firm against all forms of the extravagance by the public representatives. The ever threatening presence of heavy bodyguards shielding useless ministers from the people they represent must be cut down to zero. Who wants to kills a useless politician unless it is a personal revenge? Ministers, MEC, Councilors must use public transport system when they come to speak to the people; the cars they drive must be small cars. Elected leaders must live in the constituency areas they represent. In our campaign, we must demand that those responsible for stealing our taxpayer money should pay it back regardless of the time lapse, there is R30 billion the nation is owed each year siphoned by thieves in state supply chain points. We must demand it back all of it! Because the politicians have dishonoured the office they took oath to uphold, they have lost our respect as our leaders from now on regardless of the title they happen to wear, they can no longer be addressed as 'Your Excellency' this or 'The Honourable' that. They must stand in queues in shops and in the banking halls like all of us because none of them are VIP's just ordinary South Africans serving in public office. All VIP areas at public events that are funded by taxpayer's money must banned, so too the never ending banquets at government functions. Elected officials must serve the people rather than themselves. Excessive bonuses in the SOC public sector businesses should be circumscribed to frugal levels.

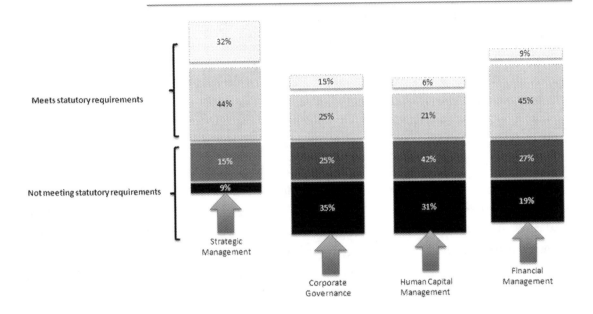

The Presidency Performance Assessment Tool

Distribution of final scores in key performance areas of government as at April 2013

Source MPTA Report. Statement of management practice in the Public Service

Political heads of ministries who do not deliver on the 12 outcomes must be sacked from government at our call and behest even if they are powerful ANC insiders. Delivering the outcomes must be based on what impacts the lives of the citizens at community level rather than what is important to government's programme. To restore semblance of discipline to the public service these outcomes should be cascaded down to the lowest ranked officials in the local government administration. At a national level, regular elections without real political alternatives do not constitute true democracy. We should be careful to get out of an experience only the wisdom that is in it not the fad. One of the most urgent campaigns citizens are conscientised to wage is to put to bed the sunset clause that made provision only for proportional representation in a closed party-list system. The youth must increase the numbers of people in major campaigns promoting civic action demanding long overdue changes including the abolishing of the proportional representation Act as it stands at the moment.

Some elements of the *Sunset clause* were dispensed with when due for review after the 1999 election but the ANC government saw it fit to retain this arrangement in particular because it suited its political agenda better. Many political analysts have correctly pointed out that the current party-list system has destroyed public accountability of the political leadership, has promoted ill-discipline among MP members as we have watched them over the years absent from parliament sleeping during house debates, defrauding, floor crossing for personal gain and disdain for any form of direct accountability from electorate. As a result, the distance between the elected and the electorate has widened, and completely removed parliament from direct relationship with the electorate such as found in constituency-based system. This electoral system has literally negated the power of one man one vote and has given it to the party national working committee who decide who comes first on the list and ensures that those on the list continue to pander to the whims of the party bosses.

Parliament, as an institution of public representation, needs to reform its procedures and practices to create the space for its members to hold the Executive and party leaders to account and in turn the replacement of lists with constituencies would allow for floor crossing—regulated by suitable checks and balances making MPs directly accountable to their constituencies not their party bosses. Constituency based politics has a better chance of creating a platform for healthy politics. The will of the people would be better served when individual MPs are allocated speaking time, debate members' statements as a right, as opposed to parties receiving these as privileges. Such reforms will transform Parliament from being a mere rubber stamp of the president and his cabinet to a genuine forum for citizen agenda.

Reforming parliamentary procedures will have the added benefit of promoting a more dynamic, yet less antagonistic, interaction between MPs and parties in Parliament. The imperative of the citizens to take charge of the destiny is now. The urgency of the moment cannot be over-emphasized. Citizens who want to bear the responsibility for themselves and who have assumed ownership of their own country must come together wherever they are at home, at work, at universities, in civil society organs and change the system that continues to deny us freedom and oppress us through poverty and inequality. Young citizen's transition movements are the way to influence public policy in the country's politics.

The greatest impetus for national salvation will come from young voters, since, as voters profile change, so will the political dynamic compelling parties to respond and adapt if they are to remain relevant, inevitably leading to new alignments in our political landscape. The manifestation of this will come in the form of parties either being completely transformed, or new parties being born consistent with the spirit of the new South Africa, without any association to the divisions of the old South Africa and imbued with the insights from 20 years of experimentation, this new movement will be better placed to deal with the real affairs that is the cornerstone of the current stagnation—deep inequality and insecurity. As young citizens, the responsibility of stewardship and citizenship demands more from them to ensure alternative voices have the space to emerge and be heard. Our responsibility as the older generation is to protect the welfare of our young with care and forethought. The Constitutional Court has already affirmed this right when it delivered its 2006 seminal judgment on the duty of government to listen to ordinary citizens. In Doctors for Life judgement, Justice Ngcobo insisted that it was a constitutional requirement that there be public debate about the merits of legislation before it could be passed, he said, parliament never intended to limit ordinary citizen's participation in political decision making to their right to vote.

Mandela said, 'Poverty, and breakdown of family life has secondary effects. Children wander the streets of township because they have no schools to go to, or no money to enable them to go to schools . . . This leads to a breakdown in moral standards, to an alarming illegitimacy, and to growing violence which erupts politically.' The wounds inflicted upon the people of South African by a century of colonization and racial oppression is still festering, the communities have not been delivered from the clutches of race hate. South African black and white communities are living aliomemetically without holding one another's hand in part because of the afflictions of apartheid and in part because there is absence of authentic leadership to model this.

The moral and psychological decay is also part of the reality of the white South Africa. They too face similar dilemmas; we can say that apartheid made all South Africans prisoners of a psychological casuistry from which we are unable to escape. According to Ramphela, the scarring of the black psyche is a consequence of colonial and racial subjugation. They struggle to find closure on many issues related to the past because the wounds are still gaping and the depth of trauma is yet to surface. South Africans don't have experience of themselves as citizens of this democracy. White men leave this country and black people remain behind gripped by the same inferiority complex inculcated many years ago. They are prepared to be recipients of crumbs from a state that does not regard them as humans. Setting black people free from the violence of marginalization and degrading poverty is the prerequisite to transformation and modernity.

Although in 2009 a new Department of Women, Children, and People with Disabilities was created, budgets are blown each year on women's day events with little impact on women's real lives. At present, 42% of Ministers in Government are women and women make up 45% of the National Assembly. Yet, few of these women dispute legislation that is passed which will be disempowering other women. The Traditional Courts Bill is another tool that will limit women's rights in the interests of a minority of traditional leaders. It is oppressive lawmaking at its best, or in this case, it's worst. It is difficult to feel free when they are threatened with a culture of sexual violence from men, and this is a reality that many women face. Unequal gender relations disempowered men too by limiting them to roles where they are unable to be active fathers, caring brothers, or non-violent friends. It is important that advertising, which promotes a diversity of ideas of what a woman can be, is aired and promoted from early childhood stage before boys become men. South Africa's fertility rate has declined significantly over time. Besides creating a larger demand for household-based services such as housing, water, electricity and sewerage, the changing household composition is eroding cumulative household earnings, thus increasing the number of households falling under the poverty line. Life expectancy in South Africa is 49 years and infant mortality rate is 4.78 deaths per 1000 people. Poverty continues to be the scourge that disproportionately impact Africans, rural households and female-headed households are a norm.

Mandela quite rightly said, 'Freedom cannot be achieved unless the women have been emancipated from all forms of oppression.' The freedom of some should never be founded on the lack of freedom of others. Women's lives have undoubtedly improved on paper in many respects since the advent of democracy. Many women are made more vulnerable by their dependence on survivalist activities, characterised by insecurity and low wages, in the informal sector, violent raping of women at will continues unabated. But it is clear that there is a long way to go. As unemployment has risen, larger numbers of the poor are living on the margins and are dependent on temporary work or social grants; from there, many have descended into homelessness.

Homelessness on the streets in South Africa is a slow-moving tragedy that arouses anxiety in government and civil society, but one that is overshadowed by the size of the population in shack housing and as a result homelessness is an obscured human tragedy. Ten percent of South African population is inadequately housed in shack dwellings. Estimates of street children suggested more than 200 000 live on the streets, which is a significant number. For the developmental state, the street homeless are the proverbial skeletons at the feast, the excluded poorest who enter unobserved and stand by gaunt and starved, terrifying to the invited guests but deprived of any capacity to join the party of the descent.

Children who are sexually active have once again been placed under the spotlight. Recently, a high court ruled against the provisions of Sexual Offences Act, which Act criminalised consensual sex among children. The Judge held that criminalisation would constitute an unjustified intrusion of control into intimate and private sphere of children's personal relationships in a manner that could cause severe harm to them. Parents have been left confused by the ruling. They are concerned that the ruling might give their children carte blanche to have sex. The current age of consent in South Africa is 16 years and older. This ruling means if sex is consensual between 10 year olds, it is legal. According to explanation given by the department of justice on the Act, these restrictions were meant to protect children. But the researches have revealed that more children are engaging in consensual sex in South Africa any way outside of parental awareness and knowledge. The spokeswoman for the Teddy Bear Clinic was quoted praising the judgement for 'promoting the best interest of children and protecting children from being violated by the very system that is supposed to protect them.'

What kind of society is this? This is very strange thinking and it should offend our sense of morality as a nation. According to the child rights organisation, children who are under the age of consent but have engaged in sexual relationships can now seek help without fear. Those who provide counseling and guidance to such children can also do so without fear of being criminalized. 'Arresting a young child because they have engaged in sexual activities will not solve the problem. But educating and empowering children will help in dealing with the problem. Children are sexually active at the early age. 'Our findings have highlighted the sad fact that South Africa is now precariously poised on the edge of a cliff. All indications are that South Africa is stuck at crossroads in other words between the hard place and a point of no return. It's not that ANC can't see the solution. It is that they can't see the problem. Truth can be accepted and woven into a design for a living because time brings all things to pass.

Addressing parliament in 1994, Mbeki said, 'If, in time, the reality of the absence of fundamental change convinces the black majority that we have created a political democracy which is unwilling to fully dismantle the systems of racial oppression and exploitation, then we must expect that the dream deferred will, rather than wilt in the sun, explode. Hardened by their experiences, the masses will indeed say that the villainy we teach them, they will execute and, given who they are, it shall go hard for them, but they will surely better the instruction that we will have imparted to them' For Mbeki to quote the American poet Langston Hughes was all and good, but omitting to place himself at the centre of the dream of his people not so good, birds have come home to roost. The ANC has in the view of many people sacrificed the future of the young generation at the alter of expediency and has left an unbearable irony of privilege and poverty.

Xolela Mangcu asks the question 'whether or not the ANC has the common sense to recognize how far it has veered off from the original promise that our democracy held, and whether the organization will have in it wisdom and capacity to bring us back from the brink' and retorted 'but then again, getting from the brink is a task not for the ANC but for all of us South Africans.' Pallo Jordan also warned the ANC just days before its Mangaung conference 'The ANC will emerge post Mangaung united if it musters the moral courage for the serious introspection required to reclaim the moral high ground.' In closing, our remarks must come from the constitution, which in its preamble enjoins us to remain true to the spirit with which our founding fathers envisioned a future full of hope and better life for all.

> We, the people of South Africa, recognise the injustices of our past; Honour those who suffered for justice and freedom in our land; Respect those who have worked to build and develop our country; and Believe that South Africa belongs to all who live in it, united in our diversity. We therefore, through our freely elected representatives, adopt this Constitution as the supreme law of the Republic so as to—Heal the divisions of the past and establish a society based on democratic values, social justice and fundamental human rights; Lay the foundations for a democratic and open society in which government is based on the will of the people and every citizen is equally protected by law; Improve the quality of life of all citizens and free the potential of each person; and build a united and democratic South Africa able to take its rightful place as a sovereign state in the family of nations. May God protect our people. Nkosi Sikelel' iAfrika.

The Constitution's vision of democracy requires structures that enable the people to engage in representative, direct and participatory forms of democracy, which ensure that government remains accountable, open and responsive. Democracy' cannot denote mere majority rule. At a minimum, democracy stands for the proposition that the rights in the Bill of Rights are not in conflict with majority rule: they are, rather, in a 'constructive tension' with each other. Rights are necessary conditions for meaningful representative, participatory and direct democracy. In more recent cases in the Constitutional Court, African Christian Democratic Party and Matatiele 1 and Matatiele II, demonstrate growing support for the principle of constitutional democracy, that democracy means more, much more, than mere majority rule.

The Court struck down legislation that had been promulgated without the kind of public participation. The Constitution adopts a two-stage structure for analysis. At the first stage, a court must determine whether the exercise of a right has been impaired by law or conduct. At the second stage, the party looking to uphold an impugned law—but not conduct—has an opportunity to justify that limitation if it serves 'an open and democratic society based on human dignity, equality and freedom'. The limitation clause has a four-fold purpose. First, it functions as a reminder that the rights enshrined in the Constitution are not absolute . . . . Secondly, the limitation clause tells us that rights may only be limited where and when the stated objective behind the restriction is designed to reinforce the values that animate this constitutional project . . . .

Thirdly, the test set out in the limitation clause allows for candid consideration of those public goods or private interests that the challenged law sets in. Fourthly, the limitation clause could be said to represent an attempt to finesse the 'problem' of judicial review by establishing a test that determines the extent to which the democratically elected branches of government may craft laws that limit our constitutionally protected rights and the extent to which an unelected judiciary may override the general will by reference to the basic law. But the presence of s 36 serves as a reminder that the counter-majoritarian dilemma is neither a paradox nor a problem, but an ineluctable consequence. We can never truly justify a limitation of rights—we simply own up to the fact that we make hard choices that grant ascendency to one preferred vision of the good over another and that such a choice invariably requires sacrifice in the deepest, and sometimes cruelest, sense of the term? While the Court retains an important role in articulating general norms that give content to our basic law. Courts, the other branches of government and the rest of South African society are enjoined to participate in a shared project of constitutional interpretation that reveals best practices over time. Experimental constitutionalism thus displaces the standard account of the Court as the single, final oracle of constitutional interpretation. It is this constant tension, and the sacrifice at the heart of this tension, that 'affords the notion of shared interpretation its grave significance'. On this point, there can be no dispute as we all sing in unison Amen!

Where to from here?

Mandela received with applause as the effable diplomat idolized by many made inroads into building the South African nation and put in place building blocks for future leaders to build on its momentum. In the midst of turbulence and uncertainty, a credible and optimistic story makes a strong impact. There are persons so radiant, so genial, and so kind, so pleasure bearing, that you instinctively feel good in their presence; Mandela was such to many whose paths crossed his. He exudes friendship and warmth and he is an exceptionally good listener.

His very personality expresses the importance of altruism, the sense of something bigger than yourself, the sense of feeling pain for others. His personality evoked a classical stoicism in the sense that the power to achieve one's ambition, even in a world of human expedience, rests with the individual. Whether he talked to Heads of States or Waitresses serving tea at a function, he talked to all with equal reverence. A corrective action man he was. When Mandela reconciled our nation, we began to believe in ourselves again as a people.

At the start of his presidency, Mbeki soared like an eagle a highly respected intellectual. Had an ability to listen to other voices, recognized predictable elements about the future, challenged conventional mental maps about our thinking and tested strategies for sustainability. But, he would fall at the last hurdle and lie prostrate on the ground because he spun overtures of counsel from the wisdom of the elderly. As he floundered, he would finish his race emotionally mutilated. When Mbeki proclaimed he was an African born of people of this continent, we shared his pride and we were proud to be Africans again. Mbeki introduced policies that attempted to get our economy on track and we began to believe that if we liberated ourselves from apartheid we could also liberate ourselves from poverty. Oops, it turned out we are not there yet; this country has new divisions not along the lines of the classical contradiction of the oppressed and oppressor classes but as a nation of insiders and outsiders.

Zuma the ethnic social Darwinist prevaricated, dithered and lost his initial charm ended despised for his lack of judgment, which would later turn deadly threats in the face of difficulties. Precisely because of toxic intent, his charm turned poisonous nothing good would follow him. He would mostly be remembered as a leader that presided over many tragedies in the South African history than any other head of state. Moreover, a litany of contemptible scandals that brought much embarrassment to his children and disrepute to his party. Life is not a game for the ephemeral one-day performance extravaganzas but a lesson in how to finish strong.

It was never going to be enough to rely on Mandela's nation building efforts, or Mbeki's early efforts to on societal transformation to break the back of apartheid and take South Africa to a better place. We need much more concerted effort beyond these ephemeral programmes, efforts that are inclusive of all South Africans, a social contract binding upon the whole nation in order to move this country to modernity. A call to modernity requires a unifying statesman rather than a party demagogue, a leader of this generation. It does not help that a government that enjoys popular support is abusive towards its people, it does not help that its leaders turn a blind eye on the high levels of corruption that are destroying every fabric of our society both in and outside of public sector and certainly it sure does not help one bit that a small section of people are the beneficiaries of the progress the country

143

is making. From high road walked by Mandela to the low road walked by Zuma the nation has fallen on hard ground. It may be that history will judge these first 20 years of democracy under the ANC government as a period during which the nation missed an opportunity to place itself at the front door to modernity.

Yes, democracy celebrations among the elite few will go on until the next day, same celebrations will live a sour taste for many. We hope that just as history dealt its hand to the Nationalist Party, the deeply ingrained spirit of arrogance would become the one thing that would eventually humble the prideful. South Africa stands at a critical threshold in her history there is a desperate need for authentic leadership. Credible leaders are not necessarily the types who possess oratorical skill and the gift of expression, rather those who accept personal accountability and have the humility of spirit to accept the counsel of others. They are not necessarily adept at politics, but have the moral authority to galvanize the nation into positive action.

Authenticity is often used to judge, reinforce and correct our own behavious and those of others on a daily basis. Conversations about values and authenticity deepens shared understanding and enables people to increase their capacity for acting in alignment with their values thus building the trust and shared vision to succeed in today's complex world. Authentic leaders are not people who have a posture of moral rectitude yet act against their inner values or not believe in the honesty of these values. Great leaders make a positive difference and bequeath something of enduring human value.

Leadership is rather an art and a condition of the heart, than an office to hold or set of things one does. The visible signs of artful leadership are expressed ultimately in practice and quality of that leadership, it is always the results of pure intent, sincere effort, intelligent direction and skilful execution; it is never an accident but represent the wise choice of many alternatives. Governing a modern polity in an interdependent and sophisticated economy such as South Africa is a complex business and calls for the kind of leadership that can match it. Today South Africa needs transformative leadership. Transformation leadership is about credible, visionary leadership that expands boundaries of possibilities for all citizens, enabling them to contribute their talents to create a meaningful future. It is about shifting the frame of reference from old to new ways.

A transformative leader will take the nation beyond aspirations towards a lived experience in the lifetime of that leader. The transformation of our society requires an understanding of the legacy of apartheid and an even more profound understanding of the foundations of our envisaged society. Successful leaders tend to synthesise transformative objectives with transactional skills, they inspire followers to transcend self-interest in pursuit of higher purpose and common good, while transactional leaders motivate followers by appealing to their self-interests. In the words of Harvey Mackay, a mediocre man tells. A good man explains. Superior men demonstrate but great men inspire others to actualise themselves into greatness.

Apart from the absence of a coherent, scale-appropriate strategy for the second economy, a fundamental shortcoming of government efforts is the tendency to design programmes in a way that is out of kilter with the expectations of the ordinary poor person. For example, the introduction of social grants instead of alleviating poverty the grants have far damaging unintended consequences where we began to experience a consistent pattern where fathers have abandoned their roles of taking care of their babies and mentoring their sons as they should and putting bread on the table by whatever means necessary. The government failed to translate its electoral support to significantly change the social and economic conditions in general and improve the lot of black folks in particular. It failed to advance South Africa on a path to modernity and in Zuma's years; the path was effectively diverted to Nkandla Ville.

Towards the later part of the second decade, the people of South Africa have experienced bad government characterized by incompetence, arrogance, corruption, killing of its own citizens, political clientelism, and ethnic regionalism with fratricide consequences (Tsonga communities in Malamulele in Limpopo experienced cruelty at the hands of Venda leadership serves to illustrates this point). The party has lost credibility among many supporters they are on their way to find other forms of non-formal political organizations, which are supposed to be more efficient in advancing their interests or are simply descending into political skepticism and abstain from any form of involvement. This failure to progress the nation to modernity has got most people not only disappointed but feeling somewhat dejected that their trust in the black government has been abused in the manner it has. Their judgement will become apparent in the next general election results.

Time has come for those who truly believe in the honesty of the values of freedom to enjoin the younger generation cohort to the covenant of South Africa of our dreams. As we do so we have no doubt that the young people of South Africa their country is destined into greatness because of the infinite capacity hidden in them. The dawn of that greatness can be seen even as clouds of destructions obscure it. We have in recent history demonstrated our capacity to pull back from the precipice of abyss and surprise even the worst skeptics among us. Like a phoenix, young people must rise from the ashes to reenact the vision of their envisaged selves, a vision where universal freedom is attainable in their lifetime.

BOOK II

2014-2034
THE EMERGENT FUTURE

CHAPTER 5

The Phoenix Rises from Ashes

Young people in South Africa today are negotiating a complex reality wedged between a brutal apartheid they did not personally experience; a post-apartheid era where poverty and violence are their only experience and the knowledge that they will inherit a fractured future is indeed a disconcerting one

Not so long ago we were also young; we thought we could predict the likely plains and bleakness that age might bring. We imagined the loss of status, the loss of desire and desirability, never looked ahead and then imagined looking back from that future point. While as youth we luxuriated in the doldrums of adolescence, imagining that our riotous discontent with the apartheid regime was an original response. Some among us then were already looking further ahead and wider. When compared to the youth today the difference is that they are unable to learn much from the lessons life provides. We all suffer damage one way or the other. How could we not, except in a world of perfect parents and siblings? And then there is a question, on which so much depends, of how we react to the damage, whether we admit to it or repress it, and how this affects our dealings with others. Some admit the damage and try to mitigate it, some spend their lives trying to help others who are damaged and there are those whose main concern is to avoid further damage to themselves at whatever cost. And these people are the ones our future generation should be careful of.

Discovering, for example, that as a witness to our life diminishes, there is less corroboration, and therefore less certainty, as to what one may have been. Even if we have assiduously kept records of pictures, (most of us kept a record of the first elections and Mandela's inauguration speech in DVD that's for sure), one finds that one has attended to the wrong kind of records. But none of us would ever imagine what life would be 20 years post-apartheid much less about how to transition from the bitter cold times of oppression to the sunshine of freedom. It begs the question does character develops over time? Our attitudes and opinions change as young people, we develop new habits and eccentricities, but that's something more like decorations. Perhaps character resembles intelligence, except that character peaks a little later say at forty years—and after that, we are stuck with what we've got, 'life sucks!' Someone once remarked that his favourite time in history were when things were dying, because that meant something new was being born.

Does this make any sense if we apply it to our own social context? Yes, it does a lot more than that. To die when something new is born; even if that something new is our very new self is a fluttering imagination. Just as political change sooner or later disappoints, so does life. Sometimes we think the purpose of life is to reconcile us to its eventual loss by wearing us down and breaking our will. The current brand of South African politics is admittedly less about the discipline of thought and building of civil ethos than it is about the performance of mob power. Many honestly hope this kind of politics will soon die so that something new more vibrant may emerge in its place and we hope to see this during your lifetime.

At the heart of the narrative is how we marshal national will to help extricate our young from the morass. A scan of recent mainstream media articles related to youth revealed a rather chilling tale of apathy and despair mainly due to unemployment, violence, HIV infection and being beneficiaries of grant programmes. There is no mention of young people as engaged citizens tackling key social issues on own initiative. A significant proportion of young people are searching for a definition of their generation's mission, while acknowledging the burden they've inherited from the previous generation they also recognise that they are not bound by their mistakes and so must continue to search for ways to live outside those limits. The youth is negotiating a complex reality wedged between a brutal apartheid history, which most did not experience and post-apartheid era where poverty and hopelessness are the only constant. The issues that preoccupy them are what kind of future has been bequeathed to them, as it is understood in terms of decent environment, healthy economy that produces plenty of jobs and business opportunities, a much more open society that offers freedom and fewer diseases. Yet, for the most part, the older generation perceived them as 'problems' waiting to be solved, thought to be violent or apathetic, uneducated, diseased and unemployable. True, this may be a hard reality young people are experiencing at this time the origins of which are traceable to absent fatherhood and inept leadership. It is totally unfair to evaluate youth based on a worldview that was relevant yesteryear for indeed a brave new world has emerged from which the contours of their mission is to be carved. Twenty years on the country is caught in a dichotomous bind on the one hand is an intractable present and irrecoverable past, on the other things are no longer and things are not yet. The transition from apartheid to democracy brought with it enormous optimism.

Dreams of possible future are perhaps also the process of conceptualising the nation and one's inclusion in it. For young people growing up in South Africa, dreams hold a deeper significance of overcoming poor education, inequality, unemployment and poverty. Yet, in the context of persistent poverty, the social and cultural capital necessary for getting ahead, including individual's education and the environment they inhabit are not conducive to realising these dreams just yet. In this context, the presence of the dream itself functions as currency in the face of the aridity of South African myth. By dealing in dreams, young people appear to be writing themselves into the nation's narrative by constructing their own sense of opportunity and, thereby their sense of belonging. Yet the deferment of dreams in many of these young people's lives can have devastating social consequences because this amounts to a form of violence done on them by virtue of their exclusion from the nation citizenship as its active participants. As disillusionment sets in, the weapons of resistance can work against their wellbeing. That is why the renaissance of the economic freedom movement portends a resurrection of a second revolution cannot be ignored by those interested in politics.

The ascendency of youth and attempts to wrestle power from the old generation has usually coincided with periods of intense fracture of life experience and the concomitant crisis of imagination. The entropy is dramatised by expansion of spaces of vulnerability in all arenas of life including the dilemmas presented by the never-ending unemployment. Most are barely holding on the edge with so much rage at being robbed of their future. For the freedom of human spirit to have any hope at all, the realism that characterised post-apartheid life has to be broken. This break should be about the reopening of the future for all taking a conscious attempt to retrieve life and humans from a history of waste dumped on the youth by their government. Whereas many young South Africans experience this country as flawed and imperfect, they also express a deep sense of commitment to do whatever it takes to create conditions for a better life for themselves. They're outspoken on their views that this change requires each one of them to rise beyond the current hardships, to seek every opportunity they can get, to grab the initiative whenever this present itself. They don't believe that they must rely on the government to bring about changes they want to see.

The change to is less about holding ANC officials to account for their failure to leader the nation. It is well known fact that historically, youth have lead revolutions, but changing the destiny of this nation is not the same as taking to the streets and hurling obscenities at the police. It is one thing to carry screaming placards in angry street demonstrations lamenting bad government but quiet another to roll up one's sleeve and do positive things to change a situation for better. Progress has less to do with speed but much to do with direction. To move the South Africa of our dreams beyond a single narrative of an unruly, uneducated, unemployed and violent youth we need to be asking a different question and that is what contribution should the young generation be making at this time in order to realize this envisage future? It is not enough to blame the failure of government, education, parents or the society. Excuses are the nails used to build a house of failure. It is equally important that youth must be challenged to confront the circumstance they found themselves in today and turn it around rather than play the blaming game.

Sobukwe, Biko and Mandela taught us to dig deep within ourselves and find the heroes we are made to be. Sobukwe said, 'Take away the bitterness from us and help us to work for a country where we will not hate each other because hate will destroy us all. It's time to get over bitterness and come with constructive ways of redressing the imbalances of the past instead of just complaining without bringing to the fore any viable alternatives. A doctrine of hate has never taken people anywhere. It is too exacting. It warps the mind. That is why we preach the doctrine of love for Africa. We can never do enough for Africa, nor can we love her enough. The more we do for her, the more we wish to do. I am sure that I am speaking for the whole of young Africa when I say that we are prepared to work with any man who is fighting for the second liberation of South Africa within our lifetime.' Albert Einstein admonishes, 'Anyone who has never made a mistake has never tried anything new,' and Miles Davis encourages not fearing mistakes; there are none. End is not the end—in fact, it is spelt *Effort Never Dies.* If you get 'No' as an answer, remember it means 'Next Opportunity' for you. Meanrat reminds if someone says 'that's impossible', we should understand it to mean 'according to my limited experience and narrow understanding of reality, that is unlikely.' Creative minds have always been known to survive any kind of bad training. The call for the youth is to embrace new and alternative ways of living such as for example social entrepreneurship programmes in order to go around the failures of the socio political system. At the heart of this call is the idea of modernising our society. This call is made on the strength of the assumption that there is sufficient commonly shared interest amongst the youth to co—create this reality.

At the beginning of this book, we made reference to the *Mont Fleur Scenarios,* a tool used to identify four alternatives. The scenarios provided a provocative road map for this transition. At that time, South African leaders in their wisdom opted for the Flamingo scenario; however, it appears in retrospect that this was a theoretical exercise because in practice the leaders ended dumping the nation on the Icarus scenario. What were the specific details of each scenario? In 1992, the Mont Fleur scenarios team named the Ostrich, Lame Duck, Icarus and Flight of Flamingo scenarios. Each questioned: How will the South African transition go and will the country succeed in 'taking off'? Each of the four stories gave a different answer and had a different message. South Africa was in the middle of risky transition negotiations. Nobody knew how or even whether they would succeed, or if the country would remain stuck, embattled, and isolated.

According to these scenarios there were three dark prophecies to avoid: Ostrich, in which the minority white government sticks its head in the sand to try to avoid a negotiated settlement with the black majority; Lame Duck, in which there is a prolonged transition with a constitutionally weakened government that, because it purports to respond to all, satisfies none; and Icarus, in which a constitutionally unconstrained black government comes to power on a wave of popular support and noble intentions, and embarks on a huge and unsustainable public spending programme, which crashes the economy. Then there was one bright vision of a future to work towards: Flight of the Flamingos, in which the transition is successful because all the key building blocks are put in place, with everyone in the society rising slowly and in unison to the envisioned end state. Scenario thinking is an important aspect of broader approach for social change. Scenario stories are a solid tool for co sensing, for developing a shared language.

A scenario conversation turns the attention away from the present where the debate is often mired in dirty waters towards the future. It shifts from looking for 'The Solution' to exploring different possibilities, and from separate interests to common ground in the future in which all will live. Stories that make potential futures seem vivid and compelling. A youth without a full quiver of agreed upon statements may accept in advance through less formalised acculturation, soon finds itself in deep trouble, this is our warning to present-day young people. We want to introduce a further development to the Mont Fleur exercise namely, *Dinokeng Scenarios*. See www.dinokengscenarios.co.za. In 2009, the Dinokeng team came out with three scenarios, walk apart, walk behind and walk together.

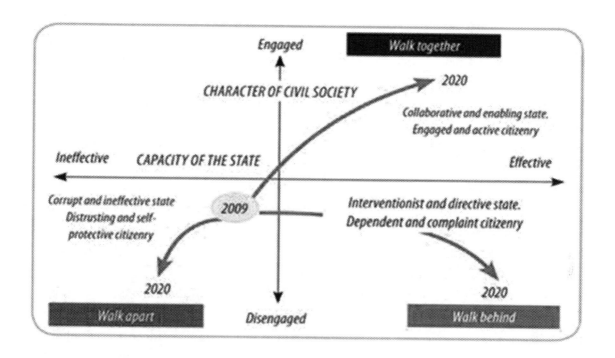

Ramphela rightly suggests that there is always the possibility of a fourth scenario and that is choosing to *walk in front* taking the lead from politicians so that in the words of Mahatma Gandhi 'You be the change you want to see in the world' can come true. This is where the role of the youth as today's partners becomes crucial but raises sharp and pertinent questions. How does youth measure their level of participation in shaping the future of South Africa? Are they engaged meaningfully in the affairs of their city or province beyond the election seasons? Do they have a sense of fear for open engagement with critical issues that impact the quality of their lives? Is their discomfort because today's 'politics are dirty,' Is it not directly their challenge to confront the reasons that caused the failure of the system that robs them of their future? Is it not in their best interest to map the way forward themselves than to be told by the powers that be what their future should be? These are tough questions but with a bit of guidance are not insurmountable for there exist precedents that can be used to their advantage.

In 1942, the ANCYL forced the hand of the older generation of the ANC leaders by unilaterally declaring an armed struggle and uMkhonto WeSizwe was formed. In 1960 Sobukwe's PAC initiated a mass defiance campaign to force an end of 'dompass' for Africans. The formation of SASO in 1968 was a direct response to the ineffectual and pedestrian student organisations of the time and black consciousness articulated a new future and sustained the newfound freedom for the students. In the 1976, high school students rose against the might of the apartheid at a huge human cost and won. In the 1980s, the author and others were a bunch of teenage boys who did not care much about politics but with time grew zealous and became part of the struggle to forge the crucible of combat under the most extreme circumstances facing death, arrests and torture but transcended those fears, survived two states of emergencies and persisted thereby opened gates to the free society we have today.

In 2005, young people of Zimbabwe dared to dream, dared to face death and took on the impenetrable mighty fortress of Mugabe and won only to be denied the prize. In 2008, Obama and a band of relatively inexperienced young people of the USA were tired of the establishment politics stood up and said 'we can' and got to change the face of America politics. In 2010, young people threw out despots in North Africa and Middle East and the Arab spring revolution gained them freedoms. In 2012, Senegalese wanted change, they entrusted a relatively young unknown Macky Sall who defeated a popular sitting incumbent president Abdoulaye Wade because they too were tired of status quo. Andries Tatane of Meqheleng Township in Ficksburg Free State was part of community that stood up and demanded a better life. Mighty men of valour from the mines of Lonmin in Marikana went to the mountaintop and demanded a livable wage and got it after laying down 44 of their own lives. 'I don't know what your destiny will be, but one thing I know: the ones among you who will be really happy are those who have sought and found how to serve' Albert Schweitzer.

Here is something young folks may want to ponder. The Middle East and Northern Africa region has one of the most youthful populations in the world, with people under 25 making up 35% to 45% of the population. So add to your thinking the fact that it is understandable that social networking and the Internet would carry with it the colossal power we see unfolding right now. The Arab revolution can be distinguished by the youth-led demonstrations and protests that began on 18 December 2010. Through highly connected networks across Tunisia, Egypt, Yemen, Bahrain and Libya, young people have shared knowledge, tactics and information about how best to stand up to the regimes that have had a stranglehold over them for decades. Although social media has been hailed as a key mechanism through which these communities of young people connected, it was the content of the knowledge they shared and the example they set which fundamentally shifted the region. Now pay attention to the power and domino effects of social of social networks and the Internet.

In December in 2010 in Tunisia, an ordinary man Mohammed Bouazizi set himself alight, a desperate act of protest after failed attempts to work as a street vendor to support his family. The scene was captured by a passerby on the video and posted on YouTube. On 11 January the protest reached the center of Tunis and the Tunisian president Zine al Abidine Ben Ali responded by sending troops to stop people from expressing their anger and to squash the uprising. The protest grew in size and in anger and Ben Ali subsequently fled Tunisia shortly after that and never returned. Tunisia became the first group of people in the Arab Spring to take to the street and 'boot out the president', driven by a single video which landed on the screens of virtually all the citizens. And so the next month Egypt revolution was born.

An Egyptian businessman Khaled Said died after being beaten by police. He stumbled upon a video that police had taken of themselves sharing the spoils of confiscated marijuana, he posted it on YouTube and it went viral within hours. A Facebook page called 'We are all Khaled Said' was created to honour Khaled's act of bravery. It featured horrific photos of police brutality, shot with a cell phone, which contradicted the official police version. The Facebook attracted over a million followers in less than a week. The Egyptians filled Cairo's Tahrir Square in protest under a watchful eye of the fully armed military, which was understandably reluctant to murder its own citizens. Eventually its president was forced out of power, imprisoned and retried again. The domino effect of this revolution without exception affected all Gulf States; and the rest is history. The question that beckons is a crucial one, surely they have taken serious note of the powers that lie within posting videos, Facebook status updates and tweeting and that Internet is a force to be reckoned with.

In Obama's words lies a simple truth, 'In the face of our common dangers, in this winter of our hardship, let us remember these timeless words. With hope and virtue, let us brave once more the icy currents, and endure what storms may come. Let it be said by our children's children that when we were tested we refused to let this journey end, that we did not turn back nor did we falter; and with eyes fixed on the horizon and God's grace upon us, we carried forth that great gift of freedom and delivered it safely to future generations.' There are only two forces that unite youth—fear or interest'; we hope interest in your future rather than the fear of what might or might not happen to you is the force that might drive you. Change is not made without inconvenience, even from worse to better. So, what does this mean for the youth in South Africa? Will WeChat, Facebook, Twitter and YouTube be their way of spreading the revolution? This is a big unknown only time will tell. The youth has everything they need to find the direction and build something far bigger than themselves. Destiny is calling—the season has arrived.

Central to writing this book were thoughts of the youth, their views on specific social and political issues and attitudes towards particular emergent phenomena. We set out to engage them in multilayered conversations. We began by conducting focused-group sessions as well as in-depth qualitative interviews with sample groups in Tembisa, Gauteng,

Pietermaritzburg, KZN and Malamulele in Limpopo over a period of time. Nearly all the youth were younger than 35 years; a fair size of the sample was in the region of 18 to 24 brackets. Participation in the conversations came from youth living in the townships, suburbs and villages, high school, university students as well as unemployed. The sample approached circa 1390 participation. The facilitation of the discussions in the regions was mainly peer driven; their voices were captured through digital photo voice. Different interests in the different age groups were observed; views were as varied as were the topics discussed reflecting geographic-specific nuances. Inspiring their conversations at the venues hung background banners with inscription from Richard Rhodes.

'All of us live by a story and you have a unique story to tell. If you speak with passion many of us will listen. Yours enlarges the circle.'

Their voices were weaved into a tapestry and its narrative embodied in the voices of Shadi and Skhumbuzo (assumed names). A verbatim translation of the conversations would fill several volumes and this need not detain us here. Below we select highlights of the crosscutting issues especially where cross-group interests were high.

It is appropriate that we give a short description of the profile of this youth as we understand them rather than the label media has given them. Young people mostly born in the 1980s or after the dawn of new democracy in 1994. They have no consciousness of the apartheid era and its sins they don't care, period! Today, are aged between 19 and 33 and constitutes over 42% of our population today. Their community is connected digitally through Google+, WeChat, Facebook, Whatsapp, wikis, flicker, YouTube, Mxit, Twitter and MySpace media; they are socially savvy and literate digital natives. This tribe is less impressed by charisma than by practical common sense; they don't care about political correctness simply because this youth is dogma-agnostic, they are the practical sort. You don't find them in political meetings mainly because theirs is a digital community. They find long-winded political sermons that are disguised as education so yesterday and plain boring because they just want functional information. These young people have been called undeserving of the great gift of a free nation given to them by the 'young lions' of the liberation struggle. #Tag 'Yeah rite dream on' they tweeted to each other.

The perception of these children about politicians is one of an ineffective, self-serving corrupt breed of struggle heroes and their attitude towards them is simply blasé. They represent the archetypal counter-culture—a new society that does not fit into the models we have created in our minds. This means it is impossible to view this group with the same lens our forebears used on our generation and the one before us. Many years since the birth of the Rainbow Nation, these young people can no longer simply be categorised as black, white, coloured or indian, they approach life, love and everything in between from a perspective vastly different to ours. Influenced by both global cosmopolitan culture and traditional belief systems, this ultra contemporary tribe are complex, three-dimensional people that cannot be accurately described using traditional demographic segmentation toolset which only sees them as apathetic, vain consumerist, apolitical, disinterested and obsessed with pop culture. They are avant-garde tribe that fall roughly into three broad categories namely:

Techno-Hippies, otherwise known as Hippie 2.0s are tech-savvy geeks with hipster tastes and hippie ideas about saving the planet. Although they are passionate about changing the world on an abstract level, they prefer passive activism to actually getting their hands dirty, and as such, have gained the nickname Slacktivists: Someone who is happy to generate awareness for a cause on social media platforms, but who isn't prepared to leave their comfortable life to implement change on the front line. It is not uncommon for Techno-Hippies to spend the morning at their local iStore buying the latest iPhone upgrade and spends the afternoon at a hippy craft market picking an up-cycled handmade case made of bamboo. Techno-Hippies are also organic vegetarians, vegans or 'raw foodists' who draw social status from publicly promoting their extreme eating habits ritzy shops, which has a 'post-manufacture story' is also popular with this group.

Then there is the [Totido] Turn-On, Tune-In, Dropout tribe. They turn on their computers, tune in to the Internet news, blogs, sites and opinions, and drop out of school in pursuit of Internet entrepreneurship and the dream of living the self-sufficient lifestyle of the modern. They have gained the nickname New Rich: youth considered wealthy not because of their possessions but because they have freedom of time and location. They are self-sufficient, self-employed modern nomads who live and work whenever and wherever they want, without being bound by the clock or serving a full-time boss. In stark contrast to the 'true believers', this tribe cares very much about what they wear; both in terms of what the appearance of their clothes looks like and also the story behind the brand. Variations of smart names as a result of local subculture are in constant flux, *Cocoanuts and Amabojwa or Cheese boys* will be a popular reference Tembisa with but not for youth in Edendale or Malamulele regions. Rainbow Gatherings are contemporary communities typically held in outdoor settings, practicing ideals of peace, love, harmony, freedom and community as a consciously expressed alternative to mainstream popular culture, consumerism, capitalism and mass media that love up-cycled items that have been re-purposed and given a second lease on life. For example, old school chairs that are given a new coat of paint and resold in up market stores as designer furniture, vintage clothing from their grandfathers.

Anyone of smart thinking who wants to engage this group as a political force must raise the bar and 'be with it.' These young people are not engaging with politics because politics does not engage with them. For them politics is strife of personal interests masquerading as contest of principles, the conduct of public affairs for private advantage. Politics ignores and excludes them, which has an effect of channeling an incredibly energetic expression of social identity, idealism and culture at the expense perhaps of any political engagement. The issues that preoccupy the youth of today are what kind of future the adults have left for them? This future is understood in terms of a decent environment and a healthy economy that produces plenty of jobs and careers, a much more open society that offers lots of freedom and fewer diseases. Unless something with a compelling value is presented to them the theory that they are apolitical, vain consumerist becomes a self-fulfilling prophecy.

Prior to engaging in discussions we made our entrée by sensitising the youth to the need for creating a pool of shared meaning in the discourse, which would eventually lead to a shared view. However, young people do not act according to norms and values, but mostly according to their self-interests and there is unavoidably a tension between the two therefore, we had to navigate this balance with great care. Norms and values are founded in a system of meaning. If one group pursues its own interests at the expense of the interests of others in the group, and if the system of values and norms valid in a particular group prohibits that pursuit in principle for others, then this pursuit must be legitimised before the meaning-giving entity, since no group can permanently endure their right of existence being questioned by others. The simple reason for this is that there exists a nuanced sub-cultural difference between groups regardless of the age and location. Given the diversity of group interests, then, we asked them what a good conversation might look like that would lead to a shared pool of meaning and for an inclusive consensus to exist. In their everyday experiences, each one of them entered conversations with own opinions, feelings, theories and experiences about the topic at hand, and this was ok with us.

When two or more people enter conversations, by definition they don't share the same pool. Opinions differ. This unique combination establishes their personal pool of meaning, which propels their own sense of action. We have seen the consequence of what happens when the pool of meaning is dangerously shallow. Where people purposefully withhold meaning from one another (for example university graduates withholding useful information from others thereby to undermine the input of others in the group) or where meaning does not exist because the frame of reference is not a shared one (see the definition of different tribes and their subculture). The ideational culture comprises a system not of shared ideas, rules and meanings in the spectrum of the tribes and is expressed in the ways that the youth live it. This is also the way in which youth provide 'standards for deciding what is, . . . for deciding what can be, ... for deciding how one feels about it, . . . for deciding what to do about it, and . . . for deciding how to go about doing it.' Such subcultures are networked, tribal and fluid. They are learning cultures because they deal with ambiguity and uncertainty originating in the environment.

Not knowing how to stay in dialogue youth often relies on psychological violence, i.e. subtle verbal attacks. A person will act as though they knew everything, hoping others will be taken in by their arguments. Some tried to discredit others, hoping people won't believe their arguments. At times, they tried to use humour to insinuate their way in. It was particularly when stakes were high, where opinions varied, and emotions ran strong that the groups were often at their worst in each of their personal pools of meaning and to get others to share their pools and thus create a shared meaning. We discovered that learning is more about providing space and time for new meaning to emerge as opposed to the application of the existing information. In conversations, they learned that a shared pool of meaning is the birthplace of synergy. Not only does a shared pool of meaning help them make better choices, but also since the meaning is shared, they were willing to act on whatever decisions they made. We deliberately set up the sitting order in such way that it was an open-plan environment, that means no upfront agenda was announced and no leader was appointed; they took part in a free flow of meaning, eventually understanding why the shared solution is the best solution. In the end, this made it possible for them to be committed to act on and defend the solution that emerged from those each conversation. That's how a consensus is built between seemingly divergent tribes and from this intricate labyrinth; we are pleased to present in this book a product of synthesis of a very honest dialogue from people who did not know each other and who did not have a shared interest at first and who were all angry about the situation in South Africa today.

What this means is that the youth in the dialogue were entrusted with the historic duty of putting in place building blocks that would constitute agreement about what was important for their future we are glad we help them do it. There were two key findings in this survey the first is that the youth of South Africa don't believe that Zuma was doing as much as he could do to improve their lives and they did not believe that the ANC represented their interests at best. Secondly, we found with great surprise that investment in education, science and technology were topics they understood very well and there was keen interest in discussing possibilities presented by these disciplines.

Recently, a separate empirical study on youth was concluded by Swartz on equality and restitution and found that youth is generally envisioned as a time for developing lofty ideals and high aspirations and expectations. The black youth were no exception and had high hopes for the future. Despite their social context, young people in poor neighbourhoods are likely to express hopes and intentions of reaching tertiary education. This is supported by another study on youth by Bray in 2010 where young people spoke of their lives with great hope for the future, for South Africa, their careers, and of desires to escape the township and help their families into better lives.

These youth spoke of being doctors, lawyers, pilots, musicians and accountants, and have having nice cars and good houses in the suburbs. In this sense, they express a will to belong to the South African social body through interaction with the notion of greater opportunity and mobility in the post-apartheid era. Furthermore, youth believe in the possibility of maintaining total control over their lives. Contrary to the view that populations in situations of poverty globally have a lower sense of control, black youth in South African related a feeling of agency that, while perhaps at odds with the reality of their current circumstances, drew attention to their drive to be part of new a South Africa. Opportunities beyond the townships and villages (Malamulele is primarily rural than it is cosmopolitan in character) that match the aspirations of the youth have to be created.

In this regard, the high aspirations of township youth can be regarded as a form of a weapon against despair. The fact that dreams appeared as the second strongest influence for these young people was surprising but corroborated the findings in De Lannoy's study in 2009. Shadi remarked: 'first, if you are a person, you should have goals. If you don't have dreams, you will never be anyone in life. So, you need a dream . . . . I see myself maybe four to five years to come, having my own office, having the chair that rolls around the office, and all. If you do have these dreams, then that is what keeps you to go on.' For Skhu, his aspiration in the music industry was 'to put my family on another level' while Shadi talked about wanting to contribute to the broader community, expressing the belief that 'someone, somewhere out there will benefit from me getting an education.' Dreams and hope, in a context of hardship, have survival value.

Maintaining hope becomes a coping mechanism in the daily experiences of deprivation. Psychologists have pointed out that: 'the dream . . . contains goals, aspirations, and values and . . . can be motivationally powerful. However, the question might be asked as to what happens when young people realise that their dreams of being a wealthy business person, a brain surgeon, a professional soccer player, will only ever be dreams? When pressed, young people conceded that possibly lack of money could destroy their dreams, as indicated by

Shadi: 'what are the chances for me to achieve my dreams? I may say two out of ten. Because for me to achieve my dreams, I need finance. I do have the determination for it, you know, but the finances are not there and it takes up the 80%, you know. The determination only takes about 20%. Even though I'm trying to get means, you know but they're not working out. Shadi said, 'I think education should be free. Some young people want to be good people but they don't have money to go to university so they can study and the become good people when they have their own jobs.'

Merton's strain theory provides one explanation for why this state of affairs could be termed quiet violence leading some individuals to anti-social behaviour. Merton argues that such behaviour ensues when cultural values 'extols . . . symbols of success for the population at large while its social structure rigorously restricts or completely eliminates access to approved modes of acquiring these symbols for a considerable part of the same population.' In other words, it is significant that in the democracy the dream coupled with a global consumer culture appears to have led young people to have unreasonably high aspirations and to believe in their endless potential to acquire 'the goods' of this new democracy, despite the lack of opportunity to fulfill such dreams, at least in socially acceptable ways. In this context, the presence of the dream itself functions as currency in the symbolic economy of the South African myth. By dealing in dreams, young people in the country appear to be writing themselves into the nation's narrative by constructing their own sense of opportunity and, thereby, belonging. Yet the deferment of dreams in many of these young people's lives can have devastating social consequences and failed dreams can even return as a form of violence against young people, excluding them from the nation, citizenship and the possibility of belonging that they so desire.

However, many young people described their distress towards not having the opportunity to be heard. Here, they attribute a lack of motivation amongst their peers because they don't know how to access the potential opportunities available to them. Young South Africans believe that if they're not able realise their potential as young people, the future livelihood of their country is at stake. 'We are still imprisoned by worldly things for example hatred, crimes and xenophobia . . . What happened to our unity? We lack originality; we fake accents and adopt lifestyles that are presented by social and media norms . . . We can sit around and complain all day but that wouldn't change anything . . . I want to challenge each and every one of you . . .' Shadi asserts. Here, young South Africans believe that change and improvements cannot happen by sitting and watching from the sidelines. The youth want to receive more support and guidance in order to achieve the changes they believe is necessary to improve the country.

There is an enormous opportunity for organisations and the private sector to step in and assist young people to recognise the potential they have to rise above their current circumstances. 'People are not living freely because crime has surrounded them . . . SA is getting rotten.' says Shadi. Crime continues to be 'a shadow' over South Africa as many young South Africans have felt the negative impact that crime has on South Africa. From their perspective, crime is not an intrinsic characteristic of the country but rather it's the symptom of a country that cannot provide adequately for all its citizens. Almost one-third of South African voters are now too young to have any direct memory of the oppression of apartheid, or of the popular struggle against it. Their loyalty to the ANC is absent compared to their parents and grandparents. Shadi admits she is disappointed in the party. 'Power changes people,' she says. 'Looking at where we are now, it is hard not to feel depressed. You see people fighting over power, people who will do anything for money or power' She believes that change will come when citizens feel the government is no longer untouchable. And Skhu angrily objected to government's destruction of his country retorting, 'zismoshela izwe lethu lezinja (*labantu*)'.

Identifying measures that have a high impact on student achievements, funding them adequately appear to be issues they would like to explore in greater detail had they were given more time. They thought this would help the next generation of students after them. The need to create renewable cleaner energy sources for the twenty first century is imperative rather than just desirable, our dependence on oil doesn't just affect our economy today; it undermines the security of their future all of them have insisted. 'To us this appears self-evident that these are the issues that ought to be the central feature of the 2030 agenda rather than social grants and BBEEE.' said Skhu. 'We young blacks must stop expecting goodies from affirmative action, employment equity or black economic empowerment programmes and realize that self-economic empowerment is the way to go. Even though our parents were but the truth is that we are not historically disadvantaged individuals because by naming ourselves this way we are saying we will never reach new heights." Was an insightful observation by Skhu.

'Youth with their energy, talent and skills contribute for the development of healthy political system. In any case, experienced people are there to guide the youth in the policy-making matters. Youth being the dominant age group should definitely have a say in the policymaking and the concerns about the present and future generations is well known to us' commented Skhu. The desire to make a difference and to find ways to work together to improve the country was a big theme. Where young South Africans see this country as flawed and imperfect, they also express a deep sense of commitment to developing the country.

This, they believe, can only be achieved by working together. Without a sense of unity across the country between all the different cultural groups, young South Africans believe we won't be able to achieve the country's potential.

Youth with its fresh ideas, perspectives and ability to adapt to the changing global political scenario, withstanding the emergencies and internal security problems could be dealt with easily. Even now, the role of youth in politics cannot be overruled due to their developmental contribution and influencing factors that attract the mass to their policy framing style. So, youth should not just indulge in politics with high enthusiasm but be central to it and write their own fate in creating a modern South Africa. This generation of young South Africans believes that relying on the government to bring about changes is not good enough. Young people want to be taken seriously and they want to be able to make a difference. They're outspoken on their views that this requires them to rise above their hardships, to seek every opportunity they have to empower themselves and to take initiative.

The challenge here for organisations and the private sector is to harness this optimism among young people and help them convert their good intentions into an action plan for change. Ultimately, the risk with young people is that their desire to achieve greatness will get displaced by disillusionment and a sense of failure that they're not able to achieve their goals. 'The ANC councilors treat us badly. They insult us, call us animals and switch off our electricity' said Shadi. 'The fact of the matter is that this country may be on the verge of going down the drain . . . We look up to our leaders but if all they bring is deception through greed and corruption, then what meaning are they bringing to democracy . . . [But] there is room for pure unadulterated change . . . Think again before you undermine our country . . . .'

Shadi expressed the view that there's more to be said and more to be done.' 'You see we did not leave the ANC. The ANC left us behind while all we ever wanted was the chance to get ahead' reflected Skhu. Civic engagement among young people seems to be relatively low. Significant proportions of young South Africans are disillusioned with their country. In a survey of Gauteng high school pupils on civic engagement, 32% said that they agreed with the statement, 'I wish that we still lived in the old South Africa'. Some 29% of African pupils agreed with this statement, compared to 44% of white students. A quarter of African respondents said they would like to leave South Africa because they do not like the way the government treats them. Some 45% of all respondents said that they felt other race groups had more advantages than they did.

Some 43% agreed with the statement, 'Government does not care what you think', and 61% thought that 'the people who run the country are not really concerned with what happens to you. There were also high levels of disillusionment with economic prospects, with 77% saying that they would find it hard to find a good job, no matter how educated they were. Some 61% felt that young people leaving school in 1990 would have found it easier to find jobs than they would, and 47% reported being worried that members of their family that were employed would lose their job in the next year. The overriding sentiment across the conversations was that youth are highly resilient and even though they highlight many issues that negatively impact the country, they remain hopeful about the possibility to improve the situation in the future. There are many issues that threaten to erode their optimism as they become adults and it is important for communities to work together to assist young South Africans realise their full potential.

The signs of entropy are there for all to see. Dramatised by the dilemmas of unemployment and the expansion of spaces of vulnerability in everyday life. Most youth are barely holding on the edge with so much rage working inside them. To stem the tide sermons of 'service delivery' and 'decent jobs' by the technocratic group will not cut it for the youth any more. For the human spirit to have any hope at all, new politics must break with the realism that characterised post-apartheid life. It should be about the reopening of the future for all. It should take the form of a conscious attempt to retrieve life from a history of waste dumped on it by careless leaders. The National Planning Commission whose mandate was 'To help define the South African we seek to achieve in 20 years' time and to map out a path to achieve this.' The preamble opening to the diagnostic report told us that South Africa would fail to meet the stated goal of eliminating poverty and inequality if the government carried the business as usual approach.

As important as this goal was to all South Africans the commission went ahead and crafted a vision statement without the youth forming the centerpiece of that vision. Inputs were later received from small pockets of groupings such as the Young Professionals Forum members among others. In theory, the NPC was expected to do something the government had never done before that is to take a different approach in doing things and mobilise the full might of society through active engagement creating a national conversation, ensuring expert's views were canvassed and, carry out its function taking on board all South Africans irrespective of the shade of their political affiliations. Yes, in theory this was possible sadly in practice they were not capable of doing. The diagnostic document highlighted that five areas covering human conditions, material conditions, nation building, the economy and the institutions of government were important. In the end, the commission's product is the NDP and this is the new 2030 agenda or is it?

Youth and modernity

In an article titled *The Role of Youth in Participatory Democracy,* Nkondlo offers a fresh perspective on youth conscientisation and modernity. The definitions of who the youth is on the African continent are so many and varied depending on country-specific context. The problem with the notion of youth is that it sometimes conveys the impression that it represents a trans-historical and trans-cultural category, whereas the concept of youth is not universal in range, hence the cultural meanings and social attributes ascribed to youth vary. But there is a developing analytical core in academic literature in which there is a significant degree of consensus on what the term youth infers. Baller characterises the notion of the youth as inferring a social shifter, something which points to the relational context in which young people define themselves. Whereas Fokawang argues that the notion of youth as a social category is a construction across time and space rather than a fixed and context transcendent category. As Richter and Panday put it, the youth is essentially a comparative self-perception, arising within a social, economic and cultural context. Young people are not only in transition, but youth itself is a transitional construct. There are of course legalistic, age-based definitions of youth and these vary from country to country. For example, Kenya and Malawi categorise the youth as 15 to 30 years of age Sierra Leone, Ghana, Madagascar and Senegal as 15 to35 and South Africa as 14 to35. To speak of the youth is to speak not only of the future of a people or of a nation, but it is to speak of hope; it is to speak of the very 'soul' of a nation. Hope is an ontological need that demands an anchoring practice. It requires a realistic practice for it to become edifying for it to become historical concreteness.

The soul of a nation, on the other hand, infers the very seat of power; the wholeness of essence and the propelling drive to higher levels. This underlines the weight of meaning and the depth of value the youth carries in a nation and to its people. Kierkegaard in his book, *Either/Or* indicates that he prefers speaking to the youth for with them there is hope that they grow to become rational beings. This he said in the early 1800s, which shows the great hope attached to the youth throughout generations of human existence. The theme the role of the youth in participatory democracy invokes both the performativity and the constantive attributable to that section of society seen as young, fresh, capable and full of life—the youth. But the question is: are we betting on the right horse? Are we throwing the weight of our expectations and hope where it deserves to be thrown? This is a very complex subject—the horizon of truth is difficult to reach, but the bottom of despair is not distant. The youth, have made us wonder where it all went wrong—is it with the mode of our politics of national liberation? Is it with us—by failing to live up to the challenge of moral example? Is it the ubiquitous post-modern materialist culture? Is it the age we are in, the age of extremes or is it simply an inter-generationally transmitted curse?

Perhaps it is a combination of some of these elements, but most importantly, the concept and life of marriage and family now faces challenges, given the changed conditions of modernity and the return of history. The changed conditions of modernity are manifested through the demands for reflexivity one finds in every social space—in marriages, the demands for freedom of choice and the space to be one's self are threatening stability—it demands that men begin to truly treat and regard their spouses as equals and give them the space and support they need. So, do youth demand their voice and serious consideration of their views? The foundations of orthodoxy in the family space are crumbling and without this foundation, what do we lean on? This is the question I won't venture to answer. But I can invoke the works of Foucault on modes of subjectivation of the self to indicate the importance of conscientization and teaching, of course without impositions, of values that could fashion the self to attain lofty goals through a modest life of self-discipline, dedication and commitment. These are values that should define the family foundations, values that the youth can carry into the political sphere. This brings to the fore the importance of foundational years of the child in the family before he becomes a youth.

But when talking about the family we must not be romantic, there are realities we need to understand and confront. These include the fact that the conventional family as we have known it is being discredited by the fact that it has tendencies which foster and sustain gender inequality where women are expected to be subordinate to and financially dependent on men, and where women's place is thought to be the home. Also, the model nuclear family is gradually giving way to other family types, such as lone-person family, single-parent families and polygamous family models. These kinds of families are likely to breed different kinds of children who become the youth of today, unless they are united by values and these values need to be the values commonly held by the society at large. This is where the notion of ethical public leadership instilling values our children can emulate becomes important.

This is how as a society of families, we can set the foundation for the construction of a deserving youth. This is a new kind of youth South Africa needs to preserve its heritage and future for. A deserving youth is the youth that is conscious of its dignity and destiny; it is a youth that has gotten right the essentials of life's philosophical strategy and is therefore able to both discover and fulfill its mission. It is a youth that has gotten to know the spiritual value embedded in emancipatory praxis and that freedom consists of discipline and selfless service to others. Most importantly, a deserving youth is the kind of youth that embraces the absurd; by this, I refer to the ethic of compassion and the ethic of respect. But the question is how to create a new constructive spirit; how to invoke a new awakening and levels of critical consciousness that are commensurate with the challenges that our society faces, among the ranks of our youth. The role of the youth in South African politics is probably as old as society's construction of the youth as a social category.

From the beginning of wars of primary resistance just after 1657 to the rise early of African nationalism in the late 1860s. To modern Nationalist movements as expressed in the formation of the ANC in 1912, to the post-1994 democracy project, the youth in South Africa has always played an important role, albeit the variations in scope and profiles of their role. But the role of the youth must also be underlined in areas of collaboration with oppressor forces, counter-resistance and counter-insurgency initiatives against own people. The *Native garrisons*, the *Native Corp,* the *Native Warder*, etc., were partially constituted by the youths and all these attest to instances of willful collaboration by the youth in oppressive institutions of the colonial and apartheid era. I mention this because there is a tendency to romanticise the history of the youth in South Africa as though it was a history of struggle against oppression and we forget to mention that it is also a history of betrayal and collaboration with oppressive systems.

In other words, the youth is not one homogenous block but is a very heterogonous social category in terms of age, culture, and political outlook; hence, the homogenising assessments of its role are incorrect. We have a situation in South Africa where effective youth participation is visible among certain youths of particular political traditions. The ANC Youth League and Young Communists in South Africa are now the visible representatives of the youth of South Africa. As a result, when we talk about youth participation in democracy, we always refer to the youth in these two political structures. We forget to mention that these are youth structures of a political party and the majority party itself is not necessarily representative of the whole youth of South Africa. South Africa is much broader, much more diverse to be expressed through one political party that happens to be in numerical majority.

The youth outside organised political structures, in village organisations, the youth in cattle deep organisations, in burial societies and Facebook communities tend to be marginalised and their voices not heard in matters of political participation. The question is how we pull together the richness and diversity of our youth in order to develop a deserving youth that have something positive to contribute to our democracy rather than lamenting a lost generation. The point I am making is that the youth's role from the very foundational moment of democratic governance in South Africa, was sometimes largely unguided, largely not informed by a clear emancipatory concept and largely lacking discipline and an ethic of compassion and respect. The role of the youth borders largely on protest politics. Of course, there are instances when the country gets constructive inputs and interventions from youth formations, such as the National Youth Development Agency. The initiatives of this formation generate a fair degree of hope, but it will take time to realise the impact of their interventions. The challenge, however, is how to extend the reach of its programmes to the deep rural communities and also broaden its services so that it is not merely a constituency-building platform by the ruling party. This view imposes a number of limits to the various forms of public participation our government has created.

To Nkondlo's perspective, we would also like to add another view—one that builds further on the idea of participatory structures that extends to the actual engagement in the body polity. South Africa is a country where not all citizens are engaged in all major issues that affect their lives. A place where adults and young people are together at the table grappling with problems, crafting solutions and jointly deciding on how resources should be allocated. Rather, this task is deferred to the structures of the ruling party. A strong democracy where all citizens, including youth, exercise their right to select those who should speak and act on their behalf and hold them accountable for the results to be delivered is an ideal that should be cherished. Imagine adults and young people working together to build a thriving a society from the ground up contributing to nation building from the street-level to city level culminating to the national level. Herein lies the power behind the potential role of youth as partners through political participation. Where young people have an equal opportunity to have a sustainable livelihood. The term nation building is used here to refer to a constructive process of engaging all citizens in building social cohesion, economic prosperity in an inclusive way just as Sobukwe, Biko and Mandela had envisaged in their contributions to building this nation.

It is a process through which all people have access to structures and mechanisms that govern their lives. Admittedly, the vision sounds unattainable and lofty for two reasons. Few societies have found adequate ways to ensure that all adults fully participate in the political process and even fewer have found adequate ways to ensure that young people share in the burdens and benefits of citizenship but not impossible. There are three frequently cited reasons for why young people are excluded from participation in societal matters. Young people are often viewed as lacking the skills needed to become part of the political process. These perceptions are often backed by popular theories on childhood development and adolescence, many of which define youth as social group that is in the stage of becoming adults. Young people are not the group we should systematically exclude in our affairs. Young people are not afforded the opportunities to share power with adults in part, because they are viewed as lacking the requisite skills. Consequently, they are not invited to the table. The very idea of youth citizenship young people participating as equals is a stretch for many adults. The irony is, however, that once at the table, young people are often viewed as a threat to adult power. Rather than work with young people to build the skills, adults either abdicate power or work to control it. This tendency to exclude young people has been well substantiated in the South African context and is not a wise thing going into the future. Therefore, youthfulness has become a major justification for excluding young people from decision-making. It is also important to emphasise that these ideas are also present in all major social institutions; from the family, the school, the community; religious institutions and so on. It is not a surprise that there are no expectations, and processes that facilitate the political participation of young people within their communities as well as at the national level. One of the more frequently used justifications for excluding young people is the entrenched myth of youth apathy—young people are frequently portrayed as lacking motivation to become involved. This myth is captured most aptly in the media hype about the Generation Y syndrome, which describes young people as a socially inept, self-absorbed group with little or no interest in the political process.

There are two conceptualisations of youth citizenship in modernity. The first is as a bundle of constitutional rights and responsibilities defined and guaranteed by membership in the state and submission to its power. The second highlights the constant struggle of marginalised persons to expose the violence inherent in their exclusion and the social origin of the state. The other are founded on public participation, in community life and decision-making, as well as other contributions to the collective. To be unable to participate directly in the functions of the collective, or to be dependent on others for social access or even subsistence, is to be excluded from full participation as a citizen. Therefore, we can say the experiences of township youth, as being formally citizens of the political nation of South Africa while simultaneously excluded from the rights and benefits, which that status is meant to confer, does not bode well for the country of our dreams. Certain socioeconomic disparity and class-based oppression are mutually supportive in shaping such exclusion. The puerile partisan politics waged by the current crop of political parties far outweighs the advantages for participation in party structures per se hence political parties are hard-pressed to find talented stock.

However, recent research reveals that young people are far from apathetic. It is true that many young South Africans over 18 do not vote or show interest in the conventional modes of political expression via political parties. Yet, young people are showing great interest in political issues and are constantly searching for different ways of expressing themselves in the body polity outside of the formal party structures. There are two dominant spheres in contemporary youth politics. The first is largely middleclass sphere whose points of political engagement are informed by the mainstream media and online platforms. Here you find debates, which titillate an educated class that believes it is part of a broader civic intellectual culture. This sphere is mostly confined to the economic elite and driven by individualism cultivated by private school systems, which instills a belief in pupils that they are natural leaders destined to be the most important voices in society. The pinnacle achievement in this sphere is the creation of a personal brand, media profile and fame. There are no new political insights to be found here just the regurgitation of mainstream media cycle.

The second sphere is the mass domain in which the majority of politically interested students and unemployed are located. The ANC affiliated members dominate this sphere. Here you find that engagement is treated as a mass mobilisation affair where issues are framed in a hodgepodge of Marxism, African nationalism and government bureaucratic speak. More and more, the aim of this sphere is to discourage questioning of the ANC current malaise and deep flaws of individual leaders. In-between these two spheres there exists a very small space where the possibility of a more independent youth public politics is emerging. We see youth led groups in townships; informal settlements in rural areas rejecting partisan politics in favour of locally informed concerns. We also see black driven middle class campus groups organising critical dialogue spaces, we see privileged suburban youth volunteering, tutoring peers without drawing attention to themselves or assuming intellectual leadership over the poor. What they all have in common is a strong understanding of freedom traditions and some desire to critically adapt them for today's community concerns. Post-apartheid youth, regardless of partisanship, have not yet seen that we must create a new intellectual tradition from the scratch. There can be no credible politics without credible ideas.

It would be a grave mistake to assume that youth do not participate in the political process at all. There are innumerable activities that seek to mobilise young people politically in neighborhoods and cities across the nation—activities initiated by young people and some initiated and supported by adults committed to youth empowerment. These initiatives cover a very broad spectrum. Examples include: organising young people in their communities as debating societies; educating young people to use the democratic process; advocating for and training young people to be part of governance structures of civil society organisations and through local government; monitoring and advocating for changes in the legislation at city and provincial level. These initiatives are unique because young people play a central role in the determination and execution of strategies. Many agree that this rich tapestry of localized youth action holds the promise of expanding the possibility for young people as equal and active stakeholders in the political process. However, such initiatives tend to be limited to the micro level and rarely transcend the neighbourhood and city level. The idea of tackling this subject arose at the International Development Conference: Global Meeting of Generations held in Washington DC in January 1999. At this forum, young people from across the world grappled with the role young people should play in the governance process of their societies as well as in international bodies such as the United Nations.

There is no other resource that matches the human being, because mankind is the corner stone of any development and civilization. Out of the human intellect, a nation is built. This can be confirmed by the fact that many countries are able to attain steady growth and development with limited natural resources through the intelligence of their people and the labour force. Young people are a crucial segment of a nation's development. Their contribution therefore is highly needed not just talked about in Cabinet Lekgotla sessions every January. Young people are social actors of change. Scholars have stated, 'time is not evaluated by what has been harvested, but what has been planted.'

The society at large has equal responsibility to provide the youth with suitable grounds and thereby bringing about a matured and responsible population for the coming generation to lead a better life. Moreover, for this reason the establishment of the National Youth Service is appropriate. Meanwhile, it is good to have these structures in place but if the youths do not make the best use of them, no beneficial result will be realised. 'As young people we must be ready and willing to take advantage of any opportunity that comes our way. It is important to note that we can't all work in offices, therefore some of us would have to train ourselves to be welders, plumbers, electricians, carpenters, craftsmen, farmers and so on' was a view expressed by Shadi. Traveling to Europe and the USA on fact finding missions does not provide relief for the youths as different societies are at different growth curves of their own ever-changing dynamics; what works for the USA or Australian society might may not necessarily work in South Africa—given our historical and cultural context so home grown solutions are a must.

The social challenges of today

Young South Africans face a number of societal challenges, with issues of causality and interrelationships manifesting in complex ways. We cannot pretend the regressive forces do not bring destruction and rob this generation of their purpose. The real issues are compromise of health, gangsterism and crime, Compounding these factors is the media young people consume and the premature introduction to pornographic material that destroys their moral backbone and encourages premature teen sex. Furthermore, once youth have left school they face the challenge of labour market entry. Among the demand side constraints, the issue of aggregate demand is chief constraint, followed by the nature of labour market demand. According to SAIRR report, many children in South Africa grow up in fractured families. Millions grow up living without one or even both of their parents. Poverty and unemployment take their toll on family life, while many are increasingly concerned about the state of public education. The consequences for young people—the country's future workers, entrepreneurs, and leaders—may be dire. Research suggests a strong link between educational success and growing up in a stable family with both parents present. A study published in the journal *Adolescence* found that secondary school pupils living with their fathers on average scored higher on a scholastic achievement test in all subjects than pupils with absent fathers.

Fractured families may therefore play a role in the educational outcomes of South Africa's youth. Combined with the effects of growing up in broken families, problems such as teenage pregnancy, HIV/ STD, drug and alcohol abuse, and crime, are at risk of becoming more prevalent. More risky sexual behaviour, including unprotected sex with multiple partners, is one potential outcome of large numbers of unoccupied young people having grown up in dysfunctional families. Once again, the absence of a parent when growing up can have a significant effect on a young person's attitude to sex and relationships. Many young people have started to have sex at a much younger age than the previous generations. Some of sexually active respondents in the lifestyle study had sex before they were15 years. In addition, a significant proportion of the sexually active young people in the lifestyle study reported using alcohol or drugs before having sex. The number of teenagers falling pregnant is disturbingly high. While South Africa's adolescent fertility rate is half that of the average for sub-Saharan Africa, it is three times higher than the average rate in East Asia and four times higher than the average European rate. Moreover, high prevalence of pregnancy in lower schools has become more of a problem than before. The HSRC has warned, 'Young mothers begin a lifelong trajectory of poverty for themselves and their children through truncated educational opportunities and poor job prospects. Furthermore, the problems facing teenage parents are likely to be passed on to their children, High numbers of young people falling pregnant indicates that many young people are having unprotected sex, which has a bearing on the HIV/AIDS epidemic.' Many young people are exposed to sexual violence, perpetrate violence against their partners and peers, and at the same time are particularly vulnerable to being the victims of crime. A recent study into violent crime described the normalisation of violence in South African society, which has contributed to a culture of violence. Violence between young people in romantic relationships seems to be surprisingly common. Approximately half of all respondents in a survey of Grade 9-12 pupils at seven high schools in Eldorado Park, Gauteng said they had been either the perpetrator or the victim of violence in a romantic relationship in the last 12 months. Exposure to criminal and violent role models in a child's family is not the only factor contributing to youth crime. Of course, many young people are not criminals, but crime affects young people disproportionately.

The use of drugs and alcohol has strong links to youth crime and rates of victimisation. Although a crude measure, looking at alcohol and drug use among the different race groups can give some indication of the lack of any clear link between poverty and the use of drugs and alcohol given that only 4% of white people live in poverty compared to 15% of Indians, 36% of coloured people, and 64% of Africans. There is clear evidence that the abuse of alcohol and drugs has a negative effect on young people, and that it is likely to contribute to victimisation rates, youth offence rates, school dropout rates, and mental health problems.

A survey conducted in the Western Cape found that 17% of children and adolescents suffer from psychiatric problems, including attention deficit hyperactivity disorder, major depressive disorder, and post-traumatic stress disorder. The lifestyle study confirms that significant proportions of young people suffer from mental health issues and low self-esteem. Rates of depression or sadness were higher among 21 to 22 year-olds. One in 20 of those who had been sad or depressed had considered suicide. Of those who had considered suicide, three quarters had devised a plan for their suicide attempt, 46% had attempted suicide once, and 32% had attempted suicide two times or more. Respondents who had experienced violence in their homes or communities were significantly more likely to feel depressed or suicidal. A study of about 2 000 15 to 26 year-olds in the Eastern Cape found 21% of young women and 14% of young men had depressive symptoms. Notably, there was a strong link between depression and sexual risk behaviour. It is possible that disrupted family life contributes to mental health problems among young people. Research conducted suggests that young people living without their mothers are more likely to be depressed.

Herold in Statistics SA estimated that in South Africa 52% were estimated to be younger than 40. New entrants to the labour market constituted 20 percent of the total population and 32 per cent of those normally considered economically active. This report also noted that out of a total of 10.1 million individuals in the 15 to 24 age cohort 3.3 million were neither employed nor attending an educational institution. The report revealed that South Africa had a worse rate of employment for youth between ages 15 and 24. South Africa's 50 percent employment rate for working age youth is lagging behind other middle-income emerging market economies, which employ about 80 percent.

The situation is compounded by the racial disparities 53.4 per cent of young black 15 to 24 year olds were unemployed by the end of 2009, which was three times worse than 14.5 percent unemployed rate of young white South Africans. On the one hand, youth unemployment is a demand-side income problem as the number of jobs created is too small. On the other hand, youth unemployment is a supply-side problem because many young South Africans lack the required skills, work related capabilities and higher education qualifications required to be used for skills economy. The 2009 CHET publication describe the post school education and work environment as being characterised by the following

Large outflow of students from schooling without meaningful opportunities, post school institution architecture that limits further education opportunities for young people, a lack of integrated and systematic 'excluded youth' and a recapitalised FET colleges sector that requires capacity building. In a well-functioning society, youth should be afforded an opportunity to be young. The rights of young people are articulated elsewhere, but a good measure of society's performance is in the first instance a successful transition to adulthood. For this to happen youth must remain alive until adulthood, make a decent livelihood as a young person and later form and support a family. So many of these outcomes depend, firstly, on labour market conditions faced by the young people when they enter the market.

Good health is as important to successful transition to adulthood as any other desirable objective. It not only underpins the ability to secure employment, but impacts on their ability to fulfill their goals in general. Youth who are involved in the gangs are likely to be missing out on vital human capital acquisition, a factor that will disadvantage them once they enter the labour market in earnest. Discouragement is a feature in the South African environment of mass unemployment and typically long periods of unemployment. What is often overlooked is that such discouragement is often self-sustaining. Lack of self-esteem and the need to feel a sense of control and competence encourages criminal activity and gang association. The youth unemployment problems have been highlighted sufficiently above, namely that they don't finish school, if they pass grade 12 they do so with inappropriate subjects that don't lend themselves to employment. There is lack of appropriate skills and work related capabilities, concerns regarding elementary communication, lack of networks, mobility and mismatched expectations. The longer the unemployment lasts, the harder it is to reverse its effects. The youth demographic dividends are gained only if youth are active in the labour market. There is strong evidence to suggest that there are institutional barriers to the labour market. Therefore, scalable interventions aimed at dramatically expanding post school employability are one of the solutions.

Mfundo from Tembisa 13 years old was keen that we talk about this new township fad called *Izikhothane,* as it was both fascinating as well as aspirational for boys his age. Since he is from a single parentage background, it means he is not from a wealthy family that could afford to splash money on him to buy fancy clothes, which he could trash as a ritual of entry to this tribe. And so, he wanted to engage with the concept for self-enlightenment if not pure fantasy. Izikhothane is an idea that evolved among school-going children [despite efforts to ascertain its origin we remain unsure of where it started though] that began to gain traction in the townships we learnt that it gained notoriety in Voslorus. As it were, township youths would buy expensive branded ware only to thrash the same in a public spectacle. The thing grew in size so much so that they were seen brandishing R100 and R200 bank notes and then shredding them in full view of others (the catch is that there must be spectators to witness the fun otherwise the thing looses its glamorous appeal). In the main, once they got it going school-going teens mostly from humble homes were the first disciples who exhibited the strongest penchant for this fetish and later emulated by their out of school cousins. Although denied by the *Sushi* trend Czars Kenny Kunene and Gayton Mckenzie but a strong correlation between this fad and the extravagance of *Sushi* culture on naked models at Sandton's ZA private lounge exist. Whatever the case, Izikhothane has become the next best thing in town, love it hate it, is with us at least for now.

service cooperate

support **H E L P** sharing

guidance boost

CHAPTER 6

The New Revolution

For I know the thoughts I think towards you, says the Lord, thoughts of peace and not of evil, to give you a future and a hope. Then you will call upon Me, and I will listen to you and you will seek Me and find Me, when you search for me with all your heart

Implicit in the discourse is that hope of a shared open society is not scattered in broken fragments but merely fractured by the misdirection of the country's leadership. Young people must remain hopeful in spite of the situation that appears to get from bad to worse knowing that the state of affairs cannot remain this way for long. God has in His covenantal faithfulness pledged to Himself to listen when sought from the heart, He has promised to give young people a future and a hope. We need to remind young people that democracy is a quest, a mission so big that it fills us with constant new energy and hope. The quest of this vision is eloquently captured in the lyrics of Don Quixote's song:

The Impossible Dream

To dream the impossible dream
To fight the unbeatable foe
To bear with unbearable sorrow
To run where the brave dare not go

. . . To be willing to march into hell

People who follow a quest have a reason to live, they constantly dream about their quest, their creative thoughts are destiny-directed, they never give up hope never stop finding new ways to follow their star, to chase their impossible dream, and to do what only they can do. They have a reason to live. Hope start with an intense desire, a longing or a need. Add to this desire a reason for it to be expected. The desires remain a mere desire until it has the added benefit of a possibility within reach. The paradox of this generation is that their job is at once much easier and much more difficult at the same time. It is made easier by the existence of a body of knowledge about what went on before their time. The job is, however made more difficult by the absence of a common obstacle around which to galvanize energy because a common cause called apartheid monster is long dead. Retrieving historical memory in the context of historical amnesia requires a certain degree inventiveness always finding new entry points that will call forth the experience of the older generation while holding the interests of their own generation beyond the one-minute sound-bites and therein lies the numb of the challenge for this generation. Sobukwe, Biko and Mandela's contributions to building our nation will always serve as the inspiration to us all. Sobukwe left us this treasure

'Education for us means service to Africa. You have a mission; we all have a mission. A nation to build we have, a God to glorify, a contribution clear to make towards the blessing of mankind. We must be the embodiment of our people's aspirations. And all we are required to do is to show the light and the masses will follow.'

In a nation where education often separates the elite from the masses, where the illiterate are often treated with contempt, where education is often used as a stepping-stone to pursuing a life of personal enrichment, wealth accumulation and manipulation of opportunities to promote self-advancement at the expense of society at large, Sobukwe's wisdom has relevance for us. In Sobukwe's generation education was not something that was used to separate themselves from the masses, but rather to identify with them and their struggles. It was a responsibility to take what they had learnt and to use it not just for self-enrichment, but to uplift and serve the poor and marginalised. Education is not just a tool to increase our capacity to earn more, but rather to increase our capacity to give more of ourselves and serve better.

Education is a tool to be used in the pursuit of social justice for all. We are also reminded that Afrika is our mission field and not just our minefield from which to make money. We all have a role to play in the development and advancement of Afrika and that those who have been privileged to get educated have a responsibility to point the way forward for those who have not, instead of just living opulently, treating them contemptuously and not caring about their plight. We the educated elite have a duty to work towards the upliftment of the impoverished majority; we cannot retreat into middle-class, comfortable suburban lifestyles.

Mandela's words too strengthens us, 'we have unparalleled opportunities to leave our mark on the momentous times in which we are living. Each of us has an important role to play in making sure that South Africa and indeed the whole African continent fulfils its potential in this era. That will take leadership—not just political leadership, but leadership in its broader, more far reaching and more empowering embodiment. All of us have a role to play in building our nation, our continent and a future for our communities. I want to encourage you to recognise and give value to your strengths as individuals and to the strengths of South Africa as a country. South Africa has so much that it should be proud of. Despite the shame of the apartheid years, the people of South Africa mobilised and turned oppression into a triumph of the spirit. The peaceful reconciliation of South Africa's struggle is one of the events that the whole of humankind referred to with pride at the end of the twentieth century. It is not a coincidence that a country that had been troubled for so long had four Nobel laureates in the same century. That is the legacy that you should take forward with pride. Those are the landmarks that should be your catalyst to carry on and to strengthen the achievements of this fledgling democracy. South Africa has begun to use its distinctiveness, its positive traditions and its amazing human resources to envision a new path for the country and the continent. I look forward to travelling that road with all of you.'

Biko's words are distinctive if not more poignant, 'our preparedness to take upon ourselves the cudgels of the 'new' struggle will see us through. We must remove from our vocabulary the concept of fear. Truth must ultimately triumph over evil. In a true bid for change, we have to take off our coats, be prepared to lose our comfort and security, our jobs and positions of prestige, and our families. We have set out a quest for a true humanity, and somewhere on the distant horizon, we can see the glittering prize. Let us march forward with courage and added determination, drawing strength from our common disappointments with the ruling elite. In time, we shall be in a position to bestow upon South Africa and give our children the greatest gift possible a more human face of freedom.' This is what hope does and this is the message of this book.

Social engagement driven by volunteer spirit

Edmund Burke once said, 'the only necessary thing for evil to triumph is for good men to do nothing.' For our part, we are in a race against the positive and negative implications of our interdependence. Despite these challenges, our spirits rises when we consider the historic duty placed before us and we do not want to do this work because we are heroes or because we want to make this world a better place. We do this as a Biblical injunction for the glory of God. Youth enters this brave new world with determination and the knowledge that they shall succeed. Civic engagement and social participation are often cited in literature as key elements to young people's development in any society. The value of this statement lies in the fact that civic engagements of sorts shaped our political consciousness as well as our social inclinations as youth activists in the 1980 and 1990s. From various researches including our own, young people have already expressed their wish in that they regard it repugnant to be subjected [because of lack of gainful employment and good education] to dependency on government grants and voucher handouts. We stand ready to help them access alternative means to overcome poverty. Youth should be offered opportunities that cultivate dependency on their innate abilities and maximize their own potential in order that self-actualisation and that a better life is indeed possible in their lifetime.

The community upliftment programme [CUP] is a proposition we put forward not only as civic imperative but also as a means to give expression to the wishes of the young people. This proposition builds on the understanding that volunteerism as an ethos of community—youth are the agents of community transformation themselves if they accept self-reliance. CUP projects seeks to channel the pent up anger of the black youth into meaningful contribution in their own lives as well as a meaningful contribution to the welfare of their communities. CUP is a blended social entrepreneurship and skills development opportunity with the sole objective of involving the youth in service of their community. Access to opportunities, skills and useful connections would become possible.

We cannot fail and her youth of South Africa not after so much effort by the founding fathers to create a common purpose society. Setting up logistical, human capital and financial support for this work is a monumental task to accomplish nevertheless achievable, we know at local community level, there is not enough money to carry mega budget projects of the size envisaged by the community upliftment programme. The concept of private-public-partnership has proven viable in some instances. This project will have high visibility in the community and the cities guaranteeing at least a minimum of 200 days per youth per annum. At this time, South Africa needs practical solutions that should work in the short to medium term. The plan is to rollout the programme in every city and village in South Africa in years ahead.

Writing in *The Star* in 2012, Temba Nolutshungu suggested a raft of pretty cool ideas that are a winning solution to the unemployment crises facing the youth. She suggests inter alia that government could transfer all state owned industries back to the poor people of South Africa. These industries were in any case accumulated by the apartheid government to affirm poor whites during their era. By giving poor people in this instance, we are referring to both black and white shares in these state owned enterprises for direct economic empowerment. We know from studied models that cooperative ownership and benefit corporations are more stable than the shareholder enterprise models and are driven by tax incentives. Transfer ownership on application, of all state owned provincial hospitals and community clinics to the residents of the surrounding communities (national government should retain teaching hospitals as national assets) the community enter into agreement with provincial government to guarantee the supply of medical services and the maintenance of the infrastructure but the community employ staff and are accountable for the efficient administration of these assets. That's the only way we can provide guarantee for the efficient delivery of services.

Utilise the government landholding to give every homeless urban family freehold title to a 200m^2 land and give freehold titles to families in rural areas. This one family one plot scheme will result in ownership of the economic asset most prized by millions of people rather than the paltry 36% envisaged by government. Once beneficiaries, own them, will improve these properties thus increasing their value and creating opportunities for trading and business. All former homeland areas should be declared economic development areas, this is where the much vaunted NDP has any hopes of succeeding. Special cost reduction benefits such as tax exemptions, substantially reduced taxes and removal of restrictive employment laws for a period of ten years to apply to SME bona fide employers will go a long way to offer a reprieve in a meaningful way to small businesses.

Allow willing jobless youth and willing small business owners an opportunity to enter into agreements on any conditions and remuneration acceptable to them on free market basis provided these terms are not exploitative and sustainable in the long run of the local economy. Also, offer unemployed youth a year exemption certificates valid for three years that would allow them to enter commonwealth ideas market and earn innovation grants while their ideas are undergoing incubation. Communities should be encouraged on an annual basis to bring forward and display emerging best young talents at the community job expo thus allowing established private sector businesses as well as small entrepreneurs to establish early relationships with potential candidates for a long-term partnership. This would make the funding of costs associated with further studies a mutually beneficial and value-adding investment for both sides in this way the current ineffectual bursary scheme programme would be effectively replaced.

To advancing its own people the government could restore public confidence in managing crime by adopting a smart strategy that essentially involves the local community youth in crime detection and prevention (a suitable name can always be found by the participants themselves). In their current form, CPF structures don't work due to flawed police bureaucratic bungling and power politics. Introducing innovative socially smart enhancements to prevention of crime the quality of life of black people is guaranteed to improve. Naturally, recruitment would be from the pool of the youth not in school and not employed achieving three things at once getting youth involved in their community affairs by detecting and activating preventative measures before a crime is committed in the community, this is creating jobs and skills in the short term, and undercutting abject poverty. The underlying focus of this innovation has to do more with providing youth related support interventions rather than combating hard-core township crime.

That skills development is an urgent priority for the youth is a matter beyond debate. Our approach comes with two pronged theme i.e. work readiness and short-term industry qualifications. Recruitment and resource centers to assess grade 12 and graduate youth who finished school recently will be set up as places of assessment centers for opportunity match; they are essentially feeder mechanism in the demonstration projects to show that youth they can be prepared for formal trades in the mainstream economy. Another related idea for capacity building is more medium-term industry qualification apex bridging schools focusing on key community uplifting programmes namely; seed and crop management, permaculture, mill righting, light current electricity, motor mechanic, renewable energy technologies, environmental management, woodwork & carpentry, small scale building construction and information and communication technologies. The apex-bridging school programme is undertaken in collaboration with EFT centers for purposes of accreditation and infrastructure sharing. This raft of hope-sustaining projects have a high results orientation solution to address unemployment in the short to medium term and are predicated on the assumption that youth are willing to volunteer themselves first then as change agents for the good of their community.

Social Entrepreneurship

A social entrepreneur is a person who helps others to envision a new possibility, appreciate its meaning, and energize them to build momentum for social change. Social entrepreneurship involves a concerted effort to systematically identify people with innovative ideas for achieving major societal transformation; and shine a spotlight on their work; and develop support systems to help them achieve significant social impact. This endevour is concerned with building platforms that enable people at every age to think and behave like change makers and to help them work together in teams and in teams of teams. It looks to forge stronger linkages across disciplinary boundaries, particularly with business, and facilitate the rapid sharing of solutions at local and city level. Social entrepreneurship is about influencing public policy for social change. The social developments are spontaneous; there is no single source of leadership, but rather, countless responses to emerging needs. Individually many of the actions seem small, but they are interconnected and mutually reinforcing.

Today's change makers share one common feature: they are building platforms that unleash human potential, they don't struggle to increase the number of people who have the opportunity to contribute their talents to the world for social impact. In so doing, they help more people to live with dignity. Taken together, they add up to more than the sum of their parts. In the past, social entrepreneurship was primarily concerned with helping social entrepreneurs build sustainable, high impact enterprises. Today social entrepreneurship looks beyond individual founders to the change-making potential of *all* people and their communities. This requires the adoption of new solutions to address societal challenges. It recognizes that social entrepreneurship is contagious, every person who starts a social change organization emboldens others to pursue *their* ideas and solutions, whether by strengthening existing solutions through their investing, philanthropy, managing, advocacy, research or teaching.

Over the past quarter of a century, the field of social entrepreneurship has gained a better understanding among the various role players. Social entrepreneurship thinking and practice has evolved considerably, and these are now being implemented in thousands of enterprises worldwide. Many of the world's leading social organizations have, achieved dramatic results through complementary nonprofit, business, and hybrid enterprises. Many people with expertise in the business sector were attracted to the field during this phase as they discovered new avenues to apply their talents. The field of social entrepreneurship is improvising its own ecosystem of supports by stimulating more change making as it grows.

This question of 'sustainability' an idea that frequently causes social entrepreneurs to focus in the wrong areas and on the wrong things. When an organization is effective, people naturally ask whether it is sustainable. Typically, the answer hinges on its ability to bring in revenues to keep it going year after year. But like the question of scale, the idea of sustainability can be considered in two ways: the sustainability of an institution and the sustainability of ideas. In thinking about sustainability, it is important to focus on the forests. Today, microfinance is no longer dependent on any one institution. People will continue to create newer and better microfinance organizations into the future because they know they can do it, they know how to do it, and they know why it is worth their effort. A field is truly sustainable when its institutions can be readily renewed and improved upon. Stark distinctions between for-profit, nonprofit and governmental organizations no longer serve society's needs. As people and capital begin to move more fluidly across the old sector boundaries, we are likely to break free of mindsets that limit our ability to imagine solutions.

Once social entrepreneurs have identified themselves and come forward into the lab database. The second leg of the endevour is to develop incubation for their ideas. Setting up of business incubators include early-stage entrepreneurship where young entrepreneurs are trained, mentored and provided with small monthly fee, helping with access to facilities such as telephones, work spaces, Internet and transport to and from home. The community of social entrepreneurs enters into MoU with private companies to bid for and carry out commercially viable projects. Experience shows that all projects that go through the incubation programme remain sustainable after three years.

Sappi's *Project Grow* is an excellent example of what we are describing here. Between 1995 and 2010, Sappi injected R305 million into the project. More than 80% of the farmers are women. More than 100% small enterprises and over 1 100 sustainable jobs have been created. Interest free loans cover farming input costs and annual maintenance of plantations, communities gain immeasurably on the upside when timber prices appreciate due to increasing demands for timber products by the likes of Telkom and Eskom. These measures would be in addition to the revised BBEEE scheme meant to encourage existing owners of capital to create access to and sharing wealth with the poor of the country. It's a win win model for all concerned.

Social enterprise is not punted as a panacea for the rampant unemployment but an alternative way to tap into the innate human potential that lies idle. It is a given that social entrepreneurship is not for every one; only 20% of the society's carry the 80% of the society. A select few will become entrepreneurs yes, but the aim is for most youth to benefit from the projects. Based on the comparative studies undertaken in early adopter countries that have experimented with this concept, our take is that youth who possess postgraduate discipline of any description in the humanities, commerce, engineering and science fields would benefit greatly from this endevour without discounting naturally inclined entrepreneurs. The principal goal is to spark innovation by charging up a network of leaders so that they can link the poles of South African society through their ingenuity to a path leading to modernity.

Leadership for social development

The latest trend in the field of civic engagement and youth development has been the emphasis on youth leadership development, which is a tricky field to define and even programmes that describe themselves as promoting leadership development do little to distinguish between life-skills and leadership training. Traditional leadership programmes—whether they are aimed at the business elite or young people—have focused solely on the development of technical skills, and self-development, rather than truly on the process-nature of what it takes to lead in a social transformative way. We move away from the individualised notion of leadership development towards systems thinking and in this instance, we use Scharmer's model as a frame of reference.

Intervention Points	Types of Knowledge		
	Technical knowledge (technical skills)	Relational (stakeholder coalition building)	Transformational Self-knowledge (identity, Will)
Whole system (multiple issues)	System-wide technical skill building/training	System-wide relational capacity building/training (multi-stakeholder dialogue)	System-wide transformational capacity building (multi-stakeholder innovation)
Institution (single issue)	Institutional technical skill building/training	Institutional relational skill building/training (multi-stakeholder dialogue)	Institutional transformational capacity building (multi-stakeholder innovation)
Individual	Individual technical skill building/training	Individual relational capacity building/training (multi-stakeholder dialogue)	Individual transformational capacity building (multi-stakeholder innovation)

Otto Scharmer's Matrix of Leadership model

Real social leadership moves through the various aspects of the matrix to ultimately reach the top right-hand block of the matrix: focusing on developing whole systems interventions that build system-wide transformational capacity. Thus, according to Scharmer the definition of social leadership is the capacity of a community to co-sense and co-create its emerging future with the individual no longer working *for* their community but working *from* it towards system-wide transformation. This version calls for youths to be situated locally but acting at a deeper systems-transforming level something that we can deliver through the Leadership Incubator net. The leadership incubator is a part of programmes that are aimed at developing a unique, high-quality local cohort of young social leaders. In placing social capital development alongside personal development, this incubation will create opportunities for young leaders to cultivate what Granovetter calls 'the strength of weak ties' that is, individuals who are not solely tied to one particular network but who can move between groups and become bearers of new ideas, information, and innovation for the benefit of the whole community.

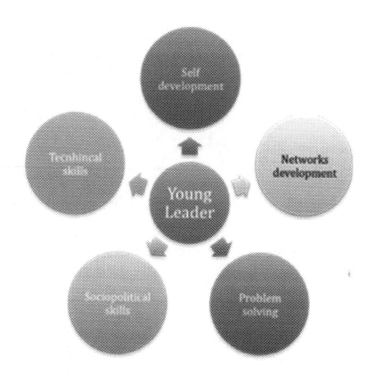

The Incubation model is uniquely placed to support and develop catalytic interventions in the community, and youth development more broadly. Its aim is to connect between 5 000 network to over alumni 20 000 by 2034 of young leaders from marginalized township communities and rural areas to one another and to points of influence and opportunity across social and economic strata. A secure leadership pipeline environment for young people to lead and supporting one another. The programme is designed to provide a wide range of leadership learning experiences to a select group of young South Africans who have not started to rise to leadership positions in their spheres of vocation and culminates in a Fellowship programme.

The Fellowship programme is a graduating school of leadership for the promising young leaders emerging from the incubation process. It is a powerful, inspirational and life changing experience for participants, and allows them many opportunities for self-reflection and growth. The active and ever growing worldwide network of Fellows means that they will have a constant source of help, encouragement and peer support as they progress in their development, and more importantly, a mechanism with which to hold each other to account in the communities they serve. Fellows are selected on the basis of their proven commitment to the concept of public good, and their abilities developed and directed to some of the toughest social problems faced by their communities.

This multifaceted learning experience, combines theory, experiential learning and practical assignments to solve community based problems in a community context. Participants will undertake a community project and collectively design solutions that potentially can be financed in the open market economy applying leadership in practical settings that will make a difference to the community they serve. The object is not to "teach" leadership in the classical business school sense, but to create a variety of opportunities to explore in depth what leadership really means for themselves, to reflect and internalise the learning, and to apply it to real life situations. The focus is on leading not leaders, responsibility not accolades. Part of this responsibility involves creating positive opportunities to enable young people to succeed.

The premise of this initiative is that new connections to information, opportunity and influence can be a powerful catalyst for innovation in highly polarized societies. If directed to the public good, these connections can strengthen development and democracy by building trust and accountability and making people less tolerant of destructive risk. They probably would come from a variety of backgrounds and occupations, but with a common denominator being that they are high achievers and have demonstrated leadership capabilities. They are drawn from the township and villages chosen on merit without regard to gender.

The taught sessions will be supplemented by mentorship with established leaders in different spheres, who are willing to share their experiences of the challenges and secrets of leadership success. There will be an regular ongoing intergenerational dialogue sessions, which will provide a unique platform for discussion between established leaders and youth protégés from across the city level. It is our hope that this will help identify new approaches aimed at encouraging greater meaningful dialogue between the generations. This is highly relevant, as young people increasingly demonstrate that their voices must be taken into account at all levels of society. They will discuss common high priority issues concerning youth, leadership and the future of South Africa and that of Afrika, a future in which the Fellows will play a leading role. Critical to the success of this flagship Leadership Incubator are avenues through which young people can experience what it feels like to take initiative, innovate and lead others in a process of contributing to the public good. The development of young leaders cannot be a once-off intervention, but rather must be a process of accumulative development of responsibilities, self-development, social capital and initiative. Ideally, the pipeline not only provides a valuable base from which to select participants for the Fellowship programme, but can also bolster the objectives of the other community initiatives. For instance a youth-leadership project aimed at developing young people, youth-led initiative where high-school students read to pre-primary school children to boost literacy would be a pipeline that reinforce both the leadership capacity of the young people and other focus areas of CUP.

Leadership development is most successfully achieved through young people having the experience of leading, and it is the aim of this initiative to support programmes and initiatives that create those learning-by-doing model at both municipal and community levels. A critical oversight in many youth leadership development programmes is the question of what happens to young people as they exit any programme beyond the scope of its programme. Alarmingly, few interventions have robust tracking of their alumni or have measured the impact that their intervention has had on the ability of young people to influence public innovation.

Thus, in order to ensure that our young participants have opportunities to exert influence beyond programmes, the CUP strategy aims to support initiatives that provide young people with direct connection to opportunity, access to influence and real decision-making power on a more extended basis beyond the lifetime of a single programme. If they want to be successful in their mandate, our NYDA can learn a lot from the Quebec Government's youth investments model for example, participation are fully determined by elected young people from across civil society providing the young people themselves with the opportunity to directly make decisions about youth development priorities and have the financial clout to invest funds accordingly. Right now South Africa desperately needs programmes that shift from tokenistic models of youth participation in decision-making towards programmes to access opportunities and influence meaningful change to ensure that high-calibre young people have the most impact on their communities, city level and beyond.

Digital age revolution and its influence

As we look into the future, it's promise and challenges, the generations Y & Z now known as Re-Generation face a brave new world, the fastest paced and exciting period in human history. Kurzweil wrote that 'technology is the continuation of the evolution by other means, and is itself an evolutionary process.' Evolution builds on its own increasing order, leading to exponential growth and accelerated returns over time.' Technology will transform the nature of work and the way they communicate, and the way they engage with one another. This generation will experience more change at a quicker rate and this change driven in part by the devices they hold in their hands, will be more personal and participatory than we even imagine.

The proportion of young people living in 'urban' centers will increase ever so much without the need for them to physically migrate to metropolitan cities because of the ubiquity of technology. The accident of birth, geography, age, social circumstance and educational status will be disintermediated to a very great extent and shaping their fortunes in the period than has ever been the case with previous generations. This is the generation that because of lack of trust between it and the state and large institutions including big businesses will expose, isolate and undermine these entities in their everyday use of technology that the power dynamics would shift in their favour for better.

Marcel Proust said, 'The real voyage of discovery consists not in seeking new landscapes but in having new eyes.' The youth has those new eyes; the trick is to find means and ways to harness this technological revolution for the greater good. The Agricultural Revolution took thousands of years to develop before it petered out. The Industrial Revolution required a few centuries to run its course. The Information Revolution, propelled by mobile technology will likely reshape our world today at the speed of lightening on the order of just decades. We live in one of the greatest times in history. When we think of the word 'power' what comes to mind? Influence, government rules and control and what impact they have on our lives as a society. When we think of the word 'power,' we certainly don't think of Facebook, Twitter and YouTube. Yet, social sites have contributed to the world becoming more integrated and have put a blur on barriers like distance between people. Interconnectivity is forming a vital part of our current society right now. Facebook, Twitter, YouTube along with Internet, have not only given rise to an environment where the world is literally at our fingertips, but has also presented itself as a pool filled with political liveliness with budding relationships between us the people, social networks and politics.

The vast majority of the young will increasingly find themselves living, working and being governed in two worlds at once. In the virtual world, they will experience some kind of connectivity, quickly and through a variety of means and devices. In the physical world, they to content with laws and rules made to keep them in check. The virtual world will not overtake the existing world, but it will complicate very behaviour. The virtual and physical civilizations will affect and shape each other; the balance they strike will come to define our world. The result, we predict is an egalitarian, more transparent and more interesting world than we can ever imagined. People and politicians will prefer the worlds where they have more control and this tension will exist as long as the Internet does. Anyone passionate about economic prosperity and social justice should consider how connectivity would help us reach the goals and even move beyond them. The case for optimism lay not in the gadgets but in the check that technology and connectivity brings against power abuses by those entrusted with public office.

There is now for the first time a real game changer. The possibility that technology has gone in favour of the ordinary folks thus placing the potential of new revolution in the hands of people is a scary proposition if it was not a page from sci-fi book. That revolution is money and it is spelled crytocurrency. Wikipedia defines it as follows; a crypto currency is a peer-to-peer, decentralized, digital currency whose implementation relies on the principles of cryptography to validate the transactions and generation of the currency itself. At present, all crypto currencies are alternative currencies, as nations are evaluating their options as alternative to fiat money Crypto currency implementations often use a proof of work scheme to guard against digital counterfeiting.

While over 30 different crypto currencies, specifications and protocols have been defined; most are similar to and derived from the first fully implemented crypto currency, Bitcoin of Canada. Most crypto currencies are designed to gradually introduce new units of currency, placing an ultimate cap on the total amount of currency that will ever be in circulation. This is done both to mimic the scarcity (and value) of precious metals. Compared with ordinary currencies held by financial institutions, crypto currencies are less susceptible to seizure by law enforcement now that is the power of revolution. Canadians were the first to raise their hands. Who is joining the revolution next maters none; a brave new world order run not by governments but by citizens has arrived. If the youth are in on it, brace yourself. As we say in local lingua franca *walala wasala*!

At every level of society, connectivity has become more affordable and in substantial ways. Young people have access to ubiquitous wireless Internet networks such as public hotspot and high-speed home networks extending to online experience that are many times cheaper. It took years for mobile-networking technology to develop and for cellular towers to go up. After mobile calls became more commonplace in a few developed countries, manufacturers added keyboards and larger screens, clearing the way for the SMS and mobile e-mail. By the year 2000, a host of sensors from GPS, which enables mobile mapping, to accelerometers that help the handset know if it's being tilted or facing down found their way into these gadgets.

In the past 10 years, alone we have seen cell phones transform into electronic Swiss Army knives with a wide variety of features. They are replacing the watch, the camera, the stand alone GPS, the alarm clock, and many other erstwhile hand tools. The smart phones of today have changed all of this. Pipeline research from Samsung, Sony and Apple reveals that smart phones are coming out in triangular form as wristwatch-like or other wearable devices with very cool 'wow' features. Within two years, the wearable devises will be trendy, with wristwatch style becoming all the rage with voice activation, holograms and imaging sensors probably real game-changers Smart phones have enabled young migrant workers in China's rural towns to find jobs, communicate with families back home, organise into groups and access information.

The technology has served to liberate workers culturally and restructure social identity. Technology has enabled them to connect with broader segments of China in ways they have never done before. Already Google has unveiled its eWallet; a mobile phone app that allows people to make purchases with their NFC enabled android phones. By simply attaching wallet account to a credit card, then wave the phone near a special NFC enabled point of purchase, and payment is done. Film and digital photography, printmaking, painting and Photoshop are another way of taking creative ideas and sharing them with others through the Smartphone technology. Artists are innovating art at the front field and doing things app creators didn't think even was possible.

According to Apple, the next big thing is mobile travel. Travel is going to be more convenient through smart technology. Apple has developed a downloadable app which when approaching the boarding and checking counters the phone will automatically send electronic identification as soon as the person is in the queue, this will trigger checkpoints to organise eboarding pass and bag checking. Outside the airport using the smart phone, one can rent a car and reserve hotel accommodation. Had Telkom for example had been in the hands of the entrepreneurs South Africa could have had accessible communication, accelerated distribution and access to Internet into every household cheaper than most providers at present. Indeed, the next moments in our technological evolution promise to turn a host of popular science fiction concept into science facts such as driverless cars, thought controlled robotic motion and fully integrated augmented reality, which promises a visual overlay of digital information onto our physical environment. The reason mobile technology is uniquely interesting to the world right now is because it represents the fifth wave of computing. The introduction of mobile phones is far more transformative than most people in South Africa realize. As youth come online, they will quite suddenly have access to almost all the world's information in one place and in the own language too. This will even be true for the illiterate youth. Mobile technology has begun disintermediation through social networking tools and will help reduce the significant numbers of school-age African children who are not receiving any formal education, simultaneously and at the same time maximising the opportunities of home based learning.

Technology really is about what happens to the entire civilization of some several billion people or more when there is useful software running on the person and in the hand of everybody, every minute of the day. Entertainment and information are the most popular activities for which smart phones are used by the youth of Africa today; music and movies are the main attractions. On the national stage though, the most significant impact of the spread of communication technologies will be the way they help reallocate the concentration of power away from the state and its institutions and transfer it to individuals.

Throughout history, the advent of new technologies has often empowered successive waves of people at the expense of traditional power brokers especially the gate keeping elites. Then as now, access to information and to new communication channels meant that opportunity to participate, to hold power to account and redirect the course of one's life with greater agency. Because of digital platform driven scale effects, things will happen much more quickly in the new digital age, with implications for every part of society, including politics, economics, media and social norms. This acceleration to scale, when paired with interconnectedness that Internet fosters will usher in a new era of globalization of ideas.

Disaster management, agriculture and health are also main systems benefiting communities across the length and breadth of Africa. Already mobile banking is the way for most rural communities of Kenya are doing business today. People pay bills, buy goods and make payments to individuals and remittances to elatives living abroad through the M-PESA technology, this technology for example is a mobile money transfer service and serves as a conduit for a fifth of the country's gross domestic product. The potential for transforming the country's dysfunctional educational system is immense, as mobile phones gain ground as tools for delivering teaching content. Mxit for example is South Africa's most recognised social media with more than 10 million active young users in the country many of whom are primary school learners. Nokia capitalised on the growing popularity of social networking and launched its own version of social responsibility initiative through *MoMath*, a mathematics-teaching tool that targets school-going age youth to learn mathematics the easy way.

In 2012, a team at a robotics laboratory in Japan demonstrated successfully that a person lying in a fMRI machine could control a robot hundred of kilometers away just by imagining moving different parts of his body. The subject could see from the robots perspective when he thought about moving his arm, the robot would move correspondingly almost instantaneously. The possibility of thought-controlled motion is certainly extending to prosthetic limbs. As connectivity spreads and new portions of the world are welcomed into the online fold, revolutions will continually sprout up more casually and more often than at any other time in history. With new access to virtual space and its technologies, groups of youth will seize their moment, addressing long held grievances with tenacity and conviction precisely because the mix of activism and arrogance is universal.

Staging a revolt used to be an exclusive reserve of armed revolutionaries with financial backing and training, not any more. Communication technologies break down age, gender, and socioeconomic barriers that previously prevented individuals from taking part. Young citizens will no longer suffer injustice in isolation this globalised feedback loop where people all around the world can comment and react will inspire many to stand up and make their feelings known and this is no longer limited to a geographic area because sophisticated translation software, streaming gestural interfaces as well as holographic projections have opened the floodgates to the information of much broader world than has been the case up until now.

Through the power of technology, age-old obstacles to youth interaction, like geography, language and limited information are mediated by a new wave of technological innovation never seen before. We accept there will be few truly new causes, merely better forms of mobilization and of galvanizing mass participation. Digital empowerment will be, for some, the first experience of empowerment in their lives, enabling them to be heard, counted and taken seriously by the political elitist cliques. Due to mass adoption of the communication technology, a democracy like South Africa is soon going to be forced to include many voices of its that it has deprived until now because that eventuality is driven by technology at an unprecedented scale fuelling one of the most exciting social and political revolution in mankind's history. Technology has given to man what control through threats, oppression, marginalization and exclusion could not real POWER.

CHAPTER 7

The Renaissance of Hope

Ex Africa semper aliqui Novi—Something new always comes out from Afrika

To address South Africa's current problems outside the context of the history of Afrika is an uninformed starting point. We look into pre-colonial history for the purpose of looking ahead more keenly because that is an essential precursor of action. A historical perspective is useful in creating a sense of momentum and in providing a view of precedence to the young generation. Afrika is mankind's past and mankind's future and no other part of the earth reveals so much of God's creation and its history clearly as Afrika does. It makes sense that there is much talk about this century being African renaissance century. Africa in first century was known in the Arabic world as *Bilad-as-Sudan;* meaning the land of black people a region south of Sahara of the Limpopo River, that which many call Afrika today we call our home.

Even though most first generation historians have been unwilling to admit that there is a rich African history to be told and that history predates the emergence of Europe, now we can proudly write this history ourselves and tell it to whoever cares to read about it. Kwame Nkruma said, 'our history needs to be written as the history of the development of our society, not as the story of European adventures. African society must be treated as enjoying its own integrity; its history must be a mirror of that society, and the European contact must find its place in this history only as an African experience, even if as a crucial one.'

According to Tobias and Anta Diop, Afrika has been the crucible of earth's history for two billion years. Nearly everything of consequence on earth started in Afrika. Afrika is the home of the first eukaryotes, the first mammals, the first hominids, the first marked enlargement of the brain, the first signs of spoken language, oldest evidence of stone tools. The cadre of the major civilisation of antiquity, pharoanic Egypt and Nubia, first hieroglyphics writing, obelisks, domestication of animals and plants, scientist in mathematics, astronomy, medicine, architecture, deep sea navigators and the first monotheistic religion with the god Ra was here on this continent (Tswana language groups still use this prefix in reference to God). And so, after sheltering the first form of *Homo sapiens* and then peopling the planet through the Isthmus of Suez and the Strait of Gilbraltar, Africa was the initiator of the civilisation.

The beginning of our rebirth as a generation must be rediscovery of our soul, captured and made permanently available in the great works of creativity represented by the pyramids and sphinxes of Egypt, the stone buildings of Axum, the ruins of Carthage and Zimbabwe, the rock paintings of the San, the Benin bronze and masks, the carvings of Makonde and the sculptures of the Shona. The discovery that the origin of the Egyptian hieroglyphic language system itself lies among black people in the Sudan was later confirmed as the mother of all Europeans writing systems. In 1978, German scientists Schmidt and Avery announced that between 1 500 and 2000 years ago, Africans living on the western shores of lake Victoria had produced carbon steel. Another team of American scientists Lynch and Robbins uncovered an astronomical observatory in Kenya Namoratunga on the edge of Lake Turkana dated 300 years BC.

Great Zimbabwe is a stone city built by Shona people in the twelfth century as royal court of Monomotapa kingdom. African in West and Central Africa developed a variety of boats. They had a marine highway 4 200 kilometers long and on that highway, one could find reed boats with sails, similar to the reed boats of ancient Egypt and Ethiopia. Scientist Bovril reported that he found Africans to be using compass and astronomical computations to guide African caravans across the desert. This was primitive nautical science. Hunter Adams III, a scientist at the Argonne Laboratory discovered that the peoples of Dagon in Mali had for centuries known the existence of our solar system and of the universe had observed and plotted its orbit between 500 and 700 years ago. Dr de Heinzelin found evidence of the use of numbers for notation count in Zaire and he said for whatever purpose the number system was used, it is the first we know of in Africa and among the first in the world.

The earliest technological leap from hunting and gathering activities to scientific cultivation of crops occurred in Africa at least 7000 years before it did on any other continent according to Wendorf's reporting in *Science* magazine in 1979. Not only were the Africans first in crop science but also were the first in domestication of cattle. Anthropologist Nelson said that the findings led them to conclude that pre Iron Age Africans in that area had a relatively sophisticated society and could have spread their mores, living modes and philosophy, eventually reaching Fertile Crescent of the Euphrates River Valley, he suggested that African technologies were exported to the Middle East through trade and cultural diffusion of information. African plant medicine was more developed than any in the world before the disruption of its culture. Approach to the diagnosis of disease, its very early knowledge of anesthetics, antiseptics, vaccination, and the advanced surgical techniques in use were among African doctors. In this century, the Ngunis in Southern Africa have

199

mastered the medicinal uses of 700 plants that are being matched with the western scientific protocols. The Ghanaian Professor Nii Quaynor is reportedly the father who pioneered Africa's first online connections with the virtual world.

Cultural contact between Egypt and the kingdom of Nubian existed from the first century. The common assumption that the peoples of Afrika were divided by the Sahara desert is without historical foundation. The Caucasoid Arabs of the North Africa and the ancient civilisations of the Monomotapa kingdom in the South flourished through trade and other cultural exchanges. On the available archeological evidence, migrations of the Bantu peoples to the south caused mixing with the *San* and *Khoi* communities who already had established presence in the region some 500 years earlier. This fact confirms the existing knowledge that there is no historic basis for Bantu peoples to lay claim that they are exclusively indigenous to the South African soil. San, Khoi, African, Dutch, Portuguese, French, Chinese and Indians all in this order are part of the migration patterns that began since time immemorial in the ancient civilisation. Voluntary movements of peoples of Arabic and European decent into Africa gave rise to creolized populations and cultures. African Americans and Afro Caribbean's and others in Diaspora recognise their Africanness through history, culture and consciousness rather than geography and skin pigmentation.

It is a mere century that the cartographers drew Southern Africa's hinterlands as a single territory. A map originating from 1876 shows a region now known as Southern Africa stretching from southern Somalia to the Cape peninsula. In the colonial carve-up that followed, lines were drawn between the Swahili coast inhabited by the Bantu tribes and Arab traders in the north divided between four colonial countries namely: Britain, Germany, Italy and Portugal. The colonial vast possessions in the hinterland eventually became present day Kenya, Tanzania, Somalia, Mozambique, Botswana, Zimbabwe, Lesotho, Swaziland and South Africa. To that mix, add subsequent dispossessions by the Dutch immigrants after the Anglo-Saxon war—we end up with a fairly mixed political heritage of the ancestral land, South Africa.

Yet, the culture and geography of these Bantu tribes, especially its swathe in the middle, have retained a distinct pre-colonial identity. Construction of this curious and exceptional situation began in seventeenth century when Dutch settlers looked upon indigenous Africans much as the English settlers in North America regarded Amerindians. British industrial imperialism, intent on exploiting the fabulous mineral riches discovered in the late nineteenth century understood that black labour, if mobilised for that purpose, would present and effective solution to the problem of extraction. It was the British, therefore, who invented apartheid and the Afrikaners simply made it to work more efficiently. They established the antecedents of the miserable homeland system, two as British 'protectorates' i.e. Swaziland and Lesotho, all designed to supply cheap migrant labour for the mines.

Mbeki said, 'It may be that it would come to pass that 50 years into the future, those who will be alive then will see this period in the history of our country, as we effect the transition from apartheid to the renaissance of Africa as the golden age of its rebirth.' Mbeki's voice is added among many before him and he was never regarded as the voice of the African renaissance in the modern era. See for example the 1920 Harlem renaissance, there too was also the rise of Pan Africanism that continues to emphasise the importance of African renaissance in the global arena. African renaissance seeks to represent the importance of Africa in the emergent New World Order. Not so long ago a black American published a book and in it were these words:

> I am an American, but a black man, a descendant of slaves brought from Africa. If things had been different, I might have been one of them [Africans] or might have met some anonymous fate in one of the countless ongoing civil wars on this brutal continent. And so I thank God my ancestor survived that voyage to slavery. Talk to me about Africa and my black roots and my kinship with African brothers and I will throw it back into your face, and then rub your nose in the images of the rotting flesh of the victims of the genocide of the Tutsis of Rwanda. Sorry, but I have been there. I have had an AK47 rammed up my nose; I have talked to machete wielding Hutu militiamen with the blood of their latest victims splattered across their T-shirts. I have seen cholera epidemic in Zaire, a famine in Somalia, a civil war in Liberia. I have seen cities bombed to near rubble, and other cities reduced to rubble, because their leaders let them rot and decay while they spirited away billions of dollars into overseas bank accounts. Thank God, my ancestor got out, because now I am not one of them.

And so it may come about that some, who harbour the view that as Africans we are people incapable of doing nothing good apart from being savages who slaughter one another with machetes, wonder how we dare speak of African renaissance! Of course the author of the book from which this excerpt is taken, knows very little about the history of Africa to talk about us with confidence at the world stage among peers. African people without the knowledge of our history, origin and culture, are like a tree without roots. Because to speak of renaissance is to speak of advances in science and technology, voyages of discovery across the oceans, a revolution in frontier knowledge. We are very proud to promote this idea of

Afrika that it should be embraced by everyone who is in Africa to renew, assert and promote Africanness as an identity, which considers others neither as an alteration, alienation nor a threat to Africa.

We carry into the world the vision of an Africa reborn, an Africa rejuvenated, an Africa re-created. We are the first glimmers of a new dawn. 'God first made us who we are, and then we out of our own will created ourselves what we want to be. The fall of Africa had a universal significance for the human race's spiritual, and moral life, so the rise of Africa renaissance is of crucial significance for healing of the spiritual character and social life of humanity and modern civilisation at large. We have begun to work to see that 21st century becomes an African century where there will be material realisation of the renaissance. We speak of Africa renaissance not as an ideological spin neither is it a redeeming psychosocial tool. The wheel of progress revolves relentlessly and all the nations of the world take their turn at the field glass of human destiny. Africa will not retreat! Africa will not compromise! Africa will not relent! Africa will not equivocate! And we will be heard because Africa has risen!' Here is why we make such bold assertions. Economists Ricardo Haussmann and Cesar Hildgo, researchers at the Harvard Center for Economic Development, not long ago produced their Atlas of Economic Complexity and, in their global rankings of gross domestic product (GDP) growth to 2020, Uganda emerges out number one. It is a shock to many we know. Even more insane is that their prediction include in the top ten—Kenya, Tanzania, Zimbabwe, Madagascar Senegal, Malawi and Zambia.

Hausmann and Hildago project that these countries will grow faster than most others in the world, including emerging market favourites Brazil and China. In fact, 13 of the top 30 countries on the list for fast growth are in sub Saharan Africa. We have started learning our lessons and the Afrika of today is very different to the Africa of the next 500 years. A McKinsey Global Institute report (2013) on the progress and potential of Africa's economies sets an 8-year prediction of Afrika's collective GDP at $2.6 trillion. If you consider that, along with predictions of African consumer spending rising to about $1.4 trillion by 2020 and 128 million households with discretionary income, it demonstrates a reduced reliance on mineral and energy exports and a greater emerging middle class in countries with healthier, well rounded economies. Economic growth in Ghana is predicted to be 7% this year and Nigeria is the same. A number of countries in East Africa are also showing significant growth, despite their current troubles.

South Africa is also waking up to the fact that the rest of the continent is modernizing fast and has begun putting in place plans for modernization starting with big infrastructure projects. There is a building of R2.3billion container terminal at City Deep Johannesburg and at Harrismith for a logistic hub development for fuel distribution. A R3.9 billion upgrade to Pier 2 at Port Durban. Phase 1 of the multiproduct pipeline, which will transport petrol diesel, jet fuel and gas. Prasa is set to renew its rolling stock and will see a new assembly line to build state of the art coach and locomotive assembly in Johannesburg. De Hoop dam in Limpopo is in the final stage of completion with Steelpoort water treatment works expected to be complete by September.

The Ingula pumped-storage scheme near Ladysmith is due to become operational in 2013. In two year's time, Medupi and Kusile power stations are ready to supply Afrika's bulk energy needs. Sere wind plant the renewable energy project is due for completion in 2014. A broadband fibre cable to improve the performance of communication network infrastructure for the 4th generation technology is nearing completion. The construction of 64 ditch Meerkat satellites for the SKA project is due to start in 2015. Two new universities, 12 new college campuses and many schools are being upgraded to take care of the surging demand for the people of the continent.

It has become self-evident that, as Africans we know where we come from and who we are and where we are headed in actual fact, we have a clear development path as to where we want to position ourselves in century global village on he 21st. If you like we are restoring the balance of our cultural exchange with the rest of the world. We assert the role of being our own prophets. Since the present generation is eager to be exponent of the millennium of hope renaissance, they will have to take stock of the failures of yesteryear. This generation would have to keep the failures as reminders of things not to do. Every renaissance is first and foremost a reawakening of thought. We dare not forget that Africa has a respectable scientific, social and technical heritage, which must be exploited to the good of her children not only to showcase the rich heritage and practices our forebears bequeath to us, but mainly to prevent us from our tendency to go to Europeans and Americans to ask what we could get at home. The goal of integration of tradition and modernity in science and technology, as well as in all aspects of our cultural life, is the achievement of an enlightenment, a specific way towards historical progress implying a genuine mastering of our social and natural environments without our losing either their soul or the conditions for the sustainability of their existence

The epoch of colonialism and white foreign rule in Africa has progressed to its logical end; the Africans dared to stand up and declare the new must be born whatever the sacrifices needed. The new African generation has learnt from the experiences of the past, they are unwilling to repeat the wrongs that have occurred; they also know that the attitude cannot be sustained where everywhere else on the globe is making progress in improving their conditions in life and they are standing on the sidelines watching. As we now work for an Afrikan Renaissance, the work of Biko assumes relevance as strong as in the time that he lived.

The African Renaissance is a fundamental change of consciousness: consciousness of ourselves, our place in the world, our capacity to shape history, and our relationship with each other and the rest of humanity. Consciousness is a key concept in political approach and vocabulary. The intervention on the level of consciousness came at a time when the political pulse of our people had been rendered faint by banning, imprisonment, exile, murder and banishment and national schism of the past 20 years. Repression had swept the country clear of all visible organisation of the people. But it was also a time when the tide of Africa's valiant struggle and her liberation, lapping at our own borders, was consolidating black pride across the world and firing the determination of all those who were oppressed to take their destiny into their own hands.

The reaffirmation of our consciousness as Africans stems from an ancient heritage that not even colonialism could destroy. Ethnic nationalism as well as self-hate has never been part of African heritage. We are therefore paying careful attention to the debate around the concept of post modernity in line with the critical evaluation of the legacy of European enlightenment to the evolution of human civilization that has brought the best and the worst in them. We are against the belief that African culture is time bound together with the notion that with the conquest of the African continent all her culture was obliterated. One of the most fundamental aspects of our culture is the importance we attach to Man. Our has always been a man centered society. Intimacy is a term not exclusive for relatively close friends but it applies to a whole group of people who find themselves together.

We believe in the inherent goodness of man. We enjoy man for himself. Our action is usually joint community oriented action. We are often prepared to have a much slower progress in an effort to make sure that all of us are marching to the same tune. The principal challenge that lies before the current and the next generation is the task of designing a renaissance that truly addresses the renewal—not just of the people and their destroyed heritage—but spiritual space in which humanity finds its highest expression and celebration of fulfilled lives. The social degeneration we are experiencing today among the youth is as a result of the real loss of African values. There is an urgent need for spiritual and moral rebirth to help reorient this young generation.

Christian religion together with the process of African westernization shares much of the blame in loosing the good African values and their significance in giving meaning to all life.

European missionaries brought the Christianity many are practicing today to Africa in the aftermath of the Dark Ages and following the Reformation Age. The religion was introduced to her people with an unbridled Western human prejudice. As we have come to appreciate the essence of the gospel as revealed to us by the Holy Spirit, we know that this western human prejudice is contra—indicated to the message of the Kingdom of God as taught in Scripture. The Christianity in whose name the European missionaries preached was no more than a religion. For example, Africans who embraced the Christian religion, were forced to add a middle 'Christian' name acceptable to missionaries as a sign of their conversion from heathenism to light, fit themselves with European attire so as to look presentable to the European missionary spiritual fathers, taught to speak a European language and learn European customs and mores because those customs and mores were thought to be highly evolved and somewhat advanced than those found in Africa at the time.

At our disposal are scientific tools including the advancing kingdom knowledge age this has given us advanced and more accurate knowledge about the theology of God than any other generation before us. We know with certainty that Christian religion is neither a way to know God nor a better way to salvation. We are absolutely certain in the knowledge that God is not a Christian neither was Christ sent to earth to start Christian religion because God does not talk about religion only a relationship with his Sons. The Kingdom of God message, which is the core message of the Bible carries a prophetic dimension of God's love for his people on earth regardless of who they may be, this message brings to us to His saving grace and with it the power of His Spirit heals our broken heartedness and reconciles us with God our Creator. Nowhere in Scripture do we read that people are required to change their identities or modify their cultural heritage except to confess Christ as the Lord and Saviour of the world and be obedient to all His commandments, thus posses the Kingdom of God. It is in this message of redemption that people throughout the earth including Africans are meant to seek God and when the opportunity is presented, receive Him with open hearts so that man's spiritual hunger may be satisfied through Christ.

Even as we acknowledge that after 500 years of colonial occupation of Afrika, and through the process of acculturation, African norms and values were destroyed and replaced by something else. We acknowledge also that spiritual and moral decadence is a problem not created by the morally bankrupt system of political leadership in the government or their predecessors, neither is this a problem created by western religion. The spiritual darkness sweeping the nation of Africa today is a matter concerning an individual in the society who must acknowledged his/her failure to repent before God and bring themselves and their children under the Lordship of Christ to receive sound mores. Although we accept that it was during this period that Africans were considered big children who needed training for a new lifestyle brought with the complements from the western missionaries. Africans were denied any reference to their own glorious history, for the colonizer Afrika's real life starts from the time of coloniser's arrival in Afrika.

Whatever customs and traditions that survived unfortunately became a mixture and hence creolized populations and cultures were born in the aftermath. In *Pedagogy of the Oppressed*, Freire addresses the situation of dominated cultures arguing that its peoples are faced with two broad types of education. One type conditions the learners to accept the ethos of domination and assimilation into the culture of those who own the power, a process that results in mental enslavement. The antithesis of this paradigm is education for conscientisation and critical reflection. This type is sponsored by those who struggle against coerced assimilation in their search for determination. Freire describes the first type as 'banking education' which treats the leaner as an object at the mercy of the teacher while the teacher acts as the 'depositor' who stuffs information into the 'receptacle'. In this type of education, the relationship between the teacher and the learners is a master versus subject exchange. In this scheme of things, the learner remains perpetual pupils for life. This type of education is costly in terms of casualties trapped in the mill and, the general masses that become the greatest sufferers as victims' institutionalized systematic erasure.

Antithetical to this model is what Freire describes as 'problem-posing and problem-solving' education. In this situation, the learner is at the centre of the educational process while the teacher serves as a resource provider. Dialogue and debate become the tools through which knowledge is shared and acquired. He concludes that problem-posing education nurtures a culture of reflection, experimentation dialogue and self-esteem while the banking education propagates a culture of dependency and negative silence. It is critical for us that we revisit as well as reconstruct some of these submerged heritages. The mental reconditioning central objective should be to rehabilitate the lost historical memory of victims of 'miseducation'. To the credit of pre-colonial time, general education and their practice were never trapped between walls of a specific building, which was named school. The community and life were the school and they lasted lifelong. Teachers and students came from and returned to the community. People collectively generated their own defining knowledge and developed skills that enhanced societal needs.

Kenya had an exciting experiment undertaken in education in the 1970s. The University of Nairobi experimented with a paradigm to eradicate colonial mentality in Kenyan youth. The experiment removed English literature and replaced it with African orature as the core. (Independent studies and practical projects in African orature were compulsory) Next to the orature were the literatures of the African Diaspora, followed by those of cultures that had similar experiences to African, such as Latinos, and Indians. At the outer core were the literatures of European countries. This experiment moved from the known to the unknown; it privileged indigenous spoken and written traditions and so validated African cultural knowledge. Only after that did it proceed to study dominating cultural canons and other global realities. The emergence of centered learners who had a solid base from which to understand themselves, their culture and surrounding reality was clear. This tested example can be used by education to create sustainable development.

African renaissance speaks of sustainable development not as envisioned in the NDP framework but as envisioned in its totality by the founding fathers themselves. It is a kind of development that moves beyond a definition that confines itself to concerns such as market economic advancement, availability of capital, superiority of infrastructure, automation of resources, acquisition of know-how and the rest of the package that goes with the notion of 'modern progress'. These are important components of development; but in all these spaces, the one factor, namely the development of a human being—if absent renders progress meaningless. If we limit our definition to one punted by the ANC that would automatically favour the wealthy and powerful that inevitably means white and European and excludes the rest of us ordinary folks. Collective advancement must be measured by qualitative soundness of societal human growth. Such growth must reflect the capacity of the group to develop their natural resources and being in control of world, sufficiently empowered to march forward as global citizens. These goals include efficiently combating famine and poor nutrition, and eradicating illness. Sound equitable sharing of the fruits of the collective labour among all actors, and equal access for all to social and economic opportunities, in brief without social justice it is impossible to give the necessary encouragement for healthy sustainable growth.

Standing on this base, African renaissance development should be able to link with the rest of the world for the task of enhancing global human development. In other words, sustainable development must, in the spirit of true African progress, embrace all people and their participation, irrespective of class and other forms of classification that are affected by discrimination. Thus, the sustainable development of a society becomes a responsibility not of the state but of the citizenry within a polity. They freely operationalise their citizenship freedom without any fear that they will be unfairly treatment by their governments. The road to sustainable renaissance also implies the necessity to consolidate the sovereignty of the peoples of the continent, their freedom to decide in their own way the kind of society in which they aspire to live without dictate or threat. No matter what the fields of specialization are, African scholars must mobilise their thinking around the issues and take a mandatory position on the desirability or non-desirability of this process, and then debate appropriate strategy and tactics to be pursued by policy makers as considered opinion of the learned fraternity of the continent to government, political leaders and African civil society.

People of Africa in the Diaspora

In light of the anger we see in the eyes of the South African youth today, it behooves us to address the question of African children from the Diaspora. First, we are categorical about the fact that no human being is illegal on earth; God gave this earth to humans to inhabit and have dominion over it. Second, Africans irrespective of the corner of the globe they may come from are the descendents of the Great Monomotapa Kingdom they can never be illegal or nonresident immigrants on African soil, they belong here and South Africa is rightfully their home too. Period. There can be no legal, moral or historical justification to discriminate against them on the basis of the fact that they were not born here. Many people including South Africans are born in one place but choose to settle some place elsewhere, there is no difference between the choice we make and the choice forced upon them by circumstances. Intrinsically humans are nomadic.

That the ANC government chooses to treat Africans as criminals serves as an indictment on their ignorance about Afrika's pre-colonial history and the orchestration of dispossession wars that scattered the Bantu peoples along the hinterland of the great kingdom. The colonial boundaries set by the Europeans in the 1800s after the scramble of Afrika, have been long declared illegal by the previous generation of African leaders thereby legitimising the movement of people and their ultimate settlement between countries. At this time, just like it was in the first century, the children of Afrika are regrouping themselves back to *Bilad-as-Sudan* a kingdom of Black Afrika and this country happens to be the nucleus from which this kingdom is consolidating and growing.

South Africa is not in a unique position in experiencing large numbers of people of Afrika migrating south. Europe, North Americas, Latin America, Australia and Asia are experiencing similar movements of people at an unprecedented scale in history. The movement of people between country borders and from rural to urban centers is the 21st century phenomenon at a global scale. These movements are not an isolated country problem to be solved at a country level; it is simply a modern day phenomenon to be embraced. The USA enlightened approach in dealing with the matter is the way every country should adopt as policy position. Another reason South Africa is experiencing rather large numbers of people choosing to make South Africa their destination of choice compared with say Botswana or Zimbabwe is the attraction to the *Brand SA* epitomized by Nelson Mandela. This brand is strong and its appeal in the continent echoes far and wide and draws everyone in.

The brand South Africa offers hope to many people including those outside of this country who feel they would rather come here than die in their war torn homelands. Added to this, we are one of few African states not in feminine, civil war or not experiencing economic meltdown over an extended period of time. Due to our country's proximity to the neighbouring SADEC countries, South Africa is the most accessible place today thanks to the availability of direct routes and cheap means of transportation. Even with the daunting prospects of living under squatter conditions in the initial stages, for the majority of Africans coming from outside—both poor and wealthy—South Africa country holds a greater promise of a better life and is a beacon of hope than they would ever find in most countries today; the squatter camp life notwithstanding is marginally tolerable in comparison with the constant threats of war, starvation and inhumane life from whence they come. Fifth, we owe them a debt of gratitude because in the era of oppression when our fathers and mothers escaped oppression and chose to live abroad their host embraced them with open arms and without question. It is our turn to be magnanimous and show hospitality to our guests. Lastly, the exiled group of men fathered many children in the host countries; mothers are now reuniting fathers with their children. Reconcile yourselves to these facts and chill.

Our appeal to young people is that adding hurt to hardship, humiliation to indignity is not in keeping with the sacred spirit of humanism of Afrika or the teachings of the sacred Scripture. Leaving their homes and extended families and everything they have built their lives around to travel to South Africa was not an easy choice but once made, this choice represents the highest price they had to pay some with their lives while others lost their children enroute to the lions of the wild. Protect and embrace your brothers and sisters in their state of vulnerability as you would your own. Turn their stay into an opportunity to forge social relationships while learning their languages and be one with them because your destiny is inextricably woven to theirs. The world has indeed become a small village and South Africa stands as its gateway. Afrika has risen as the fastest growing economic regions in the world, the economic fortunes have swung in favour of her and all her children stand to benefit from the fortunes of the economic winds of change.

DESIDERATA

Go placidly amid the noise and haste, and remember what peace they may be in silence.
As far as possible without surrender be on good terms with all people.
Speak your truth quietly and clearly; and listen to all even the dull and ignorant they too have their story
Avoid loud and aggressive people; they are vexations to the spirit.
If you compare yourself to others, you will become vain and bitter
There will always be better and lesser persons than yourself.
Enjoy your plans as well as your achievements.
Keep interested in your own career however humble,
It is a real possession in the changing fortune of time
Exercise caution in your business affairs, for the world is full of trickery.
But let not this blind you to the virtue there is; many persons strive for high ideals, and everywhere life is full of heroism.
Be yourself, especially do not feign affection, neither be cynical about love.
In the face of all aridity and disenchantment, it is as perennial as the grass.
Take kindly the counsel of the years, gracefully surrendering the things of youth.
Nurture strength of the spirit to shield you in sudden misfortune.
But do not distress yourself with imaginings. Many fears are born of fatigue and loneliness.
Beyond a wholesome discipline, be gentle with yourself.
You are the child of the universe, no less than the trees and the stars you have a right to be here
And whether or not it is clear to you, no doubt the universe is unfolding as it should.
Therefore, be at peace with God, whatever you conceive God to be
And whatever your labours and aspirations, in the noisy confusion of life keep peace with your soul.
With all its sham, drudgery and broken dreams, it is still a beautiful world.
Be cheerful. Strive for joy.

OUR SOURCES

Anta Diop, Cheik. 1974. The African Origin of Civilisation: myth or reality. Lawrance & Hill

Biko, Steve. 2012. I Write What I Like. A selection of his writings. Picador Afrika

Bornstein, David *et al.* 2010. Social Entrepreneurship: what everyone needs to know. Oxford University

Chikane, Frank. 2012. Eight Days in September: The Removal of Mbeki. Pan Macmillan

Cloete, Nico. 2009. Responding to the educational needs of post-school youth: determining the scope of the problem and developing a Capacity-Building Model. Centre for Higher Education Transformation:

De Waal, Leandra. 2006. A Profile of Social Security Beneficiaries in South Africa. Department of social work, Stellenbosch University

Gratton, Linda. 2011. The Shift: The future of work is already here. HarperCollins Publishers

Gumede, William. 2007. Thabo Mbeki and the battle of the soul of the ANC. Zebra Pres.

Gumede, William. 2012. Restless Nation: Making sense of troubled times. Tafelberg

Jobson, Janet. 2011. Interrogating Youth Leadership Development in South Africa:An overview and leadership for a winning nation strategy. The DG Murray Trust.

Khoza, Ruel. 2005. Let Africa Lead: African transformational leadership. Vezubuntu Publisher

Kondlo, Kwandiwe. 2012. The Role Youth in Participatory Democracy University of the Free State

Mandela, Nelson. 1995. Long Walk to Freedom: the autobiography. Back Bay Books.

Macdonald, Michael. 2006. Why Race Matters in South Africa. UKZN Press

Makgoba, Malegapuru (Ed.) 1999. African Renaissance: the new struggle. Mafube & Tafelberg

Mashiqi, Aubrey. 2012. Reflections on the Relationship between the State and the Party. Focus Issue 67 Helen Suzman Foundation

Maxwell. C. John. 2010. Everyone Communicates, Few Connect: What effective people do differently. Thomas Nelson

Mbeki, Thabo.1998. Africa Time Has Come: selected speeches. Mafube & Tafelberg

McKaiser, Eusebius. 2012. There is A Bantu in My Bathroom. Pan Macmillan

Miller, Calvin. 1992. The Empowered Communicator: 7 keys to unlocking audience. Nashville

Mzolo, Sipho. 2010. Understanding a Leader's Intent: a qualitative study. An unpublished Thesis

Parkin, Kate. 2006. Mandela: the authorized portrait. Wild Dog Press.

Ramphele, Mamphela. 2012: Address at Centre for African Studies, University of Basel, Switzerland,

Ramphele, Mamphela. 2012. Conversations With my Sons and Daughters. Penguin Books.

Sparks, Alister. 2003. Beyond The Miracle: inside the new south africa. Jonathan Ball.

Walden, Kate (Ed). 2006. Mandela: the authorized portrait. Wild Dog Press

Nulutshungu, Temba. *The Star*. 22/10/2012. What South Africa needs

SAIRR, 2011. Annual Report: first steps to healing South African family

SAIRR, 2013. Frans Cronje: *Democracy*

Schmidt, Eric and Cohen, Jared. 2013. The New Digital Age: Reshaping the future of people, nations and business. John Murray Publishers

Swartz, Sharlene *et al*.2012. Ikasi Style and the quiet violence of dreams: A critique of youth belonging in post-apartheid South Africa. Comparative Education 48:1 27-40

Swartz, Sharlene. 2012. Old Scars, New wounds: youth, inequality and restitution in South Africa. Havard School of Education Colloquium

Websites visited

Http//www.globalblackhistory.com. Accessed 19/10/2013

Http//www.anc.co.za/policies/html 1991/2007/2012.Accessed 07/2012

Http//www.mandelacentreformemory/articles/spechees/html. Accessed 07/2013

Http//www.afesiscorplan.org.za/article/Roleofyouthinparticipatorydemocracy.12/12/12

Http//edition.cnn.com/2012/tech/ourmobilesociety/article./accessed 12/12/12

Http//www.economist.com/leaders/21564846/southafricaslidingdownhill.accessed 12/12/12

Http//www.npc.org./documents/html/diagnosticoverview. Accessed 07/12/2012